RONALD R. WLODYGA

THE FOOLISHNESS OF GOD

Is wiser than men (I Cor. 1:25)

Volume 4

Copyright Statement

Any articles may be reproduced in whole, but not the book in its entirety under the following provisions: proper credit of book title and author must be given at the end of each article. There can be no charge of articles to the recipient. It is my desire to encourage, and inspire the Christian into further study with the fundamental belief of giving freely.

ISBN 978-0-9996000-5-4

Publication in 202 by Ingram Printing

Acknowledgements

"All scripture is given by inspiration of God, and is profitable for doctrine, for reproof, for correction, for instruction in righteousness" (2 Tim. 3:16)

"For whatsoever things were written aforetime were written for our learning, that we through patience and comfort of the scriptures might have hope" (Rom. 15:4).

THANKS BE TO GOD!

Vol. 4

TABLE OF CONTENTS

Chapter One
The Days of Noah

1. Cain and Abel—Types of the Church 2
2. Moral Decay 3
3. The Age of Sexual Immorality 4
4. The Age of Music 12
5. The Days of Lot 15
6. The Age of Sodomy 15
7. Enoch—a Type of the Church................................. 22
8. Enoch and God's 7,000 Year Plan........................... 23
9. Methuselah—a Type of the Church 24
10. The Mysterious 120 Years 27
11. The Ark and Christ's Body 27

Chapter Two
Moses and the Burning Bush

1. A Theophany 34
2. What makes God Holy... 37
3. Does God Create Calamity?...38
4. The Lesson of Uzza 39
5 More Examples 42
6. Disease A Type of Sin 44
7 God's Covenant with Abraham.................................... 46
8. Scriptures on The Great "I AM"................................... 48

Chapter Three
Why God Created Man

1. Why God Created Man 51
2. Created in God's "Image and Likeness" 53
3. Godly Character 57
4. What Man Is 59
5. The Origin of the Immortal Soul 61
6. Subject to Human Nature 62

7. The Spirit in Man 64
8. The Bonding of the Spirit 65
9. Man Created Incomplete 68

Chapter Four
   Life in the Millennium

1. Marriage—a Divine Institution 72
2. Depicts Spiritual Marriage 74
3. Abortion 76
4. Human Birth 77
6. Spiritual Birth 77
7. Spiritual Abortion 79
8. Suicide 79
9. Spiritual Eggs 80
10. Spiritual Babies 81
11. The Child of Maturity 85
12. Jesus—an Imperfect Husband? 87
13. The Perfect Man 90

Chapter Five
   The Old Covenant Marriage

1. The Lord Divorced His Wife 94
2. Jesus was Married to Israel 95
3. Jesus came to His Wife 96
4. The Pruning of God's Olive Tree 97
5. Christ to Marry His Wife 98
6. The Bride and Bridegroom 100
7. The "Mystery" of Christ's Body 101
8. The "Mystery" Solved 106

Chapter Six
   The Kingdom of God

1. The Messiah's Reign 108
2. Many Offices of Rulership 109
3. The Gospel of the Kingdom 110
4. "Born Again" 112
5. What the Kingdom will be like 116
6. How to receive Salvation 119
7. Man to be Changed 121
8. Man to become Immortal 124

Chapter Seven
To Rule the Universe

1. Our Destiny—the God Family 130
2. God--a Family 131
3. The God Family throughout Eternity 132
4. To Inherit the Universe 136
5. The Increase of His Government 137
6. The Earth--a Unique Creation. 138
7. Entering the God Family 138

Chapter Eight
Israel's Three Sojourns

1. The Egyptian Experience 142
2. Conquering the Flesh 144
3. The Bitter Waters of Marah 147
4. The Wilderness Experience 148
5. Developing the Character to Rule 150
6. Jordan—a Type of Passover 152
7. The Canaan Experience 152
8. Spiritual Warfare 154
9. Three Spiritual Burials and Resurrections. 159

Chapter Nine
The Seven Steps of Salvation

1. Repentance—The First Step 167
2. Baptism—The Second Step 172
3. The Holy Spirit—The Third Step 176
4. Faith—The Fourth Step 180
5. Grace—The Fifth Step 184
6. Service—The Sixth Step 189
7. Rulership—The Seventh Step 195

Chapter Ten
The New Heaven and Earth

1. The Marriage of the Church 199
2. Overcomers comprise New Jerusalem................... 200
3. Tabernacles and God's Dwelling............................ 201
4. The Eternal Tabernacle of God............................... 204
5. God and Man Reconciled....................................... 208

6. The Eighth Day and Eternity 208
7. Entering the "Holy of Holies" 209
8. "Spiritual Firstfruits" 211
9. To Rule over Nations 214

Chapter Eleven
Beyond the Millennium

1. Taking a Fresh Look 217
2. A glimpse into the Future 219
3. A Physical Creation 219
4. To Keep the Law Eternally 223

FOREWORD

Prophecy has been one of the most fascinating subjects to Christians of all ages. Yet it is one of the most complex subjects and I doubt if anyone has put every detail together in its proper perspective to date. I will be the first one to admit that I don't have all the pieces of this fantastically intricate puzzle in i's entirety—but for purely educational purposes, my opinions are stated.

In all candor, the only thing I want to be *dogmatic* about in this book, is that speculative aspects in regard to *my opinion* of prophetic events *are not to be interpreted dogmatically*! I do not want to speak with authority where there is no definite word of scripture to guide.

However, like the Beureans who searched the scriptures day and night to see if these things be so—it is my hope that this book will inspire you to do the same, and perhaps together we can put the final pieces of this end-time prophetic puzzle together.

Furthermore, speculative aspects contained in this book, as well as the sequence of end-time events are my thoughts, and do not represent any Church, nor am I sponsored or endorsed by any religious organization.

Though I do not press points of speculation as doctrine, I do give my opinion for reproof, for correction and instruction in righteousness (11 Tim. 3:16).

Chapter One

THE DAYS OF NOAH

The apostles asked of Jesus' return to set up the Kingdom of God on earth. "...**Tell us, when shall these things be? And what shall be the sign of thy coming, and the end of the world?**" [Greek, *age*] (Matt. 24:3).

Jesus proceeded to give His *disciples* many signs, and included *one* sign *apart* from all others—that of the antediluvian *days* of *Noah*.

Jesus prophesied of this time:

> **But as the days of Noah were,** *so shall also the coming of the Son of man be.* **For as in the days that were before the flood they were eating and drinking, marrying and giving in marriage, until the day that Noah entered into the ark. And knew not until the flood came, and took them all away; So shall also the coming of the Son of man be (Matt. 24:37-39).**

Clearly, if we want to know the conditions that will be in existence prior to Christ's second coming, we must study the conditions as they existed before the flood as recorded in (Genesis 3-6).

Cain and Abel—Types of the Church

There is a profound spiritual relationship between Cain and Abel as *types*—representing God's *true* Church and Satan's *false* Babylonish system as mentioned previously in other volumes.

This intriguing prophecy is recorded in Genesis 3:15:

And I will put enmity between thee and the woman, and between thy seed and her seed; it shall bruise thy head, and thou shalt bruise his heel.

This obscure prophecy concerns two *conflicting* philosophies of life between the seed of the woman (God's true Believers), and the seed of the serpent (Satan's false teachings and system).

Further, the way of Cain and Abel depicts TWO WAYS of religious worship toward God that would exist throughout the ages—especially prior to the return of our Savior.

Cain's offering is *typical* of FALSE religious worship of the all-loving God. Remember, Cain believed in God, and brought a beautiful offering consisting of the "fruit of the ground" (Gen.4:3). Both boys had been taught by their parents to bring sacrifices before the Eternal (Gen. 3:21).

But God did not have respect unto Cain's offering (Gen. 4:3-5). Cain's offering represented much *toil* and *sweat* [works] to produce. By contrast, the offering of Abel was a firstling lamb of his flock for a SACRIFICE to God.

To produce this lamb, Abel had to do very little—it was a *gift* from God.

In these two offerings, we have *two ways* of life, *two ways* of worshipping God—that of WORKS and that of GRACE!

The offering of Cain appeared to be more of a self-sacrifice on the surface, yet it lacked *faith* in the *blood* of Christ! Previously, God had *revealed* His plan of salvation to Adam and Eve, and the necessity for the atoning *blood* of Jesus Christ for the redemption of sins.

God had sacrificed an animal [probably a lamb], poured out its blood, and used its skins to cover Adam and Eve (*symbolic* of *covering* their sins). Thus, the Creator had *revealed* His plan of salvation by the sacrifice of a lamb [Christ], whose blood had to be shed for their sins.

Unlike his parents, Cain refused to bring an offering of *blood* and gave one based on his works.

Today, there are many religious people who are walking in the way of Cain—thinking they can work out their own salvation—without having FAITH in the atoning blood of Jesus!

The Bible clearly reveals the fault of Cain:

> **By *faith* Abel offered unto God a more excellent sacrifice than Cain by which he obtained witness that he was righteous, God testifying of his gifts... (Heb. 11:4). Not as Cain, who was of that wicked one, and slew his brother. And wherefore slew he him? Because his own *works* were evil, and his brother's righteous (1 Jn. 3:12).**

In these last days, the way of Cain is surfacing again as Jude 11 states: **"They have gone *in the way of Cain*..."**

This is the way of carnal man, who like Cain, has rejected the sacrifice of Jesus Christ, and thinks he can find salvation in himself or other false religions.

The way of Cain is typical of *false religion*. It is symbolic of the tares that are growing up with the wheat—or seed of Abel in *true religion* and *belief* in a Savior.

The Building of Cities and Moral Decay

Originally, God placed mankind in a beautiful garden, free of sin. It needed no walls to keep intruders out, or guards to retain people.

Cities are an invention of man, which always produce the cesspools of city dwelling—corruption, murder, stealing, rape, disease—SIN!

The first mention of the building of a city is recorded in Genesis 4:17:

> **And Cain...builded a city, and called the name of the city after the name of his son, Enoch.**

The Age of Sexual Immortality

Typical of city life is the breakdown of the family and sexual standards. Cain's son Lamech is the first individual to break God's marital law by practicing polygamy, Notice: **"And Lamech took unto him two wives..." (Gen. 4:19).**

The Hebrew word for "took" in this verse means "to take with violence, or take possession"—indicating a way of GET! This same Hebrew word for "took" is used in (Genesis 3:6), where mother Eve "took" of the fruit on the tree in the garden because "it was pleasant to the eyes."

The way of "get" and "take" allows one to partake of things that are not good for us, as our eyes and emotions overtake us! When the sons of God "took" [same Hebrew word] of the daughters of men, God did not approve, and sent the flood (Gen. 6:2-3). They "took them wives of all which they chose" (Gen. 6:2).

The evils of a concentrated populous and intimate working relationships between the sexes in industry, invariably has caused divorce and the breakdown of the family.

It is an established and shocking fact, that the divorce rate has gone from one in fifty, to one in three during the first 60 years of this century—and one in two during the last five years! And what about the AIDS epidemic that swept the world? Need we say more about the sexual immorality of our time?

Jesus said of the *days of Noah*, they were, **"Marrying and giving in marriage" (Matt. 24:38).**

This "marrying and *giving in* marriage" could mean the abuse of marriage. But Jesus could also be referring to a dark time that was prevalent in the days of Noah, and would prevail shortly before His second advent!

Some have looked at Jesus' reference to "marrying and giving inmarriage" to mean that everything would be going along as normal. But why would Jesus compare the end time to the days of Noah? To find the answer we need to look back into the Old Testament to find the conditions that were so evil as to bring about God's wrath. You can also find similar wording in Luke 17:26-27.

Yet, despite this promiscuous society, only Noah was "perfect" in his generations [Heb. *unblemished in heredity, ancestry, character*] (Gen. 6:9).

Invasion of the Body Snatchers?

There appears to be evidence that fallen angels had an influence on sexual immorality after the flood and is a *type* of the end-time. In Judges 1:34, we find the tribe of Dan was defeated by the Amorites:

> **And the Amorites forced the children of Dan into the mountain: for they would not suffer 'permit' them to come down to the valley: But the Amorites would dwell in mount Heres in Aijalon, and in Shaalbim: yet the hand of the house of Joseph prevailed, so that they became tributaries (Judges 1:34-35).**

Who were these Amorites that forced the children of Dan into the mountain? This is very important to our study. Although highly disputed, many Bible scholars believe the Amorites were *Nephilim* or the seed of fallen angels, whose great height was described by the prophet Amos:

> **I destroyed the Amorites, though they were as tall as cedars and as strong as oaks. I destroyed the fruit on their branches and dug out their roots (Amos 2:9).**

God had commanded the Israelites to destroy the Amorites who were described as 'tall as cedars,' and also the inhabitants of Bashan, which was called the land of giants where the giant Og lived as recorded in Deuteronomy. 3:13.

Believe it or not, Bashan is mentioned 60 times in the Old Testament. It was the name of the region east of the Jordan River, which is, in part, today called the Golan Heights. It was known as good cattle grazing land and was the very land into which the tribes of Reuben, Dan and Manasseh chose to settle (Num. 32:1-5).

Bashan was a kingdom and its king was named Og. We hear of him 22 times in the Old Testament but learn little about him, except that he and his people were the Rephaim, a remnant of the giants, also known in Hebrew as the 'walking dead.' These can be traced to Genesis 6:4 where Moses tells us:

That the sons of God saw the daughters of men that they were fair, and they took them wives of all which these chose... There were giants in the earth in those days, and also *after that* when the sons of God came unto the daughters of men, and they bear children to them, the same became mighty men which were of old, men of renown.

The controversy and explanations of this verse is found in *Halley's Bible Handbook that* states "the 'sons of God' (Genesis 6:2) are thought to have been either fallen angels...or leaders in Sethite families who intermarried with the godless descendants of Cain" (24th ed., p. 72).

The second explanation in *Halley's* gives the story of Cain and Abel and follows with the genealogical descent from Cain. In Genesis 6, we see "the sons of God" (men of Seth's godly line intermarrying with "the daughters of men" (women of Cain's ungodly line).

Thus, the giants mentioned were all destroyed in the Flood. But there would be more like them following the Flood, who were descended, just as everyone else in the post-Flood world, from Noah such as Goliath.

Interpretations from Jewish and Christian writers have disagreed about the meaning of the Hebrew word describing this event. Advocates of the Fallen Angel position view the "sons of God" as heavenly beings that married women and had children with them. These children, the *nephilim*, were "mighty men," "men of renown," and "giants." Many of the early writers on this subject believed the offspring to be demonic, but most modern scholars who hold this view reject that notion and believe they were fully human, as indicated by the words "mighty men."

Arguments for the Hebrew phrase *bene [ha]'elohim* in Genesis 6 "[the] sons of God") refer to heavenly beings (Job 1:6; 2:1; 38:7)3, as do the similar phrases *bene elyon* (Psalm 82:6) and *bene elim* (Psalm 29:1; 89:6). 1Peter 3:18–20, 2Peter 2:4–10, and Jude 6 mention certain angels who left their own abode and are now being held in "chains" or "prison" until the day of judgment because of their sin in Noah's day. Jude 14–15 also quotes from the Book of Enoch, one of many apocryphal writings from before the time of Christ that identify the sons of God as fallen angels.

Some point to Matthew 22:3 as evidence that angels cannot have sex, because Jesus said, 'they neither marry nor are given in marriage, but are like the angels of God in heaven.' This says nothing about the capabilities of angels, but how does this square with "kinds reproducing after their kind?"

Why did God order the Anakins and other tribes of similar lineage to be utterly destroyed as He Himself destroyed those who polluted the earth before the flood (Num. 13:33)?

The area in which Jesus preached as part of His ministry was heavily populated with demons, there being as many as 2000 in the one man called Legion. All of the demons knew Jesus and knew His mission (Mk. 5:7). They also knew their ultimate destiny, as they complained to Him that their time had not yet come (Matt.8:31).

Scripture tells us demons exist and that they seek to occupy human bodies and minds, unlike angels who are capable of appearing in human form without invading human bodies. Satan and his legions of demons have deluded the world and oppose God's plan by influencing world art, literature, music, education, politics, as well as religion.

Demons, which are fallen angels that were originally created by The Word, possess along with all God's created beings, personality, intelligence and are voluntary agents. It would appear that they would also have individual names like Legion, as did the angels such as Gabriel, Michael and Lucifer.

According to the Book of Enoch, the fallen angels descended on the summit of Mount Hermon and mated with human women. Here is what is written about them in the book of Enoch:

> **And the angels, the children of heaven, saw them 'handsome and beautiful daughters' and desired them... And they were altogether two hundred; and they descended into Ardos, which is the summit of Hermon. And they called the mount Armon, for they swore and bound one another by a curse (I Enoch VI.6, vs.1-5).**

The Angelic concept of an unholy union between demons and human woman were destroyed in the flood. However, according to Genesis 6:4, there was a second invasion of fallen angels who mated with the Canaanite women:

And GOD saw that the wickedness of man was great in the earth, and that every imagination of the thoughts of his heart was only evil continually (Gen. 6:4-5).

According to *Gray's Concise Bible Commentary,* this suggests that the culminating sin of the Canaanites was not different from that of the antediluvians. Observe further that the offspring of these sinful unions became *the 'mighty men which were of old, the men of renown.'* Most likely, this is where the ancient classics got their ideas of the gods and demi-gods.

Here is what the *Pulpit Commentary, Part 9: Appendix 23 & 25* says of them: *'giants. Heb. Nephilim'* Those mentioned in *Gen, 6:4 were all destroyed in the Flood; these came from a second irruption of fallen angels, 'after that': or after 'those days' = the days of Noah.*

Whatever the truth is concerning the Nephilim, the Bible tells us that there is going to come a head-on collision between the Satanic powers of pagan darkness of centuries, with strong demonic activity focusing on the supernatural as the end of this dark age draws near. To this end 'the man of sin,' or 'the son of perdition' who opposes and exalts himself against every so-called object of worship so that he takes his seat in the temple of God will proclaim himself to be God (11 Thess. 2:3-4).

Power will be given to him over all kindreds, and tongues and nations (Rev. 13:8). He will inaugurate a world-wide reign of terror, blasphemy, and murder.

He shall speak words against the Most High, and shall wear out the saints of the Most High, and think to change times and laws (Dan. 7:25).

It will be Satan's supreme and most desperate attempt to be 'like the Most High.' Isa. 14:14:

> **And then shall that wicked one be revealed, whom the Lord shall consume with the spirit of his mouth and shall destroy with the brightness of his coming. Even him, whose coming is after the working of Satan with all power and signs and lying wonders. And for this cause God shall send them strong delusion, that they should believe a lie (II Thes. 2:8-9, 11).**

> **And I saw three unclean spirits like frogs come out of the mouth of the beast, and out of the mouth of the false prophet. For they are the spirits of devils 'demons' working miracles, which go forth unto the kings of the earth and of the whole world, to gather them to the battle of that great day of God Almighty (Rev. 16:13-14).**

When Christ returns, the Devil and his demons will not be able to deceive the world any longer (Rev. 20:2-3). In Matthew 12:26, Jesus confirms the fact that Satan has a Kingdom: *'And if Satan cast out Satan, he is divided himself: How shall then his kingdom stand?'* Jesus calls him 'the prince of this world' *age* (John 12:31, 14:30, 16:11. also 1 John 5:19, John 7:7, 14:27, 1 Cor. 1:21, 11:32, 1 5:9, 1 John 3:1, 13).

Further, the apostle Paul tells of Satan's world in Ephesians 6:1;

> **For we wrestle 'contend' not against flesh and blood 'humans', but against principalities, against powers, against rulers of the darkness of this world 'age', against wickedness 'wicked spirits' in high places.**

God incarcerated those fallen angels in *Hell*, where the Greek word *Tartarus*, is used which means, a subterranean abyss or 'bottomless pit.' (Rev. 9:1,2). Genesis indicates that another group of these fallen angels descended after the flood and continued their abominable practices. They also established a form of idolatrous worship, known as the Canaanite religion of Baal and Ashtaroth.

The Prophet Daniel offered a very strange statement concerning the iron and clay in his famous explanation of King Nebuchadnezzar's dream. Some scholars believe this may be a reference to the perverted sexual relationship between physical humans and these renegade angels, notice:

> **And whereas thou sawest iron mixed with miry clay, they shall mingle themselves with the seed of men: but they shall not cleave one to another, even as iron is not mixed with clay (Dan. 2:43).**

The inspired Daniel said that *they* would mingle with *'the seed of men'*. Is it possible that he was referring to a situation similar to the one that occurred in the days before the Flood?

According to the *Encyclopedia Britannica*, Hermon means 'forbidden place.' Jerome, the 4th-century translator of the *Latin Vulgate Bible*, interpreted Hermon as 'anathema.' Evidently, mount Hermon was the port of entry for a group of wicked angels, who corrupted the human race in the days of Noah.

The apocryphal *Books of Enoch* and *Barnabus* enlarge upon the story of the Nephilim. Although these have been called apocryphal Books among the Apostolic leaders, the *Epistle of Barnabas* has been referred to by the early theologians Justin Martyr, Clement of Alexandria, Origen, Irenaeus, Tertullian, Eusebius, Jerome, Hilary, Epiphanius, Augustine, and others.

The books of II Peter and Jude add further insight about the fate of these fallen angels. The apostle Peter wrote of them:

> **God spared not the angels that sinned, but cast them down to hell (Greek, *Tartarus*, meaning a place of restraint), and delivered them into chains of darkness, to be reserved unto judgment; and spared not the old world, but saved Noah the eighth person, a preacher of righteousness, bringing in the flood upon the world of the ungodly (II Peter 2:4,5).**

Jude put it this way:

> **And the angels which kept not their first estate (Heaven), but left their habitation, he hath**

> **reserved in everlasting chains under 'darkness' unto the judgment of the great day (Jude 6).**

Both passages tell of severe punishment upon the fallen angels or what the Bible calls demons. Yet, Moses said that 'sons of God' reappeared after the Flood (Gen. 6:4). How can this be? We find the answer in Genesis 6:4 *"and also after that"*, meaning after the flood more fallen angels returned to the earth and established what Joshua called the 'land of giants.' Moses and Joshua conquered those giants, of whom, Og was king in Mount Hermon. Joshua wrote:

> **And the coast of Og king of Bashan, which was of the remnant of the giants, that dwelt at Ashtaroth and at Edrei, and reigned in mount Hermon, and in Salcah, and in all Bashan, unto the border of the Geshurites and the Maachathites, and half Gilead, the border of Sihon king of Heshbon. Them did Moses the servant of the LORD and the children of Israel smite (Joshua 12:4-6).**

It is evident from this nefarious history, the devil was determined to replace the *seed* of the woman with the *seed* of the serpent.

When the Israelite spies explored the land in Numbers 13:33 they reported seeing giants or Anakim. Here is how they described them, notice:

> **And there we saw the giants, the sons of Anak, which come of the giants: and we were in our own sight as grasshoppers, and so we were in their sight.**

The human race has never seen a battle between angels and demons before. It is a subject most theologians would rather not talk about. However, there appears to be scriptures that support a past and future battle. Scriptures tell us that the Antichrist will be possessed and not completely human.

The Age of Agriculture

Agriculture and animal husbandry is also closely associated with city growth. This was also apparent in the *days of Noah* as we read in Genesis 4:20:

> **And Adah bore Jabal: He was the father of such as dwell in tents, and of such as have cattle.**

Needless to say, one can readily see by today's advanced scientific research and machinery produced in the city—the farming business has been totally revolutionized.

The development of cattle breeding, artificial insemination, hybridization and discoveries for the prevention and cure of animal disease—surely parallels the *days of Noah*! Not all of these scientific advancements have been detrimental, however some of them have led to inferior species.

The Age of Metals

Accompanying the growth of city building was the use of metals:

> **And Zillah, she also bore Tubal-Cain, an instructor of every artificer in brass and iron...(Gen. 4:22).**

This is the first mention of the use of heavy metals in the Bible. How close the age of Noah parallels the space age we live in with all the new exotic alloys and metallurgical developments.

Today we hear of stainless steel, galvanize, rustproof, corrosion resistant, and new alloys with unbelievable tensile, flexural and shear strengths. Could we be living in the days Christ spoke of, just before His second coming?

The Age of Music

The *days of Noah* were also characterized by music. Concerning Jubal, the father of the harp and organ, God's Word says in Genesis 4:21:

THE DAYS OF NOAH

And his brother's name was Jubal: He was the father of all such as handle the harp and organ.

Music has a direct effect on our emotional system—and Satan can use music to also influence human nature in a wrong way. Suffice it to say—Satan is the "prince of the air" (airwaves). Nebuchadnezzar used music in idolatry (Dan. 3:7-15), where soft music played by string instruments made a demon go away from Saul (1 Sam. 16:16,23).

Like anything else God has created for man's good and benefit, music can be perverted by the prince of darkness!

Music can be good or bad—we wake up to it, make love to it, and eat to it.

Satan is LITERALLY the "prince of the air" (Eph. 2:2). That is, he controls the air and what is going on in the air. Perhaps he broadcasts through wave-lengths just as the ones coming over the air to TV or radio? Satan's influence goes into our mind and impacts our human spirit and causes us to have moods of rebellion, resentment—HE APPEALS TO HUMAN EMOTIONS! Satan appeals to human nature (vanity, lust, greed, jealousy, envy, hatred).

In (Ezekiel 28:13) we read of Lucifer's creation having "tabrets or tambourines and pipes" (percussion instruments). Lucifer and the rest of the angels were created with musical ability; for all the angels [including Lucifer] sang together at the creation of the earth (Job 38:7).

David, the sweet Psalmist, loved music (11 Sam. 23:1), and all the Levites were singers (1 Chron. 15:16). Their instruments were mostly strings. This is not to say that percussion instruments are the work of the Devil!

Lucifer, God's supreme creation of angelic being, must have had exceptional musical ability; but like everything else he has done in perversion since his rebellion—he can use music in a wrong way. God created Lucifer to play music for Him. Lucifer knows God likes music and is trying to be like Him, only Satan can pervert music!

Scientists tell us that music controls and influences our emotions and Satan has used this medium to appeal to human nature as he did Nebuchadnezzar.

Listen to some of the music and see what it does to those

listening to it—how many "freak out." It makes one wonder who really "writes the songs that make the whole world sing?"

It is also very interesting to note that drugs have been used by many musicians of today, and that the Greek word *pharmakeia* from which we get the modern word "pharmacy", was used in connection with "sorcery" or "witchcraft" (Gal. 5:20, Rev. 18:23).

Doctors tell us music can be helpful or potentially harmful depending upon one's emotional, physical, physiological, mental, and spiritual responses to music. One of the more obvious ways music can be harmful is within the lyrics

The volume of music can cause stimulation of the heartbeat, respiratory rate, movement, etc. Depressing, scary music with curse words certainly would not be beneficial for most children. Music videos can also be harmful for children if it has sexual content in it.

The drum was used to drown out the screams of little children as they were being sacrificed to Molech, one of the false gods of Satan (Jer. 7:31). So loud and prevalent were these screams that the place where they occurred became known as the "valley of the drum" (11 Kings 23:10).

On the contrary, music can be a source of pleasure and contentment, and there are many other psychological benefits as well. Music can relax the mind, help one to sleep better, energize the body, and even help people better manage pain.

The Age of Violence

Another evil facet of city dwelling is crime and violence. This again was portrayed in the *days of Noah:*

> **And Lamech said unto his wives, Adah and Zilliah... hearken unto my speech: for I have slain a man to my wounding, and a young man to my hurt. If Cain shall be avenged sevenfold, truly Lamech seventy and sevenfold (Gen. 4:23).**

The antediluvian age was reminiscent of unprecedented violence, murder and atrocity:

THE DAYS OF NOAH

> **And God saw that the wickedness of man was great in the earth, and that every imagination of the thoughts of his heart was only evil continually (Gen. 6:5).**

Certainly, anyone who reads the newspaper of today, would have to admit we live in an age of unparalled VIOLENCE, (hostages, crime, mass murder, bizarre murder, sadistic murder, and ritualistic murder which fill the headlines of our newspapers regularly.

The statistics are shockingly overwhelming as to the increase in crime, juvenile delinquency, runaway children, teenage prostitutes, child molestation, child abuse, etc. Truly we are reliving the *days of Noah!*

The Days of Lot

When Jesus gave the signs of His coming to His disciples, He made special recollection to the *days of Noah* and also to the *days of Lot*. Jesus prophesied of the *days of Lot*:

> **Likewise, also as it was in the days of Lot, they did eat, they drank, they bought, they sold, they planted, they builded: But the same day that Lot went out of Sodom it rained fire and brimstone from heaven, and destroyed them all. Even thus shall it be in the day when the Son of man is revealed (Lk. 17:26-30).**

This scripture tells us that Jesus will come as a thief in the night, when no one expects Him—Business and everyday life will be going on as usual!

But there were other things going on the *days of Lot* that were not normal—that is the sins of Sodom and Gomorrah.

The Age of Sodomy

The first mention of the sin of "sodomy" is recorded in Genesis 19:4-5:

> **They had not lain down to rest before all the**

> **townsmen, the inhabitants of Sodom, beset the house, young and old from every quarter, shouting to Lot, 'Where are the men who came to visit you tonight? Bring them out to us *that we may rape them.*'**

The subject of homosexuality is very sensitive and yet it is vital to find out what the Creator God has to say about it. Does God ordain it? How should Christians treat homosexuals (there are Christian homosexuals)?

Clearly, God does not approve of perversion in sex of any kind, including same sex marriages, and transgenderism. Our society is very confused about sexual identification. In an interview that college students were asked, "how many genders are there," their answers ranged from 6 to infinity!

Sex trafficking and abuse of children. Human trafficking is one of the most heinous crimes on earth. Right now, traffickers are robbing a staggering 24.9 million people of their freedom and basic human dignity—that's roughly three times the population of New York City according to the secretary of state in 2019.

Jaco Booyens, is a producer and director, known for *We Are Brothers*, and *8 Days* (2014) which tells the story about Sex trafficking, especially of children. "It is a diabolical scourge that still affects the modern world, but the depth and scope of this evil are worse than you probably imagine. In his book, Booyens recalls how his sister became a victim of sex trafficking when they were growing up in South Africa, which made the issue very personal for him. "I didn't jump on a bandwagon by reading a book or a movement that I felt led to," he said in an interview with Mark Levin on Life Liberty and Levin, August 18, 2019. The filmmaker explained. "It was dire."

"What is the typical outcome of this experience?" Levin asked. "Death. The average lifespan of a child that's trafficked is seven years. Because with it comes addiction, physical abuse, emotional abuse; suicide rate is through the ceiling, because how do you get out?" Booyens explained.

Shockingly, the United States leads the world with the lowest average age of trafficking victims: 12, Booyens says. He also notes that a child trafficking victim in the United States will bring a pimp $200,000 to $250,000 per year tax-free: "Now you have a real problem — a real problem. Because now, like I say, the demons come out. Because there's so many takers."

And those takers come from all walks of life. While Booyens said that he's glad that the high-profile arrest of billionaire sex offender Jeffrey Epstein put attention on the issue of sex trafficking, he has a big problem with what he sees as a widespread assumption that supporting the sex slave market is only a problem among the ultra-wealthy.

"Are the wealthy involved in this? Yes," Booyens says. "So is the middle class, so is the lower class. This thing is so sick, Mark, you could almost order a child as you order pizza — you like cheese, I like pepperoni, etc., etc.," Booyens concluded. "The audience may be shocked, but this is a fact."

We must also ask why God obliterated Sodom and Gomorrah with fire and brimstone! All the inhabitants were destroyed except Lot and his two daughters.

In speaking of the time before the flood, the apostle Paul says in Romans 1:20-29:

> **Because that, when they knew God, they glorified him not as God, neither were thankful; but became vain in their imaginations, and their foolish heart was darkened (Vs. 24). Wherefore God also gave them up to uncleanness through the lusts of their own hearts, to dishonour their own bodies between themselves: (Vs. 26) For this cause God gave them up unto vile affections: for even their women did change the natural use into that which is against nature: (Vs. 27) And likewise also the men, leaving the natural use of the woman, burned in their LUST one toward another; men with men working that which is unseemly.**

Notice, the apostle says that sexual relationships of men with men and women with women is not a natural lifestyle that God approves of, but is shameful because of their vile affections!

The Bible is very clear that it is an abomination for men to have sexual relationships with other men (Lev. 18:22), and for women to have sexual relationships with other women. God's word also declares it is also an abomination for men to dress like a women and visa versa (Deut. 22:5).

Today, we are witnessing the acceptance of life styles contrary to the word of God by all nations and Jesus proclaimed the consequences.

Sexual promiscuity was prevalent in the pagan Greek and Roman world in which deviant sexual behavior was accepted as normal. It is no coincidence that the Greek god Eros and his Roman counterpart Cupid are depicted as naked boys.

Suetonius, a Roman writer in the second century AD, compiled a catalogue of this disgusting behavior in his *The Twelve Caesars*. He states that Emperor Tiberius kept groups of boys for his personal perverted pleasures. Nero publicly married a transvestite man and had relations with other men and women.

History shows that individuals and societies that condone and adhere to these perverted sexual acts of ignoring our Creator's laws will come to a bitter end!

Jesus said that social conditions at the end of the age, prior to His second advent would be as the days of Noah and Lot (Lk. 17:26-30). In Noah's day, "all flesh had corrupted their way" as a result of rampant wickedness, and God brought that world to an end with a great flood (Gen. 6:5-13).

Let us beware of the *days of Lot* and this present age of open sexual unrighteousness. Yet today, people seem to be complacent about it, and don't even know that it not a lifestyle that honors God.

How well Isaiah prophesied of our time when he said that they would, **"...declare their sin as Sodom and hide it not" (Isa. 3:9).**

The Sin of Ham?

In Genesis 9:21-25, we read of a most bizarre account in which Noah planted a vineyard soon after the flood and got drunk from the wine. The account further says that Noah's son Ham, the father of Canaan saw the nakedness of his father, and told his two brothers who then covered Noah's naked body.

Most commentators believe that this was an act of homosexual transgression, either that Ham gazed at the exposed body of his father maliciously, or committed some act of sexual indecency with him.

However, there are several keys to the understanding of the enigmatic account. Firstly, the phrase "saw the nakedness of his father" is paramount to understanding this episode.

Leviticus 18 contains a list of all the forms of incest that were prohibited under Mosaic Law. The general principle is found in verse. 6: "None of you shall approach any one of his close relatives to uncover nakedness." The phrase "to uncover nakedness" is clearly a euphemism for a sexual act. The phrase "to see the nakedness of" is used in Leviticus 20:17, again as a euphemism for incest, notice: "If a man takes his sister...and sees her nakedness, and she sees his nakedness, it is a disgrace. Again, we read in Leviticus 20:11: "And the man that lieth with his father's wife hath uncovered his father's nakedness." These scriptures clearly mean having perverted sexual relations.

But why was Noah's grandson Canaan so horribly cursed because his father Ham saw his father Noah unclothed?

Notice Genesis 9:24 for the answer: "And Noah awoke from his wine, and knew what his younger son had done unto him. Someone did something to Noah while drunk and the question is WHO? There was an illicit sexual act committed here. Noah was very drunk and did not realize that someone had taken advantage of him and committed an act of sodomy with him.

This confusing verse can easily be cleared up once we realize that Canaan was not Noah's son but Ham's! The pronoun "his" in this verse properly refers to Ham's son, not Noah's. The answer is found in Genesis 10:6: "And the sons of Ham; Cush, and Mizraim, and Phut, AND CANAAN." Canaan was Ham's youngest son! So, Canaan was not punished for what Ham did, he was punished for his own sin!

Love Homosexuals

The late apologist, Ravi Zacharias gives his opinion on how Christians should treat practicing Homosexuals:

> **Loving our neighbors and clearly communicating the gospel are sacred privileges of disciples of Jesus. But not all of our neighbors want to be loved and some really don't want to hear the gospel. This is especially true in regards to the homosexual community where conflict abounds**

between Christians and those who view sexuality outside the lines of God's original design. How can we as Christians think through this social issue?

Zacharias provides 'three panels' of an answer concerning homosexuality. First, is the sociological problem. This problem is seen in how our culture relates to authority. We value autocracy, which means a law to oneself and that no outside and objective authority has power over you. The notion of owing allegiance to God, our moral lawgiver is exchanged for our own glory and perceived right to choose.

Second, is the theological problem. Our race, ethnicity, and sexuality are sacred attributes of being made in God's image. Sexual immorality then is the 'de-sacralizing' of what God has made and intended for a specific purpose. The full picture of the biblical concept of love can be explained through the Greek words *agape* (unconditional love), *phileo* (friendship love), *storge* (parental love), and *eros* (sexual love). Zacharias contends it is only marriage between a man and woman that can embody all of these facets of love.

Third, is the relational problem. As Christians we must be courageous in loving those whom we disagree. It is far easier to isolate and disparage those who sin than to engage them with the gospel (*The Christian View of Homosexuality in an interview by Andrew Hess, July 20, 2015*).

Perhaps Christians should heed the wisdom of Solomon as he recorded the seven things God hates in Proverbs 6: 16-19: a Proud Look, a Lying Tongue, Hands that Shed Innocent Blood, a Heart That Devises Wicked Plans, Feet That Are Swift in Running Into Mischief, False Witnesses That Speak Lies, Those Who Sow Discord Among Brethren.

The Age of Pride, Ungodliness, Idleness

There are yet other parallels of Sodom and Gomorrah and the days in which we live. Not only do we see similar moral conditions, but trends in their economics are also very similar.

The New Testament book of Jude states that Sodom and

THE DAYS OF NOAH

Gomorrah were an example of cities destroyed by fire for "having given themselves over to sexual immorality and gone after strange "flesh" or unnatural uses of sex (Jude 1:7).

Besides sexual immorality, the prophet Ezekiel lists three distinct sins of Sodom:

> **...Behold, this was the iniquity [sin] of thy sister Sodom, *pride, fullness of bread,* and abundance of *idleness* was in her daughters... (Ezekiel 16:48,49).**

The three infamous sins of Sodom that would characterize the despicable age before Christ's return are: 1) pride, 2) fullness of bread, and 3) abundance of idleness.

Anyone with "opened eyes" can surely realize that these same *three sins* are prevalent in our western world today.

Man takes PRIDE in his own achievements and accomplishments, without giving God the credence He deserves. This is all *vanity* and *ungodliness*!

Men *pride* themselves in their own wisdom and intellect, as though they are the discoverers of God's laws themselves. They boast of discovering the laws of heat, light, gravity, etc, when in fact they have merely stumbled upon God's existing laws!

It is the *pride* and *ego* in man that makes him think he can solve all of the world's ills—through science and without God.

The sin of "fullness of bread" is also evident in our western world. New farming technology has led to over-production and surpluses of food. Our government actually pays farmers a subsidy for not growing food! This is indeed preposterous, since the same government spends billions of dollars to produce greater yields per acre on soil conservation, soil erosion and the use of fertilizers.

The government spends millions to build dams for better irrigation to provide water for non-productive land. Then it gives subsidies to farmers for not growing food on land that is productive! This is all called "scientific farming" when in reality it is "sinful farming"—the same sin of Sodom.

As a result of modern technology, this easy push-button and computer age has produced the third sin of Sodom—"abundance of idleness."

Most of man's IDLENESS is spent today on more pleasure

seeking, more sports, more T.V., more recreation, more alcoholics, more fun—more SIN!

Too much spare time has divided the family and produced more delinquents and unhappy marriages!

Once again the voice of Jesus thunders—**"Beware of the sins of Sodom"!**

Enoch—a Type of the Church

Again, Jesus emphasizes: **"As it was in the *days of Noah*, so shall it be in the days of the coming of the Son of man."**

We have just recorded how city dwelling spawned the sexual, agricultural, metallurgical, and musical revolution. How violence and corruption were the end result of man's inhumanity to man during the days of Noah.

Next, we come to the event that took place before the flood came to *destroy* the inhabitants of the earth—except for Noah and his family. This was the preaching of the GOOD NEWS [gospel] of the Messiah coming to the earth.

Recall how Enoch is a *type* of Christ and the Church. His life represents what the Church [Christ's *spiritual* body] would be doing just before our Lord's return. Before any kind of destruction upon the earth, God has *always* given ample warning through His chosen servants—so the *righteous* could escape and the wicked could repent!

Jude informs us of Enoch's preaching:

> **And Enoch also the *seventh* from Adam, prophesied of these, saying, Behold, the Lord cometh with ten thousands of His saints: To execute judgment upon all, and convince all that are ungodly among them of all their ungodly deeds which they have ungodly committed, and of all spoken against him (Jude 14, 15).**

Noah was also a preacher of righteousness warning the ungodly to repent (11 Pet. 2:5).

Enoch and Noah are *types* of the "Two Witnesses", who will once again preach God's final warning before the earths end-time destruction!

THE DAYS OF NOAH

Now this is important!

There are three *types* of individuals that existed in the *days of Noah* before the flood came. They are:

- The ungodly majority of people who perished in the flood.
- Noah and his family of *eight* who were mostly righteous but went through the flood.
- Enoch who was righteous, and was translated or removed prior to the flood (Heb. 11:5). Was this a *type* of Rapture or supernatural protection?

In these *three categories*, we have three *types* of individuals that will exist before Christ's second coming, and the Tribulation!

The first category entails the multitudes of **wicked** who will perish—even as they did in the *days of Noah*!

Noah and his family are a *type* of **the Nation of Israel** who will have to go through the time of judgment upon the earth or the Great Tribulation. Many of them who *repent* during this time, will be granted *supernatural* protection or be *sealed* (Rev. 7:2-4)—just as Noah's Ark was *sealed* with pitch (Gen. 6:14).

Indications are that only 1/10 of the nation of Israel will survive the Tribulation (Isa. 6:9-13). Sodom and Gomorrah suffered the Eternal's vengeance because of their heinous sins and were left in ashes (11 Pet. 2:6; Jude 7). The same fate awaits the unrepentant as a result of their similar sins!

Enoch represents the third category of people who will receive God's protection from the *entire* Tribulation!

Even as Enoch was *translated* before the day of judgment, so God's people will also be MIRACULOUSLY protected during the Tribulation (Rev. 12:14).

Enoch and God's 7,000 Year Plan

Enoch's son Methuselah is recorded to be the oldest human being that ever lived, being nearly 1000 years old [actually 969] at the time of his death.

The birth of Methuselah had a profound impact upon Enoch's life, for:

> **Enoch walked with God after he begat Methuselah three hundred years [the rest of his life] (Gen. 5:22).**

What was it about Methuselah that changed his father's life? The answer is in Methuselah's longevity as *revealed* by the meaning of his name.

Jude mentions a seemingly irrelevant fact about Enoch's life that gives us part of the answer to *why* Enoch walked with God after begetting Methuselah:

> **And Enoch also, the *seventh* from Adam, prophesied of these, saying, Behold, the Lord cometh with ten thousands of his saints (Jude 14).**

Why did Jude mention the fact that Enoch was *seventh* from Adam? What difference did it make if Enoch was third, seventh or tenth from Adam?

This is of great prophetic significance!

The fifth chapter of Genesis lists the obituaries of the ten generations from Adam to Noah. Enoch was *seventh* from Adam in this genealogy in which *all* died a natural death *except* Enoch who was "translated."

Six generations of DEATH followed by a generation of LIFE is *symbolic* of the 6,000 years of *death* and destruction of mankind—followed by 1000 years of *rest* and peace of God's soon coming government!

Can you begin to see why Enoch represents a *type* of the Church—that will be spared the coming judgment upon the world by being *supernaturally* protected?

Methuselah—a Type of the Church

Now we come to the incredible reason of Methuselah's long life of nearly 1000 years. Why he caused Enoch to "walk with God."

The answer is astounding!

Before any destruction upon the earth, God has always revealed these things to His servants so they could warn those that would listen and *repent.*

God had told Abraham and Lot of Sodom and Gomorrah's calamity. He had prognosticated through His prophets—Israel's and Judah's doom. And the Creator has forecast the end of this atrocious age in Armageddon as well, always warning those that would heed in advance!

Likewise, God had revealed things about the impending flood to Enoch just as He did to Noah!

Remember, Enoch is a *type* of the Church and therefore the Church is a *type* of Enoch. Just as Jesus gave His disciples many *signs* that would occur prior to the coming judgment upon the earth, and the ushering in of the Millennium—so God gave Enoch a *sign* that would occur just before the flood would come.

The distinguishing *"sign"* God gave Enoch was that his son Methuselah would die prior to the coming flood!

Methuselah's *death* then became "the yardstick of time" that would determine when the flood would begin!

Here is another point of conjecture.

According to Arthur I. Pink, author of *Gleanings in Genesis,* the name Methuselah means "when he [Methuselah] is gone, then it will happen."

Pink writes in his book:

> **The name Methuselah strongly implies that Enoch had received a revelation from God. The name Methuselah signifies, 'When he is dead it shall be sent; i.e., the deluge' (Knobbier). In all probability then a divine revelation is memorialized in this name. It was as though God said to Enoch, 'Do you see that baby? The world will last as long as he lives and no longer! When that child is taken out, I shall deal with the world in judgment. The windows of heaven will be opened. The fountains of the great deep will be broken up and humanity will perish.'**

The following Biblical facts conclusively prove that the flood of Noah came exactly 969 years after Methuselah's birth.

- Methuselah lived 187 years when his son Lamech

was born (Gen. 5:25)
- Lamech was 182 years old when Noah was born (Gen.5:28).
- Methuselah was 369 years old when Noah was born (187 plus 182 = 369).
- Noah was 600 years old when the flood came (Gen. 7:11).
- Methuselah was 969 years old at the time of the flood (369 plus 600 = 969).

Actually, God extended Methuselah's life 120 years when God made His judgment upon mankind.

...yet his days [mankind] shall be an hundred and twenty years and then the flood shall come (Gen. 6:3).

Normally, Methuselah would have died at the age of 849, but God extended his life 120 years as a *sign* of the flood. Methuselah was a contemporary of Noah's, and may even have helped in the construction of the ark.

Jesus reminds us again, **"As it was in the days of Noah, so also it shall be at the end time."**

Truly, Enoch and Methuselah are *types* of the Church—as the flood is a *type* of the Tribulation!

The Church is to preach the Gospel, just as Enoch did before the day of judgment. The Church could be *supernaturally* removed from the coming Tribulation, even as Enoch was supernaturally *translated!* To carry the *parallel* one step further, the Tribulation could begin once the Church leaves—even as the flood came only after Methuselah was *removed* from the earth as God's antediluvian *sign!*

As long as Methuselah was alive, the world had an opportunity to *repent* and be spared the coming judgment—even as Ninevah did after Jonah brought God's warning. But when Methuselah died, the door of physical salvation in the ark was shut and the flood came!

As long as God's Church remains in the world preaching the gospel—individuals may become a part of it and escape the coming Tribulation through God's mercy. This also *parallels* the days of Lot, as Jesus said: **"As it was in the days of Lot...the** same day that Lot went out of Sodom it rained fire and brimstone from heaven, and destroyed them all. Even thus shall it be in the day when the Son of man is revealed" (Lk. 17:28-30).

The Mysterious 120 Years

As we have seen, the Days of Noah are but a *type* of the end-time age, and that Methuselah was given an additional 120 years to live in order that the gospel could be preached.

Some have thought these days represented mankind's allotted life span on the earth after the flood, but we know from the scriptures, this is not true. Mankind's allotted life span is recorded in Psalm 90:10, **"The days of our years are threescore years and ten (70); and if by reason of strength they be fourscore years (80)..."**

In other words, the average age of man would be approximately 70 years, with some attaining 80 if blessed with exceptional health. Of course, we know today that many have lived to be centenarians, including the patriarchs Abraham [175] (Gen. 25:7); Isaac [180] (Gen. 35:28); and Jacob [130] (Gen. 47:9).

Besides 120 additional years to preach the gospel, what could these 120 years possibly represent prophetically?

Could it be that God has revealed His 6,000 year plan for mankind through these 120 years?

Take note! If the "Days of Noah" are a *type* of the end-time, and the flood a *type* of the tribulation, and Methuselah a *type* of the Church preaching the gospel—then could these 120 years possibly represent the end of God's 6,000 year plan? And could it be that God will once again grant an additional 120 years to preach the gospel as He did during Noah's day?

The Ark and Christ's Body

There is yet additional and *exciting* analogies to Christ, found in the ark Noah was told to build.

Three arks are mentioned in the Bible and all three have very much in common, for all are *shadows of Christ!*

The ark of Noah, the ark of bulrushes in which the baby Moses was laid, and the Ark of the Covenant which rested beneath the Mercy Seat in the Holy of Holies in the Temple, are all *pictures of Christ*! Each of the three arks had the following points in common:

- **Judgment**—Each of the arks represented *judgment* of life or *death*. Noah's ark was a haven for only eight people that escaped the judgment of God by a flood. Only the baby Moses was safe in the "ark of bulrushes" as death sentence was passed upon all of the Israelite children. The ark of the covenant contained the 10 commandments by which the Israelites were judged. The death penalty was imposed for breaking several of the commandments. The Mercy Seat, located just above the 10 commandments, represented the meeting place of the law and mercy for breaking the law. Thus, is contained a "shadow" of Christ judging for breaking the law and granting mercy.

- **Life or Death**—Everyone outside of Noah's ark received either *life* or *death* by the flood. The same held true for the Israelite babies that were sentenced to death by Pharaoh. Only the baby Moses was spared. The death sentence was imposed on Israelites that broke certain commandments such as murder and adultery. The tablets of the Commandments were placed in the Ark of the Covenant. Keeping of the Commandments meant physical life for the Israelites, spiritual life for the Christian. The budding of Aaron's rod in the Ark of the Covenant was *symbolic* of "life" through the *resurrection*. The manna was *symbolic* of "spiritual food" that is necessary to give "life", and without which Christians will die.

- **Safety**—There are two Hebrew words translated "ark" in the Old Testament, and both mean a "box" or "chest" for safekeeping of valuables. Of course, the "ark of the covenant" *protected* the 10 Commandments. The ark of Noah *protected* his family from the flood, and the ark of Moses *protected* him from the brutal satanic attack of Pharaoh.

THE DAYS OF NOAH

Noah's Ark—a Type of the Crucifixion

That the ark of Noah was a *type* of Christ's crucifixion is a most phenomenal truth and will now be made quite apparent. The ark pictured the *judgment, death* and *resurrection* of Jesus Christ!

Here is how God instructed Noah to build the ark:

Make thee an ark of *gopher wood*; rooms shalt thou make in the ark, and shalt pitch it within and without with pitch (Gen. 6:14).

Atonement

God told Moses to use *gopher wood* in constructing the ark. Gopher wood is a product of natural growth and development and is *symbolic* of the BODY of Christ. Jesus came to *perfection* through a *growth* process. The *shittim wood* used in making the Ark of the Covenant also represents the body of Jesus Christ.

Physically, Noah's ark was an *unattractive* sight, looking much like a prodigious black coffin. Recall this same analogy in the Tabernacle! Jesus was also unattractive to the natural physical eye as recorded in Isaiah 53:2:

...he hath no form nor comeliness, and when we shall see him, there is no beauty that we should desire him.

The fact that the same Hebrew word translated "ark" for Noah's ark, is also translated "coffin" in (Genesis 50:26), proves unequivocally that Noah's ark was a *picture* of the death of our Lord! Those within the ark were saved, even as Christians in the "ark of Jesus" will also be saved eternally!

God told Noah to *seal* the gopher wood by covering it with and without with *pitch*. The Hebrew word in (Genesis 6:14) translated "pitch" is *kapher*, and its verb *kaphar* is translated *atonement* in at least 70 other places in the Old Testament. The root idea is "to cover." The ark in which the baby Moses was laid was sealed with "slime" and "pitch" to make it waterproof. The Hebrew word for "slime" means "tar," a mineral form of pitch.

We read in Leviticus 17:11:

> **For the life of the flesh is in the blood... to make *atonement* for your souls: for it is the *blood* that maketh an atonement for the soul.**

The Hebrew word for *atonement* here is *kaphar;* the same word translated *pitch* in (Genesis 6:14). It is the BLOOD which makes *atonement* for, or "covers", sin as (Hebrews 9:22) states:

> **And almost all things are by the law purged with blood, and without [the] shedding of blood is no remission [of sins] (emphasis mine).**

Therefore, we could justifiably rewrite (Genesis 6:14) as follows:

> **Make thee an ark of gopher wood and cover it within and without with pitch which is *symbolic* of the atoning *blood* of Jesus Christ, the Messiah.**

Here is another fascinating analogy. The Hebrew word for "Mercy Seat" [the *covering* of the Ark of the Covenant], comes from the same Hebrew word "kapher" and has been rendered by some as just "covering." Here is the beautiful meaning. The sprinkling of the blood upon the Mercy Seat (Lev. 16:14) was God's divine way of picturing the *Merciful Covering* of our sins!

Furthermore, the "gopher wood" of the ark *represented* the body of Christ with all its human frailties. And the *pitch* is *symbolic* of Christ's "atoning blood"—shed for our sins, that precludes us from the death penalty!

The Resurrection

Just as Noah's ark [representing Christ's body] was buried in a watery grave for forty days and nights before coming to "rest" upon Mount Ararat (Genesis 8:4)—so the body of Christ was "lifted up" from the grave by a *resurrection!*

Peter refers to this event as a *type* of the mystical *death* and *resurrection* of Christians in Christ in (1 Peter 3:21).

Now let's read the Genesis account:

THE DAYS OF NOAH

> **And the ark *rested* in the *seventh month*, on the *seventeenth day* of the month, upon the mountains of Ararat (Gen. 8:4).**

Once again, the seemingly irrelevant facts of the *day* and *month* the ark came to rest, will prove to be very *significant* in understanding this fantastic analogy.

The date of the *seventeenth day* of the *seventh month*, is the day Noah's ark came to rest on Mount Ararat. We will now prove this is *the very same day*, that the body of Christ was resurrected centuries later!

God gave the Israelites two calendars, one civil and one religious. The religious calendar was used to determine their holy days, and started with the seventh month of their civil year. God's Passover is held on the fourteenth day of the first month (Nisan), which is the seventh month of their civil calendar.

Recall, Jesus Christ was crucified on the Passover—the fourteenth day of the *first month* of the religious calendar. He arose three days later on the *seventeenth* day of the first month of the religious calendar—or the *seventeenth day* of the *seventh month* of the civil calendar used by Noah!

Therefore, the ark rested upon Mount Ararat the very same day Jesus rose from the dead centuries later!

What a remarkable coincidence! But is it really?

More Analogies

There are yet further *analogies* to the ark of Noah and the RESURRECTION of Jesus Christ.

The Hebrew word translated "rested" (Genesis 8:4) means to "settle down" or "to sit down." The Hebrew word *Ararat* means "high" or "exalted" mountain. In other words, Noah's ark, *symbolic* of the body of Jesus Christ, "sat down" upon the "exalted" mountain. This was a beautiful *Rembrandt* of the future *picture* of Jesus Christ "sitting down" at His Father's right hand, after His *resurrection* from the dead.

We read of this prophecy in Hebrews 1:3:

> **...When he [Jesus] had by himself purged our sins, *sat down* on the right hand of the Majesty**

on high.

On the 17th of Nisan, the renewed earth emerged from the flood waters, and centuries later, our Lord rose from the dead!

The resurrection was the anniversary of the crossing of the Red Sea, and the resting of the Ark on Mount Ararat (Gen. 8:4). The 17th of Nisan pictured the renewed earth emerging from the waters of the flood—as the redeemed in the ark emerged from the waters of the sea. The whole was a *picture* of the resurrection of our Lord from the dead!

The Door of Salvation

Continuing the relationship of the ark to that of Jesus Christ, we read of the DOOR of the ark:

> **...and the door of the ark shalt thou set in the *side* thereof...(Gen. 6:16).**

Jesus is also called a door. Notice:

> **I am the *door*: by me if any man enter in, he shall be saved, and shall go in and out, and find pasture (Jn. 10:9).**

When the door of Noah's ark closed—no one could enter into the ark and therefore perished in the flood. Likewise, Jesus will keep the "door of salvation" open through Him as long as the Father allows. But when the Father shuts the door—it will remain shut! (Rev. 3:7).

It is also very interesting where the location of the door of Noah's ark was placed—in the *side*. This is also significant in that our Lord was pierced in the *side* which opened the *door* of salvation to mankind!

What beautiful pictures of the *death* and *resurrection* of our savior Jesus Christ!

Chapter Two

Moses and the Burning Bush

The bush that was burning but not consumed in the account of Moses, we see God's revelation of many vital spiritual lessons. In this unusual story, we see God's self-revelation of who He is as Moses would eventually ask, and what all Christians would eventually ask, "Who Are You?"

The account of the burning bush is a story about the holiness of God. Through the manifestation of His presence in the bush and that what Moses experienced at the burning bush is what God's people experience today: a holy, transcendent, all-consuming God who comes down to dwell with His people.

Why was the bush burning and yet not being consumed? Moses was the mediator of the old covenant. As a mediator, he stood between God and the people of Israel. Moses *foreshadowed* the greater Mediator who would come of the new covenant, Jesus, our Savior!

THE FOOLISHNESS OF GOD

A Theophany

The definition of a theophany is an appearance of God in the Old Testament. The word theophany is a compound word of the Greek words *theo*, which means God, and *phaino*, which means "to appear." That is, a theophany refers to God appearing. But a theophany does not mean that people actually saw God.

The first theophany in Scripture may have occurred in Genesis 3:8 when we are explicitly told that Adam and Eve heard God walking in the Garden of Eden.

The theophany in the Burning Bush of Exodus 3:2-6 is most interesting. Here we find the angel of the LORD appeared to him in a blazing fire from the midst of a bush; and he looked, and behold, the bush was burning with fire, yet the bush was not consumed. So Moses said, "I must turn aside now and see this marvelous sight, why the bush is not burned up." When the LORD saw that he turned aside to look, God called to him from the midst of the bush and said, "Moses, Moses!" And he said, "Here I am." Then He said, "Do not come near here; remove your sandals from your feet, for the place on which you are standing is holy ground." He said also, "I am the God of your father, the God of Abraham, the God of Isaac, and the God of Jacob." Then Moses hid his face, for he was afraid to look at God. Exodus 3:2-6 (NASB)

At the end of the passage we learn that this angel of the Lord was the God of Abraham, Issac and Jacob. He was Jehovah God. Acts 7:31-32, 35 also teaches us that the angel of the Lord appeared to Moses in the bush. Other examples of theophanies in the Old Testament can be found in Exodus 13:21-22; 24:9-11 and Judges 6:11-23;

What Moses saw in this fire was a supernatural, visible manifestation of the glory of God. He had a momentary encounter with the Holy, and the closer he got, the more afraid he became. The first thing that God reveals about Himself is that He is personal, "I am who I am." His character is one of self-existence, transcendence, and His aseity (the quality or state of being self-derived or self-originated; specifically : the absolute self-sufficiency, independence, and autonomy of God).

MOSES AND THE BURNING BUSH

Self-existence means that He depends on nothing and no one for His existence. Only God has the concept of self-existence. God is self-existent, eternal, and pure, or transcendent! When we consider the transcendence and aseity of our God, we will respond in worship and awe—just as Moses did at the burning bush.

In His interaction with Moses, God reveals not only His majesty but His mercy. The great I AM establishes a covenant with Moses that will lead to the redemption of sinful man.

The Theophany of Moses' encounter with God in the burning bush and others demonstrate God's Shekinah glory revealing God's transcendent character that is above and beyond our scope and that He alone is holy.

God wants Moses to go on a journey to take His people out of Egypt and into the promised land because He hears the crys of His people, notice: "And the LORD said, I have surely seen the affliction of my people which *are* in Egypt, and have heard their cry by reason of their taskmasters; for I know their sorrows.." (Ex. 3:7).

But what was Moses' response? It is much like many of us who don't have faith when we don't know who God is: "And he said, Certainly I will be with thee; and this *shall be* a token unto thee, that I have sent thee: When thou hast brought forth the people out of Egypt, ye shall serve God upon this mountain. And Moses said unto God, Behold, *when* I come unto the children of Israel, and shall say unto them, The God of your fathers hath sent me unto you; and they shall say to me, What *is* his name? what shall I say unto them? And God said unto Moses, **I AM THAT I AM:** and he said, Thus shalt thou say unto the children of Israel, I AM hath sent me unto you (verses 12-14).

Do we as Christians know who God is? What His character is? Are we like our first parents who sinned and then hid themselves from God? Moses didn't know who God was as He asked Him what is your name? Moses knew the God of Abraham, Isaac and Jacob—but did he know who "I AM THAT I AM"?

Our relationship with God is in His name, His character—who He is! He is holy and there is none like Him! What does it mean to be holy? God reveals more of His character in Isaiah 45:3-7 in speaking to the Gentile King Cyrus in a prophecy that would take place 150 years before he would fulfill this prophecy of Israel's deliverance, notice:

> **And I will give thee the treasures of darkness, and hidden riches of secret places, that thou mayest know that I, the LORD, which call** *thee* **by thy name,** *am* **the God of Israel. For Jacob my servant's sake, and Israel mine elect, I have even called thee by thy name: I have surnamed thee, though thou hast not known me. I** *am* **the LORD, and** *there is* **none else,** *there is* **no God beside me: I girded thee, though thou hast not known me: That they may know from the rising of the sun, and from the west, that** *there is* **none beside me. I** *am* **the LORD, and** *there is* **none else. I form the light, and create darkness: I make peace, and create evil: I the LORD do all these** *things.*

We find many things about God's character in these verses as to WHO is the great I AM! Most Christians have no problem of WHO Jesus is from the N.T. versus— but do we know the God who creates evil or calamity as many versions translate the Hebrew word "raah"(resh ayin hey) which means "evil." The word *ra'* is used throughout the Old Testament with several meanings. It is used many times to mean something morally evil or hurtful (Job 35:12, 1 Sam 30:22, etc.) but it is also used to mean an unpleasant experience (Gen 47:9 and Prov. 15:10). It is used to describe fierce beasts (Lev. 26:6), and even spoiled or inferior fruit (Jer 24:3).

The Word of God tells us that God is not the author of evil as James 1:13 states "Let no one say when he is tempted. 'I am being tempted by God'; for God cannot be tempted by evil, and He Himself does not tempt anyone." We know also that God is not a God of confusion (1 Cor 14:33).

We would also have to answer the question, "Did God create the Devil?" The answer to that question is an absolute NO for God created Lucifer, a shinning star or light bringer of truth who BECAME the Devil by his own choosing!

MOSES AND THE BURNING BUSH

What Makes God Holy?

So how do we explain all of these seemingly contradictory Scriptures on the nature of God, and the Hebrew word *ra'?* The story of God's plan for King Cyrus presents a clue into God's character and nature that perhaps most Christians do not understand. If we only think of God as a God of love, understanding, forgiving and merciful — We would not understand His character of revenge and WRATH upon the wicked!

In Isaiah 45:5, God gives a future message to Cyrus (His anointed) as He further expounds upon His character as He did Moses: "*...That they may know from the rising of the sun, and from the west, that there is none beside me. I am the LORD, and there is none else.*"

God emphasizes WHO He is three times in this chapter as I AM THE LORD, AND THERE IS NONE ELSE, THERE IS NO GOD BESIDE ME..." (versus 5, 6,18). This was the same message that the God of Israel gave to Moses as He spoke these words: "And God spake all these words, saying, I *am* the LORD thy God, which have brought thee out of the land of Egypt, out of the house of bondage. Thou shalt have no other gods before me " (Ex. 20:1-2).

What is it that makes God *holy* and that He wants us to know WHY there is none like Him? IT IS HIS HOLY AND RIGHTEOUS CHARACTER! As finite beings we simply cannot understand God's character of being infinite, omnipresent, omnipotent, sinless; omniscient; etc. God always existed, is everywhere, all powerful and all knowing, has never sinned and never changes! God alone is self-existent!

Contrariwise, human beings get heavier, older sin and die! God's character does not change! Human beings grow in knowledge and science, but God has all knowledge and wisdom! God is the Creator and sustainer of the Universe! Everything in the Universe had a beginning, except God who has always existed! That's why there is none like Him!

THE FOOLISHNESS OF GOD

Does God Create Calamity?

One of the hardest things for Christians to comprehend is, "why does God allow bad things to happen to good people if He knows everything and is all powerful to prevent disaster." After all couldn't He have prevented some of the most horrific tragedies in history such as WW1, WW2 and the holocaust or the calamity of the Twin Towers on 911?" If God could have prevented these atrocities, why didn't He?

Furthermore, can we believe that God can allow calamity or judgment upon sinners or rebellious nations? Let's look at some biblical examples. In Chronicles 13 we read of a very sorrowful event that even King David could not comprehend as God struck down Uzzah who was just trying to steady the special cart made by David and the Ark was being returned from captivity by the Philistines.

The Ark was brought by the Israelites throughout their travel in the desert and during wars. When they set to conquer Canaan under the leadership of Joshua, they carried the Ark with them, and the Jordan River split allowing them to pass into the land of Canaan (Josh. 3). In the Battle of Jericho, their first battle in the conquest of Canaan, they carried the Ark and marched around the city for days with armed men and the seven priests sounding the seven trumpets. On the seventh day, the wall of Jericho fell and the Israelites took over the city (Josh. 6). After the conquest, Joshua set up the Ark, together with the tabernacle, in Shiloh (Josh. 18). The Ark remained in Shiloh until the battle between the Israelites and the Philistines during the time of Eli.

When the Israelites were defeated by the Philistines, they took the Ark to Eben-ezer hoping to win the next battle. However, they were defeated again, and the Ark was taken by the Philistines (I Sam. 4:3-5, 10, 11). In Shiloh, the High Priest Eli fell dead upon hearing the news of the Ark's capture (I Sam. 4:12-18).

The Philistines brought the Ark with them to their capital city, Ashdod and put it in the temple of their idol god Dagon. However, on the next day, the statue of Dagon had fallen to the ground. The same thing happened again the following day. Soon after, the city of Ashdod suffered misfortune as plague after plague struck the city.

MOSES AND THE BURNING BUSH

The Ark was moved to the city of Gath and then Ekron, but the plague continued (I Sam. 5:1-12).

After keeping the Ark for seven months, the Philistines decided to return it to the Israelites together with offerings of expensive gifts upon the advice of their diviners and priests. The Ark was brought back to Beit Shemesh and then transported to Kiryat Yearim, where it stayed for twenty years (I Sam. 6:1-18, 21; 7:1-2).

This was supposed to be a jubilant parade for the return of the Ark until one of the Ox's stumbled and the Ark tilted and was in danger of falling off into the mud. In respect for the Ark, Uzzah placed his hand to steady the Ark, and was instantly struck down by the hand of God and executed!

King David could not comprehend God's judgment of this event at first as I'm sure most Christians have had problems understanding similar things in their lives and friends that seemingly happen to good people. One of the nicest supervisors I have ever worked with was a man who had an experience that would be a parent's worst nightmare, and turned him off to Christianity completely. One day, as he had done for years, and was waiting to put his young daughter on the school bus at his house, an out of control car hit and killed her before his very eyes. "How could this happen," he thought. I'm sure you have heard of similar stories! Let's look at some biblical examples in God's Word that will help us understand the holiness of God.

The Lesson of Uzza

Over the past decades, many have left God's Church, and we must ask ourselves why? Let's expound on one of the reasons for the astounding exodus. In (1 Chronicles 13) we read a vital lesson given to us in God's Word that will help explain. Starting in verse 9 of (1 Chronicles 13) we read:

> **And when they came unto the threshingflore of Chidon, Uzza put forth his hand to hold the ark; for the oxen stumbled. And the anger of the LORD was kindled against Uzza, and he smote him, because he put his hand to the ark: and there he died before God.**

THE FOOLISHNESS OF GOD

This incredible story of Uzza contains a deep spiritual lesson for us today. The inspired apostle Paul informs us that the things that happened to ancient Israel were for *our* example (1 Cor. 10:6).

But what possible lesson can we glean from this obscure event mentioned in the Word of God? Why was Uzza struck down by God for merely trying to help out in securing the ark?

The answer to this startling and tragic story for our benefit is contained in Uzzah's genealogy! Here is a brief synopsis of Uzzah's heritage:

Gen. 46:11 The tribe of Levi was separated to bear the Ark of the Covenant by COMMANDMENT of God. The sons of Levi were (Gershon, Kohath and Merai). See also (Num. 3:17; Deut. 10:8).

Ex. 6:18 The sons of Kohath were (Amram, Izhar, Hebron and Uzziel). See also (1 Chron. 23:12).

Ex. 6:20 The sons of Amram were (Moses and Aaron). See also (1 Chron. 23:13).

1 Chron. 15:5 Uzziel was the *chief* son of Kohath.

Num. 3:2 The generations of Moses and Aaron. Aaron's sons were (Nadab, Abihu, Eleazor and Ithamor).

Num. 3:30-31 Elizaphan, the son of Uzziel (the son of Kohath) shall be in charge of the Ark.

Num. 3 Each of Kohath's sons were given charge over some part of the tabernacle—but ONLY Uzziel's son Elizaphan was in charge of the Ark!

Num. 18:1-7 Aaron's house was given charge over the sanctuary.

Num. 4:15 When Aaron and his sons made an end of covering the sanctuary (their responsibility), the sons of Kohath (Uzziel's) were to bear it. But they were NOT permitted to touch any of the *holy vessels*, lest they die! ANYONE who was not given AUTHORITY

MOSES AND THE BURNING BUSH

to touch the "holy" Ark was STRUCK down by the Eternal! They were to carry the Ark with staves through rings so they would not touch the Ark (Ex. 25, 27, 30). They were not to carry the Ark on a cart, because the Ark could fall, if the Ox stumbled!

1 Sam. 5 The head and palms of the Philistine's god Dagon were cut off when the Ark of God fell into the hands of the Philistines. Many of the Philistines were destroyed in their cities as well.

1 Sam. 6:19 God smote 50,000 men of Bethshemesh because "they looked into the Ark of God."

1 Chron. 15:2 When the Ark of God was recaptured—David said none should carry the Ark except for the Levites: "...for them hath the Lord chosen to carry the Ark of God and to minister unto him forever."

1 Sam. 7 Abinadab's son Eleazor was *sanctified* to bear the Ark. But by whom?

11 Sam. 6:4 Uzza was Abinadab's son, who was smote because of his ERROR (rashness or irreverant act). But what error was it?

1 Chron.2:13 Uzza was David's nephew, as he was the son of Abinadab, David' brother.

1 Chron. 13:11 David was displeased when Uzza was smitten down, for the Lord made a *breach* upon Uzza.

1 Chron. 15:13 The *breach* was made upon Uzza because the Levites did not seek God after DUE ORDER! "And the children of the Levites bare the Ark of God upon their shoulders with the staves thereon as Moses COMMANDED according to the word of the Lord" (1 Kings 8:8; 11 Chron. 5:9).

Num. 15:10 David appointed (the chief son of Uzziel) to bear the Ark. Recall how Kohath's son Uzziel was given this responsibility by God in (Numbers 3). See also (1 Chron. 15:11-12). Originally, it was the Kohath's responsibility to carry the Ark with poles that went through iron rings and never touched the Ark. Remember, the Ark represented the very throne of God! It represented the "holiness of God."

God warned the Levites not to touch the Ark, lest they die: **"And when Aaron and his sons have made an end of covering the sanctuary, and all the vessels of the sanctuary, as the camp is to set forward; after that, the sons of Kohath shall come to bear** *it***: but they shall not touch** *any* **holy thing, lest they die. These** *things are* **the burden of the sons of Kohath in the tabernacle of the congregation" (Num. 4:15).**

When the holy Ark was falling, it was touched by the sinful hand of man. That is the lesson God was demonstrating in the account of Uzza.

Understanding this history, there are two possible reasons WHY God struck Uzza down for touching the Ark: 1) Uzza was not a Levite as we can tell from his genealogy, and 2) DUE ORDER of family genealogy was not followed as God COMMANDED in carrying the Ark. Both reasons would necessitate a *breach* or violation of law of "due order" and consequently rebellion!

The Eternal gave strict instructions that ONLY the Levites could touch the "holy things" of God! The Sabbath, the Altar, the Tithe, the Ark and the Levite priest were all "sanctified" or "set apart" by God for His Holy use by Israel. This is recorded in (Exodus 29). These were all "holy things" of God!

But was there any one thing inside the Ark that was considered sacred or "holy" by God!

Yes, indeed!

It was Aaron's "rod that budded," which was a "sign" of authority! Let us pay heed to the authority that God Almighty has ordained in His Church!

More Examples

There are several Old Testament examples of trying to usurp the authority of God's chosen leaders. The noted account of Korah's *rebellion* in Numbers 16 stands as a stern warning to all of us today!

MOSES AND THE BURNING BUSH

When Korah tried to take over Moses' seat of authority along with 250 princes of Israel, they were swallowed up in an earthquake!

We must remember that God's ministers sit in Moses' seat of authority today, and have rule over us (11 Cor. 10:8, 12, 13; Heb. 13:7, 17).

When Moses' sister Miriam started *murmuring* against her brother because of the Ethiopian woman he married—she became leprous (Num. 12:1; 10:11).

A man was struck down dead for picking up sticks on the Sabbath (Num. 15:32-36).

King Uzziah of Judah was also smitten with the plague of leprosy when he transgressed against God's *instructions* and burned incense in the Temple (11 Chron. 26).

His sin was similar to that of Uzza who was struck down for touching the holy Ark and not following due order. These men tried to fulfill holy ordained offices of the priesthood in which they were not called. The same can be said of Saul's rebellion when he offered up burnt offerings when it wasn't his *responsibility* (1 Sam. 13:9-11).

Aaron's sons Nadab and Abihu were *devoured* before the Lord, by a consuming fire from the Lord when they offered "strange fire" before the altar of the Lord.

Like many today who think there are no RULES or REGULATIONS to follow in properly worshiping the holy God above—these unholy priests, **"..,took either of them his censer, and put fire therein, and put incense thereon, and offered strange fire before the Lord which He commanded them not"** (Lev. 10:1).

Rebellion was the sin of these two eldest sons of Aaron as they neglected to fill their censers with live coals from the altar fire which had come from the Lord. This was similar to Cain making an offering without blood.

Nadab and Abihu did not perceive that it was the fire from God that had fed upon the sacrifices, and that the fragrance from their incense could not please God, unless it came through the sacrifice consumed in judgment on the altar. Thus, they failed to connect *worship* with *atonement* and thought they could offer incense without a *sacrifice!*

On the Day of Atonement, only the High Priest could enter the Holy of Holies symbolic of where God dwells. It symbolically separated sin from God's presence. There is a reason why there were thousands of bloody sacrifices in the Old Covenant. Why only on the Day of Atonement only the High Priest could enter through the curtain into the presence of God! The High Priest symbolized the atoning work of Jesus Christ. The book of Hebrews informs us that only the sacrifice of Jesus is what saves us! God wanted to impress this upon us through these thousands of sacrifices! That's why He is the Great I Am and there is none like Him!

These examples in the Word of God are for our Christian admonition, and may God help us to be submissive to His government—lest we be smitten down like Uzzah, Korah, Miriam, Nadab and Abihu!

Disease—Types of Sin

Jesus performed countless miracles throughout His 3 1/2 year public ministry. Among them were the raising of the dead, healing of the deaf and mute, blind and palsy.

Each of these diseases are *types* of "sin" that Jesus will conquer in His triumph over Satan and sin!

The wages of sin is death (Rom. 6:23), yet Jesus proved His power over sin and death by raising three individuals back to life!

Jesus healed the blind man to relate the *spiritual blindness* of the Jews (Jn. 9:14). To these BLIND Pharisees Jesus exhorted: **"...If ye were blind, ye should have no sin: but now ye say, we see; therefore your sin remaineth" (verse 41).**

To non believers, Jesus likened their condition to DEAFNESS: **"Therefore speak I to them in parables: because they seeing see not; and hearing they hear not, neither do they understand" (Matt. 13:13).**

Leprosy had the connotation to the sin of rebellion through DEFILEMENT of God's governmental structure.

Moses' sister Miriam was stricken with leprosy as a result of rebellion [murmuring] against God's chosen servant Moses—because he had married an Ethiopian woman (Num. 12:1,10-11).

King Uzziah of Judah was also smitten with the plague of leprosy when he *transgressed* against God's instructions and burned incense in the Temple (11 Chron. 26).

MOSES AND THE BURNING BUSH

His sin was similar to that of Uzzah who was struck down for touching the Holy Ark and not following due order. These men tried to fulfill holy ordained offices of the priesthood in which they were not called.

Uzziah was made a king by the people at the age of sixteen after his father was murdered. He was sixteen years old when he began to reign, and he reigned 52 years in Jerusalem. The Bible says that King Uzziah sought God in the days of Zechariah, who had understanding in the visions of God.

King Uzziah's reign was one of the most successful and most prosperous reigns in the kingdom of Judah. The Lord helped him to have conquests; he defeated the Philistines, the Arabians, and the Meunites.

King Uzziah was a good king. However, when God blessed him and he became great, rich, and famous, he became proud. Though he did not forsake the Lord at the height of his power, he was driven by pride to transgress against the Lord by attempting to do something which he was not permitted to do.

One day King Uzziah entered the temple of the Lord to burn incense on the altar of incense. But Azariah and eighty priests who were men of valor went in after him and they resisted him and said to him, "It is not for you, Uzziah, to burn incense to the Lord, but for the priests, the sons of Aaron, who are consecrated to burn incense. Go out of the sanctuary, for you have done wrong, and it will bring you no honor from the Lord God." Then Uzziah became angry with them. Now he had a censer in his hand to burn incense, and when he became angry with the priests, leprosy broke out on his forehead in the presence of the priests in the house of the Lord, by the altar of incense. And Azariah the chief priest and all the priests looked and saw that he was leprous in his forehead. And they rushed King Uzziah out of the temple quickly, and he himself hurried to go out, because the Lord had struck him. Being a leper, he lived in isolation – in a separate house- and he was unclean and was excluded from entering the house of the Lord to worship for the rest of his life. He died with leprosy for he was a leper to the day of his death.

What was Uzziah's fate for usurping God's holy office? **"And Uzziah the king was a leper unto the day of his death, and dwelt** in a several house, a leper: for he was cut off from the house of the Lord..." (verse 21).

Job was smitten with boils from the sole of his foot to his head until he learned not to be so SELF-RIGHTEOUS (Job 2:7).

As a result of Korah's rebellion, the plague broke out among the people, for their *murmuring* hearts had caught the infection of Korah's sin (Num. 16). Thus, the plague's spreading action impressed upon them the infectiousness of HERESY!

God's Covenant with Abraham

We read of a most unusual request that God instructed Abraham to make in Genesis 15:9-17:

> **So the LORD said to him, 'Bring me a heifer, a goat and a ram, each three years old, along with a dove and a young pigeon.' Abram brought all these to him, cut them in two and arranged the halves opposite each other; the birds, however, he did not cut in half...When the sun had set and darkness had fallen, a smoking firepot with a blazing torch appeared and passed between the pieces.**

This event reminds us of the miraculous "Burning Bush" that would appear to Moses! God explains the meaning and consequences of this seemingly strange event in Jeremiah 34:18-20:

> **The men who have violated my covenant and have not fulfilled the terms of the covenant they made before me, I will treat like the calf they cut in two and then walked between its pieces. The leaders of Judah and Jerusalem, the court officials, the priests and all the people of the land who walked between the pieces of the calf, I will hand over to their enemies who seek their lives. Their dead bodies will become food for the birds of the air and the beasts of the earth.**

MOSES AND THE BURNING BUSH

God told Abraham to cut a sacrifice in half, then, a smoking firepot/blazing torch (God) passed between the pieces. This represented the agreement to the covenant God made with Abraham and then passed down to his Issac and then his Jacob. In essence they signed a covenant with God in blood and sacrifice! But the leaders did not follow the terms of the covenant and God reminded them that they promised to the terms of the covenant to their death.

In the Old Testament, the English phrase "make a covenant" is most often a translation of the Hebrew **kārat berît**, which literally means "cut a covenant." Why does biblical Hebrew regularly speak of "cutting" covenants? Certainly, this idiomatic wording is used metaphorically in some cases, but more importantly it seems to reflect ancient covenant-making practices. In our day a contract often becomes legally binding when the parties sign a document detailing the terms of the agreement. In a similar way, ancient covenants often became binding by killing and cutting an animal. This may sound foreign to us in modern society, but the phrases "cut a deal."

Typically, both parties in the covenant would walk between the pieces and the burning torch (symbol of God) passes between the pieces. The person passing through is saying, in essence, "so may it happen to me (be cut in half) if I fail to keep this covenant." This is why we would say there is an unconditional element to this covenant with Abraham. Only God is obligating himself to the agreement. That doesn't mean he did not require anything of Abram, but that he would make sure Abram would keep his part of the covenant.

All of these examples were written to teach us vital spiritual lessons! Christians must learn from these examples of how God desires to be worshipped! Let us not become spiritually blind! It is not how we wish to worship God—but how He desires to be worshipped! It is not in what pleases us, but what pleases Him!

Indeed, God is just and merciful and loving—but He also, because of who He is has wrath upon those who will not worship Him the way He desires! The history of the nation of Israel is not only one of redemption from slavery and oppressors—but one of how to worship God. It contains vital lessons for us Christians! That is why there is none like Him, the Great I AM!

THE FOOLISHNESS OF GOD

Scriptures of The Great "I AM"

1. "**I am** El-Shaddai—'God Almighty' Gen. 17:1).
2. "**I am** the God of your father, Abraham" He said. "Do not be afraid, for **I am** with you and will bless you (Gen. 26:24).
3. "**I Am** Who **I Am**. Say this to the people of Israel: **I Am** has sent me to you" (Ex. 3:14).
4. And God said to Moses, "**I am** Yahweh—'the Lord' (Ex. 6:2).
5. "**I am** the Lord who heals you" (Ex. 15:26).
6. "**I am** the Lord your God, who rescued you from the land of Egypt, the place of your slavery (Ex. 20:2).
7. "**I am** merciful" (Ex. 22:27).
8. "Yahweh! The Lord! The God of compassion and mercy! **I am** slow to anger and filled with unfailing love and faithfulness" (Ex. 34:6).
9. "If you obey my decrees and my regulations, you will find life through them. **I am** the Lord" (Lev. 18:5).
10. "Be still, and know that **I am** God! I will be honored by every nation. I will be honored throughout the world" (Psalm 46:10),
11. Therefore, this is what the Sovereign Lord says: "Look! **I am** placing a foundation stone in Jerusalem, a firm and tested stone. It is a precious cornerstone that is safe to build on. Whoever believes need never be shaken" (Isa. 28:16).
12. "Don't be afraid, for **I am** with you. Don't be discouraged, for **I am** your God. I will strengthen you and help you. I will hold you up with my victorious right hand" (Isa. 41:10).
13. "**I am** the Lord; that is my name! I will not give my glory to anyone else, nor share my praise with carved idols" (Isa. 42:8).
14. "**I, yes I, am** the Lord, and there is no other Savior. First, I predicted your rescue, then I saved you and proclaimed it to the world. No foreign god has ever done this. You are witnesses that I am the only God," says the Lord" (Isa. 43:11-12).

MOSES AND THE BURNING BUSH

15. "From eternity to eternity **I am** God. No one can snatch anyone out of my hand. No one can undo what I have done" Isa. 43:13).
16. This is what the Lord says— your Redeemer and Creator: "**I am** the Lord, who made all things. I alone stretched out the heavens. Who was with me when I made the earth?" (Isa. 44:24).
17. "Remember the things I have done in the past. For I alone am God! **I am** God, and there is none like me." Isaiah 46:9
18. "I, yes **I, am** the one who comforts you. So why are you afraid of mere humans, who wither like the grass and disappear?" (Isa. 51:12).
19. "**I am** a God who is near," says the Lord. "**I am** also a God who is far away. No one can hide where I cannot see him," says the Lord. "I fill all of heaven and earth," says the Lord (Jer. 23:23-24).
20. "For **I am** the Lord! If I say it, it will happen" (Ezek, 12:25).
21. "**I am** the Lord, and I do not change" (Malachi 3:6).
22. Jesus answered, "**I am**. And in the future, you will see the Son of Man sitting at the right hand of God, the Powerful One, and coming on clouds in the sky" (Mk. 14:62).
23. Then Jesus said, "**I am** He [the Messiah]—I, the one talking to you" (Jn. 4:26).
24. "**I am** the bread that gives life" (Jn. 6:48).
25. "**I am** the light of the world. The person who follows me will never live in darkness but will have the light that gives life" (Jn. 8:12).
26. Jesus answered, "I tell you the truth, before Abraham was even born, **I am!**" (Jn. 8:58).
27. "**I am** the good shepherd. The good shepherd gives his life for the sheep" (Jn. 10:11).
28. Jesus said to her, "**I am** the resurrection and the life. Those who believe in me will have life even if they die" (Jn. 11:25).
29. Jesus answered, "**I am** the way, and the truth, and the life. The only way to the Father is through me" (Jn. 14:6).
30. "Believe me when I say that **I am** in the Father and the Father is in me. Or believe because of the miracles I have done" (Jn. 14:11).

THE FOOLISHNESS OF GOD

31. The Lord God says, "**I am** the Alpha and the Omega. **I am** the One who is and was and is coming. **I am** the Almighty" (Rev. 1:8).
32. "**I am** the One who lives; I was dead, but look, **I am** alive forever and ever" (Rev. 1:18).
33. "**I am** coming soon. Continue strong in your faith so no one will take away your crown" (Rev. 3:11).
34. The One who was sitting on the throne said, "Look! **I am** making everything new!" Then He said, "Write this, because these words are true and can be trusted" (Rev. 21:5).
35. Jesus, the One who says these things are true, says, "Yes, **I am** coming soon." Amen. Come, Lord Jesus! (Rev. 22:20).

Truly, from the Days of Noah unto this day can we say that we have learned WHO the Great "I AM" is as we see a world much like the days of Noah? Have we learned that God's ways are not our ways as stated in Isaiah 55:8-9: "For my thoughts are not your thoughts, neither are your ways my ways, saith the Lord. For as the heavens are higher than the earth, so are my ways higher than your ways, and my thoughts, than your thoughts."

Chapter Three

> *So God created man in his own image, in the image of God created he him, male and female created he them*
> —Gen. 1:27.

WHY GOD CREATED MAN

Many have wondered what is the PURPOSE of this life? Why the Great Creator God placed them on planet earth. Can these things be known? Is it merely to be saved? Saved for what purpose? Has God revealed them to us through His prophets, ministers, or His Son? The answer is an astounding YES! Notice: **"For he (God) has made known to us in all wisdom and insight the mystery of His will, according to His purpose..." (Eph. 1:9-10, RSV).**

God has indeed revealed the secret things unto His servants the prophets (Amos 3:7).

It is true we cannot understand everything of God's plan, for: **"...the secret things belong unto the Lord our God: But those things which are revealed belong unto us and to our children for ever" (Deut. 29:29).**

We will now see what things God has revealed to us and to our children!

Jesus came to REVEAL the way into the Kingdom of God! Prior to Jesus' time the people had only **"...the law and the prophets" (Lk. 16:16)**—but now **"grace and truth"** were added (Jn. 1:17).

Jesus brought the light of the gospel into the world. He came with *new information* that had not previously been revealed. Until God sent Jesus Christ with the message of the gospel, the plan of God had been somewhat enigmatic to the religious world.

A blanket of "darkness" had been spread over the Jewish people concerning the real meaning of the scriptures. Paul pointed out that **"God gave them a spirit of stupor, eyes that should not see and ears that should not hear, down to this day" (Rom. 11:8).**

Nobody had really understood, with full comprehension, the marvelous plan of God up until that time. Even Paul confessed that, **"...we know in part" (1 Cor. 13:9, KJV).**

Though we still see through **"a glass darkly" (1 Cor. 13:12),** we do see much more clearly than in ages past! God has indeed *revealed* the essential elements of His MASTER PLAN to His Church!

God's incredible plan is being worked out through the agency of His Son Jesus Christ. It was established even before the creation of the first man on earth. Jesus said, **"Come, O blessed of my Father, inherit the kingdom prepared for you from the foundation of the world" (Matt. 25:34).**

God did not reveal the entirety of His plan to the earthy patriarchs of the Old Testament. Many of the prophets earnestly desired to look into the things which we can now understand. Notice what our Savior and Creator said: **"For verily I say unto you, that many prophets and righteous men have desired to see those things which ye see, and have not seen them; and to hear those things which ye hear, and have not heard them" (Matt. 13:17).**

Jesus *has* revealed to us what has been hidden since the foundation of the world, for He said: **"...I will utter things which have been kept *secret* from the foundation of the world" (Matt. 13:35).**

God's plan was "finished"—that is, established—at the very

beginning, notice carefully: **"...His works were finished from the foundation of the world"** (Heb. 4:3). God knew, even before creation, that His Son Jesus Christ would have to come to this earth and be revealed to man. Peter wrote of this time: **"He was destined before the foundation of the world but was made manifest at the end of the times for your sake"** (1 Pet. 1:20).

God knew that He was going to select a people, an *ekklesia* [church or group], to exemplify His way of life upon the earth. He knew long before He created man through Christ: **"Even as He chose us in him before the foundation of the world, that we should be holy and blameless before him"** (Eph. 1:4).

Our great magnanimous God knew that Jesus would have to die in order to pay the penalty for human sin. The Lamb was **"...slain from the foundation of the world"** (Rev. 13:8).

Every human being, from Adam to the last human being ever born, will have his or her opportunity to become a part of God's great plan of salvation! God is not willing that any should perish, but that **"...all should come to repentance"** (11 Pet. 3:9).

Why God Created Man

Just how God was going to reproduce His PERFECT RIGHTEOUS CHARACTER into billions of beings is a most incredible revelation. God is perfect in body and mind and was now going to reproduce this **"image"** and **"likeness"**—HIS CHARACTER into billions of others. Beings that would be flawless in character and incapable of sinning—yet free to choose!

God is a Spirit Being that personifies perfection in KNOWLEDGE, WISDOM, REASONING AND CREATIVITY—in essence CHARACTER!

God was now going to make man, His *grand design,* out of physical rather than spiritual material—out of the "dust of the ground."

How is it possible that human beings, full of sin, could ever become *flawless* and perfect in character?—this answer is most incredible!

Did God Create Man Perfect?

Many Christians blindly assume God created Adam and Eve spiritually perfect. They, therefore, can only conclude that God was "surprised," and even sorrowful, to discover that the "perfect" humans whom He had just created had sinned.

According to this faulty reasoning, God then supposedly scratched His head and began thinking out a way to "repair the damage."

This traditional concept of the "fall" of man actually makes God into an unknowing Being. But God is Omniscient!

What, then, is the truth? What really did happen? Did God create Adam and Eve "perfect" like God? Insofar as being perfect specimens of humanity, and insofar as being without sin at the moment of their creation, He created them. But unlike God, they were also created with a potential capacity for weakness—the ability to sin—to choose the wrong course of action. And so, God did create a perfect man for His purpose—to be able to CHOOSE—nothing else! Just as a hammer is a perfect hammer for its purpose, but cannot be used as a saw, man was created for one purpose only—to CHOOSE!

Why an imperfect Man?

Some ask: "Why didn't God create men so that they could not sin?" Well, the simple fact that God didn't do so, is testimony to the fact that perfect Godlike character is not created instantly. Rather, it is the end product of a process of development.

God can create sinless creatures; and He has, in fact, already done so. Horses, cows, dogs, cats, frogs, snakes, etc., all are sinless. They always do exactly what they were created and designed to do.

But when God creates a being with its own Godlike mind, having its own free will, then that very power of volition inherently includes the ability to make wrong choices—the power to sin—to will to go the wrong way.

God is perfect. He has perfect character. And He can certainly create beings who have the capacity to develop perfect character. But this can only be done through the crucible of time, experience and free choice—which means that sin and suffering are always possible.

WHY GOD CREATED MAN

God did not want to fill the universe with dumb, mindless creatures devoid of willpower. Neither did He want to create mechanical automatons or robots.

Man created in God's "Image" and "Likeness"

God is creating His supreme masterpiece by two distinct steps: Man, the clay material creation (Gen. 1), is only the first phase of what is to become God's finished spiritual creation.

God created man in the clay image of Himself, from the dust of the ground. We are only in the form or **"image"** of God now, but not of the radiant composition, not of the same **"likeness"** or Character.

One can go to Florence Italy and see a statue or image of David, and it would be a *likeness* or *image*; but not the very same material. We are merely the clay model and God Almighty the Master Potter. He has made us of matter so He could *reform* and *shape* us into the final *image* that it was His original purpose to make (Isa. 64:6-8).

"Image" of God

Originally, God created man in the clay image of Himself. That is, man looks like God. Most people think it is impossible to know what God really looks like. But God has made it possible.

It is true that no human being has ever seen the Father's shape (Jn. 5:37). But remember, the second person of the God-head, who later became Jesus Christ in the flesh, has seen the Father. So, let us read how Jesus describes what the Father, the first person of the God-head looks like (Jn. 1:18).

Christ said **"...if you have seen me, you have seen the Father (Jn. 14:9).** True, Jesus was speaking primarily in a spiritual sense, but there are other scriptures that indicate the Father appears like a man! Christ indicated that He has the general form and stature of a mortal man! Didn't God say that the invisible things including the God-head, could be clearly seen by the visible creation? (Rom. 1:20).

God breathes (Gen. 2:7), has fingers (Deut. 5:22), and arms and ears (Isa. 59:1). Our heavenly Father has a heart (Gen. 8:21), a face, eyes, nose, and a mouth (Ps. 139:5, 16; 1 Pet. 3:12; Isa.

59:1-2). God has hair as white as snow, feet like fine brass, as if they had been burned in a fire, eyes like a flame of fire (Rev. 1:13-17; Dan. 10:6). His voice is as the sound of many waters (Rev. 1:15).

In (Genesis 1:27) we read, **"In the image of God...male and female created he them."** Therefore, "in the image of God" does not demand one sex or the other. Each is equally "in the image of God." To be male doesn't make one more in the likeness of God than to be female—each equally reflects God.

Because both male and female are "in the image of God" it must be because of what each has in common—two arms, two legs, a human body shape, a head with two eyes, two ears, a nose, a mouth—and most important of all a mind!

Color of skin is not a factor, any more than color of eyes, hair or age.

In God's first phase of creation then, we see how God has created man in His "IMAGE" physically, out of the dust of the ground. When this first phase is completed, man is going to be composed exactly of the very "image" of God who is composed of SPIRIT! (Jn. 4:24).

"Likeness" of God

In the beginning, God did not place within man a divine nature whereby he would also resemble God inwardly—SPIRITUALLY. We do not yet possess God's nature, CHARACTER or LIKENESS!

Adam had a fleshly, carnal nature within him—and like begets like. That's the kind of nature the human race was born with! So, man resembles God in *external* "form" and "shape" only—not in spiritual CHARACTER.

God Himself could not create beings with the power of choice and then give them instant godly character! To develop this godlike *character* takes time and experience. This is why God created men with the capacity for weakness.

If God could have created man with inherent, perfect, godlike character, He would have assuredly done so. Our Creator is a God of infinite love and mercy. He certainly would not have made man subject to "vanity" or "temptation" with the awful potential of sinning and suffering—if this could have been avoided!

Instead, God is creating this perfect character in and through those who now VOLUNTARILY yield to Him and His process of salvation. This process [of repentance, acceptance of Christ, and of godly living] continues throughout our lifetime through the indwelling of the Spirit of God. In this way, we are to come unto a perfect man, unto the measure of the stature of the fullness of Christ (Eph. 4:13). This process of developing GODLY CHARACTER was something which the Creator thought out long before man was created.

And so, the second phase of God's creation, "LIKENESS", has to do with the SPIRITUAL, the MIND, ATTITUDE, OR CHARACTER development!

Godly Character

Turning our attention to (Isaiah 55:8-9), we read of God's *character*. There, Isaiah records the mind of God that each of us will have eventually:

> **For my thoughts are not your thoughts,**
> **neither are your ways my ways, saith the Lord.**
> **For as the heavens are higher than the earth,**
> **so are my ways higher than your ways, and my**
> **thoughts, than your thoughts.**

God is Holy (Ps. 99:9). The word "Holy" means pure of heart or free from sin.

God is Spirit (Jn. 4:24). God is Love (1 Jn. 4:8). Love is a GIVING attitude, rather than a *getting* attitude.

God cannot lie (Tit. 1:2; Heb. 6:18).

God is merciful and gracious, slow to anger, and plenteous in mercy (Ps. 103:8).

God looks not on the outward appearance, but on the heart or attitude of a person (1 Sam. 16:7).

God forgives all our iniquities, and heals our diseases (Ps. 103:3).

God's power and understanding is infinite (Ps. 147:4-5). How unsearchable are His judgments, wisdom, and ways, who is His Counsellor? Who hath known the mind of God (Rom. 11:33-34).

God calls the stars by their names (Ps. 147:4-5). He knows

THE FOOLISHNESS OF GOD

the number of hairs on our head (Matt. 10:30). God knows the number of steps we take (Job 14:16, 31:4). With God all things are possible (Matt. 19:26).

God laughs (Ps. 2:4, 37:13, 59:8), and likes wine (Judges 9:13; Matt. 26:29; Eccl. 9:7). He enjoys eating and drinking (Gen. 18; Lk. 15:23). God likes dancing (Jer. 31:4; Lk. 15:25). God faints not, neither gets weary [tired] (Isa. 40:28).

God gets angry (Ps. 7:11). Seven things the Lord hates: A proud look, a lying tongue, hands that shed innocent blood, a wicked heart, mischievous feet, a false witness that lies, he that disseminates discord among brethren (Prov. 6:16-19).

God says the whole earth is His (Ex. 19:5; Job 41:10). God owns all the gold and silver (Hag. 2:8). God sets up the bounds of nations (Acts 17:26; Deut. 32:7-8), and gives His Kingdom to whomsoever He will (Dan. 2:20-21, 4:17, 25). God breaks down, and builds again, the deceived and deceiver are His. God makes judges fools, sets up kings and removes them, overthrows the mighty, takes away understanding from the aged, weakens the mighty, increases and destroys nations (Job. 12:9-25).

God creates evil (Prov. 16:4; Isa. 45:7; Amos. 3:6). The Hebrew word here is also translated as "disaster" and "calamity" in some Bibles. God does not create evil, but allows evil to exist by His permissive will. In other words, God could stop evil if He so desired, but chooses to allow it to exist to fulfill His divine good purpose.

God takes responsibility for the deaf, mute, and blind (Ex. 4:11). God determines the outcome of wars (Ps. 33). God hardened the Pharaoh' heart [though Pharaoh did it to himself] (Rom. 9:15-26).

God is not the author of Confusion (1 Cor. 14:33).

God can change His mind. There are countless examples in the Bible where God changed His mind because of prayer and one's righteous relationship. Abraham talked God out of destroying all the righteous people in Sodom and Gomorrah (Gen. 18:20-33). Moses talked God out of destroying all of Israel (Ex. 32). God changed His mind about King Hezekiah because of his prayer of repentance, and God granted 15 additional years to his life (11 Kings 20:1-6). See also Num. 11:1-2; 14:12-20; 16: 20-35; 41-48; 1Kings 21:27-29; 2Kings 13:3-5; 21:27-29; 1 Chron. 21:15).

God works in mysterious ways. God sent Joseph into

WHY GOD CREATED MAN

slavery to preserve Israel during a famine (Gen. 45:5).

Every good and perfect gift is from God above (Jas. 1:17). God will finish His Creation that He started (Phil. 1:3; Ps. 138:8).

God cares for us (1 Pet. 5:7), and will not fail, nor forsake us (Deut. 31:6). Like as a father pities his children, so the Lord pities them that fear Him (Ps. 103:13). God is our comforter (11 Cor. 7:6), and loves us (1 Jn. 4:19). He wants to save the whole world (Jn. 3:16-17), and is not willing that any should perish (1 Tim. 2:1-4).

God has the ability to look inside a person to see what makes him tick (1 Sam. 16:7).

God does not change His Mind or attitude toward sin (Mal. 3:6; Heb. 13:8).

To be created then in "the likeness of God," means to be developing in the very nature of God—HIS FANTASTIC MIND!

What is Man?

Turning to (Genesis 2:7), we find where the creation of man is recorded: **"Then the Eternal formed man of the dust of the ground and breathed into his nostrils the breath of life and MAN became a living soul."** Notice, *man became a living soul*; that is what man is—a soul!

There is no mention here that man *has* a soul, but that man *is* a soul!

When God placed Adam and Eve in the garden, He issued this command to the two living souls:

> **And the Eternal God commanded the man, saying, Of every tree of the garden thou mayest freely eat: But of the tree of the knowledge of good and evil, thou shalt not eat of it: for in the day that thou eatest thereof thou shalt surely die.**

When God said Adam would surely die for taking of the wrong fruit, He was directly informing man of the penalty for sin. The apostle Paul wrote, **"For the wages of sin is *death*; but the gift of God is eternal life *through* Jesus Christ our Lord"** (Rom. 6:23).

Ezekiel was directed by the Holy Spirit to write, **"The soul that sinneth, it [the soul] shall *die"* (Ezek. 18:4, 20).**

Death is the absence of life, the cessation of life—not the continuation of life under different circumstances.

Notice the two opposite states given in (Romans 6:23). God tells us the wages of sin is DEATH, but on the other hand, the GIFT OF GOD [not something we were born with] is eternal life through Jesus Christ!

If eternal life is the Gift of God, and comes only through Christ, how is it that humans have assumed they already possess eternal life in the form of an "immortal soul"?

John 3:16 is often quoted concerning salvation, but few connect the rest of the verse: **"For God so loved the world, that he gave his only begotten Son, that whosoever believeth in him should not perish, but have everlasting life."** To perish means to cease from living!

Man is a Soul

The Hebrew word in (Genesis 2:7) for soul is *nephesh* and means "a breathing creature, i.e. animal or vitality" and is also rendered in the English as "any, appetite, beast, body, breath, creature... man, me, mind, mortality." (See No. 5315, *Strong's Exhaustive Concordance).*

Nephesh cannot mean, under any circumstances, *anything* immortal, eternal, extra-physical or possessing life other than temporary and mortal! In (Genesis 1:24, 20, 21, 2:19, 9:10, 12, 15, and 16) the Hebrew word *nephesh* is used to mean "creature." In (Leviticus 21:11, Numbers 6:6, 9:6,7 and 10; 19:11, 13 and 16) the Hebrew word *nephesh* is translated "dead body."

God told Noah the life of any animal, or *nephesh* was in the blood! **"But flesh with the life [Heb. *nephesh*] thereof, which is the blood thereof, shall ye not eat" (Gen. 9:4).** Here, the word "life" comes from the same Hebrew word *nephesh* which is elsewhere rendered "soul" or "body." In (verse 5) the same word is used for our English word "life," this time in reference to *Noah* and every man! The life of man and the life of animals is the same! MORTAL life!

In (Isaiah 53), concerning the prophecy of the coming Messiah to die for the world, God shows it was the *soul* of Christ that was given for us: **"Yet it pleased the Eternal to bruise him,** he hath put him to grief: when thou shalt make his soul [*nephesh*] an offering for sin."

The origin of the "Immortal Soul"

The *Jewish Encyclopedia* states under "Immortality of the Soul" that the thought came to the Jews from contact with the Greek philosophy of Plato, who got his beliefs from Babylonians and Egyptians.

Recall, the Jews were taken captive, first by the Babylonians, and that empire was swallowed up by the Medo-Persians and finally the Greeks.

Herodotus, the Greek historian who lived in the 5th century B.C. admitted: "The *Egyptians* were also the *first* that asserted that the soul of man is *immortal*" (*Euterpe*, 123).

It was the Greek Socrates, who travelled to Egypt and consulted the Egyptians on this very teaching, who, after his return to Greece, imparted the concept to Plato, his most famous pupil. Plato wrote in his book the *Phaedo*:

> **The soul whose inseparable attribute is life will never admit of life's opposite, death. Thus, the soul is shown to be *Immortal*, and since immortal, *indestructible*...Do we believe there is such a thing as death? to be sure. And is this anything but the *separation of the soul and body*? And being dead is the attainment of this separation, when the soul exists in herself and separate from the body, and the body is parted from the soul. That is death—Death is merely the separation of soul and body.**

Plato, the student of Socrates, did not believe death was really death! Rather, he conceived it as a separation of the "soul" from the body.

After Plato came Aristotle, who perpetuated the theory, then Virgil (70-19 B.C.).

Justin Martyr, an early Catholic philosopher turned professing Christian (A.D. 160) said he expected immortality from the promise (*Ante-Nicene Fathers*, vol. 1, pg. 176).

Origen, an early Catholic teacher in Alexandria, Egypt

started Neo-Platonism in A.D. 200. He used the Bible to prove Platoism. He said, "Souls are immortal as God himself" (*Ante-Nicene Fathers*, Vol. iv, pg. 314, 402).

Arnobius, an early church father during Constantine's time said the same thing as did Origen (*Ante-Nicene Fathers,* Vol. vi, pg 440).

Thomas Aquinas, an Italian scholastic teacher and theologian (A.D. 1225-1274) stamped the doctrine of the "immortality of the soul" on the Christian world.

Fifty years later, Dante Aleghieri wrote the famous poem "The Divine Comedy," which was his imaginary concept of hell, purgatory, and paradise.

In 1513 during the Protestant Reformation, Pope Clement V declared anyone who didn't believe in the doctrine of the immortality of the soul was a heretic. Martin Luther didn't believe it (Defense, Proposition No. 27; *Historical View* pg. 344; *Life of Luther*, Bohms' edition, pg. 133 (Michelets). See also (*The Outline of History*, by H.G. Wells, pg. 386). So, Luther was branded a heretic by the Pope!

"Luther held that the soul died with the body, and that God would hereafter raise both the one and the other" (*Historical View*, pg. 344).

Luther states in Michelet's *Life of Luther,* Bohn's edition, pg. 133, "It is probable, in my opinion, that with very few exceptions indeed, the dead sleep in utter insensibility till the day of judgment...On what authority can it be said that the souls of the dead may not sleep...in the same way that the living pass in profound slumber the interval between their downlying at night and their uprising in the morning?"

Man created subject to Human Nature

We have seen *what* God is and *what* He looks like—His "image" and "likeness." But man is not the same now *physically* or *mentally* in his entirety.

God formed man in His "image" out of the dust of the ground (Gen. 2:7). This is an entirely different composition than God, for God is of spirit composition (Jn. 4:24).

Man is of the earth, earthly (1 Cor. 15:47), earthly *physically* as well as *spiritually* or mentally in comparison to God's divine nature. If Adam were already perfect in character—a perfect

WHY GOD CREATED MAN

masterpiece of God's creation—why did God tell him that if he ate of the tree of the knowledge of good and evil he would surely die? (Gen. 2:15-17). It would have been *impossible* for Adam to sin if he were perfect! But man is not perfect—in body or mind, as is God!

Instead, the Bible tells us man's **"...carnal mind [the one Adam had] is enmity against God: For it is not subject to the laws of God, neither indeed can be" (Rom. 8:7).** This nature in man is the opposite of God's nature. This *human nature* does not want to acknowledge God's laws. Man also has a heart: **"... that is *deceitful* above all things, and desperately wicked" (Jer. 17:9).**

More of this human nature in man is found in Proverbs 14:12: **"There is a way which seems right to a man (Adam used this reasoning) but the end thereof is the way of death."** Proverbs 3:5 tells us, **"Trust not in your own understanding."** In (Psalm 39:5) and (Isaiah 40:17), we are told that man in his best state is altogether vanity. Human nature was made subject to vanity: but will be delivered from it (Rom. 8:20; 11 Pet. 2:18; 1 Pet. 4:12). While in this state of mind, **"...we are all as an unclean thing and our righteousness is as filthy rags"** [to God]... (Isa. 64:6).

Many have supposed that "human nature" was instilled in each human being at birth, but they are grossly mistaken. Jesus clearly shows us in (Matthew 18:1-3), that little children are innocent and naturally good. Notice: **"Verily I say unto you, except ye be converted, and become as little children, ye shall not enter into the Kingdom of heaven."**

After God had created everything, including mankind, He said it was "very good" (Gen. 1:31). Did God bless Adam and Eve and expect them to live in accordance with His ways and laws by creating a satanic, diabolical nature in them? Of course not! Adam and Eve were created with as innocent a nature as the little children Jesus held in His arms!

Many have also erroneously assumed Adam and Eve to have been created with an evil nature and passed it on to all of mankind through heredity—but this is simply not true as the doctrine of "original sin" demands!

Originally, Adam and Eve did not *have human* nature and neither did their offspring. How then, did all of mankind, including our first parents acquire it?

THE FOOLISHNESS OF GOD

The apostle Paul explains the mystery of *human nature* in (11 Corinthians 11:2-3). Let's read it: **"But I fear, lest by any means, as the serpent beguiled Eve through his *subtilty*, so your minds should be corrupted from the simplicity that is in Christ."**

This scripture informs us, the Serpent beguiled Eve or DECEIVED Eve! It was by *deception* that the devil got Eve to distrust the instruction God gave them. Notice further how Satan deceived Adam—through Eve: **"And Adam was not deceived [by Satan], but the woman being deceived was in the transgression" (1 Tim. 2:14).**

Satan deceived Eve, but Adam knew better and rejected the knowledge of what was good and what is evil. In other words, they decided for themselves what was right and wrong!

It was at this time that Satan's *rebellious* spirit entered their minds and their eyes were opened (Gen. 3:7). The truth of God had vanished from their minds and was now replaced by Satan's evil and perverted mind.

It was at this time that they realized they were naked, and covered themselves with fig leaves thinking sex was shameful (Gen. 3:7). Their minds had become twisted and warped like Satan's!

The evil HUMAN NATURE that had now become a part of them did not come from God—but from Satan! Adam and Eve were not created with an evil rebellious mind and neither was Lucifer!

The Spirit in Man

God says of man in Genesis 3:19: **"...for dust thou art, and unto dust shalt thou return."** When we die, our physical body goes back to the ground—but there is also a non-physical spirit in mankind that goes back to God. The Bible is clear that this spirit is not God's Holy Spirit!

Turn now to (Job 32:8) to learn more of the spirit in man: **"There is a *spirit in Man*: and the inspiration of the Almighty giveth them understanding."** Again, we read of Man's spirit in Zechariah: **"The Lord formed the *spirit of man* within him" (Zech. 12:1).**

It is by the spirit that God has put into each human being that the transition from *flesh* and *blood* to *spirit* can take place at

WHY GOD CREATED MAN

the resurrection!

The composition of man is *physical*—flesh and blood. But God is composed of *spirit*, a different composition than *matter*. Since matter cannot be converted into spirit composition, God has used a most unique method of changing mortal flesh and blood humans into immortal and eternal spirit.

It is by this unique nonphysical "spirit in mankind" that makes them different than animals and makes possible the transition from *human* to *divine*.

Although each human is *not* born with human nature, they are born with this unique nonphysical component in them. It is through the five senses that the physical brain sees and feels pain. It is the "spirit in man" that lifts the physical brain from the animal level to the plateau of man.

Do not misunderstand! The "spirit in man" is not the same as "the Holy Spirit." It is the Holy Spirit that raises the level of man to the plateau of divine (see volume 1, pg 8)!

Although "the spirit in man" cannot reason or think by itself, it bestows power to the brain to think and have *personality*.

The Bonding of the Spirit

Let's realize how this *human spirit* works hand in glove with God's Holy Spirit. Notice in 1 Corinthians 2:11-16:

> **For what man knoweth the things of a man, save [except] the spirit which is in him? Even so the things of God knoweth no man, but the Spirit of God. Now we have received, not the spirit of the world [Satan's spirit], but the spirit which is of God; that we might know the things that are freely given to us of God. Which things also we speak, not in the words which man's wisdom teacheth, but which the Holy Spirit teacheth; comparing spiritual things with spiritual. But the natural man [the man who only has the spirit in man] receiveth not the things of the Spirit of God: for they are foolishness unto him: neither can he know them, because they are spiritually discerned.**

More understanding of God's Holy Spirit uniting with the "spirit in man" is found in Romans 8:16: **"The Spirit [God's Holy Spirit] itself beareth witness with our spirit [the spirit in man], that we are the children of God."**

There is indeed a "spirit in man" and this spirit can unite with either God's Holy Spirit to impart spiritual truth and understanding, or with Satan's spirit to cause confusion, doubt, deception, lust, greed, vanity jealousy and rebellion of God's way of life.

To the Church at Ephesus, God said through the apostle Paul: **"And you (who)...in time past...walked according to the prince of this world, according to the prince of the POWER OF THE AIR, the spirit that now worketh in the children of disobedience..." (Eph. 2:1-2).**

Satan is called here **"the prince of the power of the AIR"**! We could not have understood what this meant before the advent of communication by air waves. However, this is exactly *how* Satan works to deceive man—by *broadcasting* through the air in MOODS or attitudes! Music is transmitted through the air, and television wavelengths that we cannot see. We all know there are invisible wavelengths in the air such as ultraviolet rays.

The spirit in every human being is automatically tuned in on Satan's wavelength. You don't hear anything because he does not broadcast in words—nor in sounds, whether music or otherwise. He broadcasts in ATTITUDES! He broadcasts in attitudes of self-centeredness, lust, greed, vanity, jealousy, envy, resentment, competition, strife, bitterness, and hate. This is termed *human nature*, but is SATAN'S NATURE and can be inculcated into man by being tuned into Satan!

There is a wonderful Biblical illustration that demonstrates how Satan's spirit and God's spirit internalize with "the spirit in man." When God wanted to cause captive Jews in ancient Babylon to return to Jerusalem to build the second Temple, He put it in the mind of Cyrus, king of Persia. We read of this most fascinating account in Ezra 1:1: **"...the Lord stirred up *the spirit of Cyrus* king of Persia, that he made a proclamation throughout all his kingdom, and put it also in writing."** Notice, God did not speak to Cyrus by words, but caused him to know God's will by stirring up his "human spirit."

Utilizing this same principle, Satan, prince of *the power of the air* and master counterfeiter of God's truths, stirs up the spirits of humans, injecting into them carnal attitudes. Satan instills moods, and impulses of selfishness, vanity, lust, and greed, attitudes of resentment against authority, of jealousy and envy, of competition and strife, of resentment and bitterness, of violence, murder and war.

The apostle Paul recognized that Satan appeals to "the spirit in man," and recorded the following for our admonition, notice:

> **Do you think that the scripture saith in vain, the spirit that dwells in us [the spirit in man] lusteth to envy? (Jas. 4:5). For I know that in me [in my flesh] dwelleth no good thing... (Rom. 7:18). For the flesh lusteth against the spirit, and the spirit against the flesh: and these are contrary the one to the other: so that ye cannot do the things that ye would [what your mind wants to do] (Gal. 5:17).**

Paul describes what Satan's spirit will cause as "works of the flesh" and what will be the penalty for those who succumb to Satan's influence:

> **Now the works of the flesh are manifest, which are these: adultery, fornication, uncleanness, lasciviousness, idolatry, witchcraft, hatred, variance, emulations, wrath, strife, seditions, heresies, envyings, murders, drunkenness, revellings, and such like: of which I tell you in the past, that they which do such things shall not inherit the Kingdom of God (Gal. 5:19-21).**

Paul continues to warn those under Satan's influence, that (effeminate, nor abusers of themselves with mankind, thieves, covetous, extortioners, liars, those who practice filthiness, foolish talking, jesting, whoremongers), none of these has any inheritance in the Kingdom of God (1 Cor. 6:9; 1 Tim. 1:10; Eph. 5:3).

Finally, John gives us this warning: **"The fearful, unbelieving, abominable, murderers, whoremongers, sorcerers, idolaters, and all liars, shall have their part in the lake of fire" (Rev. 21:8).**

Human Nature is subject to jealousy, greed, vanity, envy, selfishness, but God did not put these evil feelings in us when we were born.

God had not completed the creation of Man at the creation of Adam and Eve. The physical creation was completed, as our first parents had this "human spirit" at their creation. But now must follow the *spiritual* creation. This required a second spirit in man—God's Holy Spirit! When God's Holy Spirit unites with the spirit in us, we can understand spiritual things, not just physical things (see Rom. 8:16; 1 Cor. 2:11-16).

When we die, the spirit in us [not the Holy Spirit] goes "upward" back to God (Eccl. 3:21, 12:7; Lk. 23:46; Acts 7:59). The spirit in animals goes "downward" when they die. It is our personality or MIND that is restored, despite the fact that the body decays. God will at the resurrection put our SPIRIT or MIND back in a body—only it will be a spiritual body (1 Cor. 15).

It is as though our MIND or SPIRIT is like a computer diskette, and our body as a computer. Upon death, God has filed our diskette—US, what we are—to be put in a different computer [different body] at the resurrection! Steven understood that his spirit would go back to God as recorded in (Acts 7:59).

Man Created Incomplete

There are *four* main stances that science uses to explain human behavior (human nature). They are the, 1) *Behavior* approach—this stance believes there are no absolutes (right or wrong). They believe a person is what he or she is and you cannot, and should not try to change him. 2) *Cognitive*—this approach contends our minds actively receive information and transform it into truth. 3) *Analytical*—this school believes our unconscious instincts determine our behavior. 4) *Humanistic*—this stance says that human nature is basically good—just leave man alone and he will solve all his problems.

But each of these schools of thought *fail* to realize that human nature is not good, and cannot be changed by man alone! Human nature cannot be changed by man, anymore that the Ethiopian can change the color of his skin, or the leopard his spots (Jer. 13:23). Only the omnipotent God can change human nature through His Holy Spirit!

The apostle Paul had this to say about the psychology of human nature: **"For I know that in me [that is in my flesh] dwelleth no good thing: for to will is present with me; but how to perform that which is good I find not" (Rom. 7:18).**

That is why people are doing their "own thing" today and don't even know that "alternate life styles", is SIN!

Such people are deceived and have yielded to their human nature, without realizing: **"There is a way which seemeth right unto a man, but the end thereof are the ways of death" (Prov. 14:12).**

God did not place within man the living spiritual attitude that only He has—the attitude characteristic of His Holy Spirit! God's Holy Spirit imparts the spiritual love and power man desperately needs to develop God's character, and fulfill His *Royal* spiritual law of love.

Our loving and gracious God has promised that He will begin to share His very own divine nature with us. He has promised to do this by *begetting* us with His Holy Spirit—provided that we will truly repent of disobeying His way of life, completely surrender our own will to His will, and have faith in the cleansing blood of Jesus Christ. Then the All-loving God will place His Holy Spirit of life and power within us, thus making it possible for us to begin living by His eternal, Royal law of love and begin developing the very nature and character of God.

Chapter Four

FAMILY LIFE IN THE MILLENNIUM

In this chapter we will explore how the All-wise Creator God designed the physical family around His SPIRITUAL FAMILY— the Church today, and it's *family* life as a *type* of millennial life!

Sound incredible? It's true!

We will plainly show how the husband and wife roles, the children and family relationship, and the entire egg-fetus cycle to birth, vividly portray the Christian experience.

Through unambiguous scriptures, we will show positively how the *physical* husband and wife relationship *picture* the Church as the *glorious* affianced Bride of Christ.

Furthermore, it will be explained how the human begettal of embryo-fetus development to birth, graphically illustrates the spiritual birth of a Christian.

Finally, we will show that the relationship of these three elements of a family—father, mother (wife) and children, are the same entities in the God Family!

Animals Don't Marry

Have you ever wondered *why* human beings get married? It's not to have sex—for that can be done without marriage, and is being done more and more in today's promiscuous society!

Furthermore, it's not to reproduce, for that also can be done without marriage. Animals don't get married—yet they have sex and reproduce.

Why then is marriage a DIVINE INSTITUTION ordained by God Almighty? Let's read on, to find the answer!

A Divine Institution

To comprehend the great awesome purpose for marriage, we must first realize that sex and marriage are God-ordained. The reason God created the woman is found in Genesis 2:18:

> **And the Lord God said, it is not good that man should be alone; I will make an help meet [mate] for him...But for Adam there was not found an help meet (mate) for him...**

God then caused a deep sleep in Adam, and took one of his ribs:

> **And the rib, which the Lord God had taken from man, made he a woman, and brought her unto the man. And Adam said, this is now bone of my bones, and flesh of my flesh: she shall be called woman, because she was taken out of man. Therefore, shall a man leave his father and his mother, and shall cleave unto his wife: and they shall be one flesh (Gen. 2:22-24).**

Clearly, God's original purpose for creating man and woman was to become ONE, or *complete,* through sexual copulation!

It was through the marriage institution that God joined male and female together, each being *incomplete* without the other. Together, they could learn to share and give—in essence, to LOVE!

Through sex, they would learn to love one another and also fulfill God's second purpose for sex as recorded in Genesis 1:28: **"Be fruitful, and multiply, and replenish the earth and subdue it..." (Gen. 1:28).**

By raising children, both would learn the responsibility of teaching and training them godly principles. The results would

THE FAMILY OF GOD

be a tranquil and happy home.

When two marriage partners love each other, they will *give* themselves to each other in every way. They will express this love through the sexual union.

The apostle Paul commanded each partner to fulfill this responsibility, realizing Satan can tempt you if you're negligent. Paul says directly and candidly to mates who are fasting:

> **Let the husband render unto the wife due benevolence: and likewise also the wife unto the husband. The wife hath not power of her own body, but the husband: and likewise also the husband hath not power of his own body, but the wife. Defraud ye not one the other, except it be with consent for a time, that ye may give yourselves to fasting and prayer; and come together again,** *that Satan tempt you not for your incontinency* **(1 Cor. 7:3-5).**

Sexual intercourse is the *ultimate* expression of physical love for two marriage partners in its highest human form. When two partners are united in mind and heart, it is only natural that they be united in body. God has made this union sacred through the marriage institution.

Sex Not Shameful

When God created sex in Adam and Eve, He told them to be *fruitful* and *multiply*. He said it [sex] was very good, notice: **"And God saw *everything* that he had made, and behold, it [including sex] was very good."**

While both were naked, Adam and Eve did not think sex was a sin: **"And they were both naked, the man and his wife, *and were not ashamed*"** (Gen. 2:25).

Only after our first parents sinned did sex become shameful to them in their eyes: **"...and *they* sewed fig leaves together, and made themselves aprons" (Gen. 3:7).** However, it wasn't God who told them that they were naked and made sex shameful: **"And he (God) said, who told thee that thou wast naked?...And the woman said, The serpent [Satan] beguiled me, and I did eat" (Gen. 3:11-13).** Notice, it was SATAN who made sex shameful in man's eyes, not God!

Sex is a natural God-given blessing as the apostle Paul states in Romans 1:27: **"And likewise also the men, leaving the natural use of the woman..."**

Paul says here without reservation, that sex is a natural thing between a man and a woman!

The writer of Hebrews further writes of the marriage union: **"Marriage is honourable in all, and the bed undefiled [not defiled or wrong]..." (Heb. 13:4).**

Paul told Timothy that in the end times there would be some, **"Forbidding to marry..." which was a doctrine of demons (1 Tim. 4:1-3).**

Depicts Spiritual Marriage

The physical union of a man and a woman in marriage is a *type* of spiritual union and marriage between Christ and His Church. This is a most fascinating truth.

Spiritually, Christ is going to marry the Church, His own spiritual body! At the time of matrimony, they will become ONE flesh!

Here's what Ephesians 5:22-23 says of this analogy:

> **Wives, *submit* yourselves unto your own husbands, as unto the Lord. For the husband is the head of the wife, EVEN AS Christ is the head of the Church: and He is the Savior of the body. Therefore, as the Church is subject unto Christ, so let the wives be to their own husbands *in everything*.**

This was God's intended purpose for woman since creation, as He said: **"...thy desire shall be to thy husband, and he shall *rule* over thee" (Gen. 3:16).** See also (Col. 3:18; 1 Cor. 11:3; Gal. 3:16; Tit. 2:3-5).

God's apostle to the Gentiles who was no male chauvinist as some claim, continues the husband's role in Ephesians 5:25:

> **Husbands, *love* your wives, even as Christ also loved the church, and gave himself for it: That he might sanctify and cleanse it with the**

> **washing of water by the Word, That he might present it to himself a glorious church, not having spot, or wrinkle, or any such thing; but that it should be holy and without blemish. So ought men to love their wives as their own bodies. He that loveth his wife loveth himself.**

Not only Paul, but Peter gave strong admonition to husbands and wives. Peter wrote in (1 Peter 3:1) to the wives:

> **Likewise, ye wives, be in *subjection* to your own husbands; that, if any obey not the word, they also may without the word be won by the conversation of the wives; while they behold your chaste conversation coupled with fear.**

To the husbands, Peter wrote these words in verse 7:

> **Likewise, ye husbands, dwell with them according to knowledge, giving *honour* unto the wife, as unto the weaker vessel, and as being heirs together of the grace of life; that your prayers be not hindered.**

It is indeed unfortunate that all husbands and wives don't heed the advice of these inspired apostles! See also (1 Pet. 3:25,28; Col. 3:19).

From this spiritual relationship of husband (Jesus) and wife (Church), can the earthly husband and wife roles be understood. Just as Jesus was the HEAD of the Church and gave Himself by serving, helping, training, providing, educating and protecting— so is the earthly husband's role to perform for his wife.

A Christian wife should also be a *faithful* wife, even as the Church should be to Jesus in applying God's ordained laws and principles.

Through the marriage union, man and woman are made ONE through the understanding of their marital roles. By fulfilling each role, we learn the spiritual relationships between Christ and HIs Church! Both husband and wife should submit to one another in the fear of the Eternal in fulfilling their respective marital responsibilities (Eph. 5:21).

Women to keep in Silence?

Although the relationship between a husband and a wife depicts spiritual roles between the Church and Jesus Christ—we must realize that on a human plane, it was never God's intended purpose to have the male role dominate the female in such a way that she have a non-leadership responsibility.

Some have interpreted the apostle Paul's words, **"But I suffer [permit] not a woman to teach, nor to usurp authority over the man, but to be in silence" (1 Tim. 2:12)**, to mean that God was addressing authority in the Church. However, Paul was not addressing (2:1-2) authority in the Church, but rather (2:8-9) glorying, or self-exaltation which was a greater problem in the Church at that time.

The problem was not who had the right to speak per se, rather authority, for some women wanted to rule over the men. Verse 12 is not forbidding women to speak or teach in the Church, but that they should not try to usurp the authority from those God had chosen. The Bible tells us that women are in fact to be teachers of good things (Tit. 2:3). Women had authority over the younger (1 Tim. 5:14).

In God's command to His creation, He told both man and women to have dominion [power, supremacy, rulership] over the creatures (Gen. 1:26-28). As marriage to God in His spiritual family will produce "one flesh" with power to rule— both male and female have been given dominion to exercise authority over the earth even as God!

Abortion

Inceasingly, pressures have been accelerating in the western world to make abortions legal.

Should abortions be made legal? Or is it considered *murder* as some religions advocate?

At what stage in a woman's pregnancy is the unification of a male sperm with a female egg, considered "a life"? And if it is a life, does God consider it *murder* if a woman decides to have an abortion?

In 1973, the Supreme Court allowed abortion in the U.S. in the well known Roe versus Wade decision. But what was their decision based upon? They said, *"We need not resolve the difficult question of when life begins...the judiciary at this point in the development of man's knowledge is not in a position to speculate as to the answer."*

So, they admit that man is incapable of understanding when life begins! Furthermore, they admitted as to who has the right to make this decision according to the 14th Amendment of the U.S. constitution, *"If this suggestion of personhood (when life begins) is established, the appellant's for the fetus' right to life is then guaranteed specifically by the 14th Amendment...nor shall any stated deprive any person of life, liberty or property, without due process of law, nor deny to any person within its jurisdiction the equal protection of the law...congress shall have the power to enforce, by appropriate legislation, the provisions of this article."*

The answer to this controversial question can only be answered by the giver of life, not congress or anyone but—God Himself! The Almighty One who forbids murder in His Ten Commandments, is the only one who can tell us WHEN a life starts and IF terminating a life is considered as murder!

Human Birth

Many Bible oriented individuals have come to realize that there is a *duality* of human experiences to divine principles. It is through the *human* conception of embryo-fetus development to birth that *spiritual* birth can be understood.

Scientists tell us that human conception takes place when a male sperm enters the ovum or "egg" produced by the female and is fertilized!

By understanding "physical birth," we can relate this to "spiritual birth" in what the Bible calls being "born again" and RESURRECTED!

Spiritual Birth

The term "resurrected from the dead" refers to the regeneration process that begins when we receive God's Holy Spirit and begin repenting of our sins. At the end of our lifetime, IF we have been faithful to God, our bodies will be transformed to spirit at the resurrection of the dead as many scriptures verify.

It is only at this precise juncture that Christians will be *changed* completely to spirit and born of the spirit. Jesus was the firstborn of many brethren (Rom. 8:29). It is by this same process that Christians are BORN into the family of God and inherit the Kingdom of God.

The Bible terms the condition Christians are in now as spirit-led sons of God. A Christian's spiritual life begins when God's Holy Spirit enters him from God the Father. This is the "sperm" of "spiritual life" even as physical sperm from the male impregnates the female ovum in human begettal. As the Christian begins the conversion process, he is if uninterrupted, eventually resurrected or born into God's family.

Notice this spiritual relationship as outlined by Paul in his epistle to the Romans:

> **For as many as are led by the Spirit of God, they are [now] the sons of God. For ye have not received the spirit of bondage again to fear; but ye have received the Spirit of adoption [sonship], whereby we cry, Abba, Father, The Spirit (of God) itself beareth witness with our spirit, that we are the children of God: and if children, then heirs; heirs of God, and joint-heirs with Christ; if so be that we suffer with him, that we may be also glorified together (Rom. 8:14-17).**

John continues this saga of a Christian's fate in 1 John 3:1:

> **Behold, what manner of love the Father hath bestowed upon us, that we should be called the sons of God...Beloved, now are we the sons of God, and it doth not yet appear what we shall be: but we know that, when he shall appear, we shall be like him: for we shall see him as he is.**

Before human birth takes place after conception, there is a period of time or gestation in which the embryo-fetus "grows and "develops" in the mother's "womb"—even as a Christian must "grow" and "mature" before his body can be changed into spirit essence.

The human embryo-fetus is fed by the human mother via the umbilical cord. Christians are also fed and nourished with spiritual food from the Church—the "Mother of us all" via God's ministry (Gal. 4:26; Heb. 12:22-23).

Both physical and spiritual mothers *protect* their infants from any harm that may come their way. Of course, the mother Church protects Christians from satanic attacks by educating them in "Satanic warfare."

Spiritual Abortion

As already noted, a Christian is not completely changed into spirit *until the resurrection,* in which he will receive a new *spiritual body*. However, during spiritual gestation, a Christian can actually commit the "unpardonable sin" and NEVER enter the Kingdom of God. Though this individual had inherent "life" in him from God the Father—it does not mean he is eternally saved!

The question remains, understanding this *spiritual analogy*, can we then apply it to the physical as well?

Scientifically, we know from the moment of *conception,* human life is started and then enters the gestation period toward actual birth. This new *life* receives nourishment from its mother as it awaits actual birth. To interrupt or ABORT this *life* process sooner than its natural course is considered MURDER by many!

Many Christians believe that God, the giver of life is the only one who has the right to take a life—and anyone who interrupts the physical birth process willingly, has committed what is tantamount to murder!

Suicide

Today, unfortunately, people commit suicide for many reasons. Children who are bullied or who feel different from their biological sexual orientation have taken their lives. The ratio of Police officers who commit suicide compared to being shot is an alarming two to one! Shockingly, approximately 20 of our retired military commit suicide every day!

Oftentimes people kill themselves because they think the

world has treated them unfairly! They feel that they have gotten a rotten lot in life and think the world owes them something. They feel they have been "ripped-off" by the world and become despondent.

When people get to feeling so depressed, they will do one of two things—kill themselves, or kill others to alleviate this feeling of frustration.

However, the Bible tells us that the only one who has the right to take a life, is the one who gave it—God Almighty!

The Germ of Eternal Life

First, notice that the Holy Spirit—the germ by which we begin the "Born Again" process, comes from the Father. God has masculine characteristics. That's why we call Him "Father." Christians are called the "begotten" children of God (1 Jn. 5:1).

Our heavenly Father then, has the power to beget us as His children—and begets us through the vehicle of His Holy Spirit. When we are BEGOTTEN by God's Spirit, we receive His germ or "seed" which Peter calls the "incorruptible seed" by the Word of God, which liveth and abideth [in us] (1 Pet. 1:23).

While in the flesh, we have God's spiritual seed impregnating us—but only when we are literally changed to spirit beings will we become total spirit essence (Jn. 3:5-8).

Realize also that an attribute of God's Holy Spirit is perfect character. The Holy Spirit is the germ of eternal life, and transmits that possibility into us. It is the Spirit of obedience—of perfection! Just as physical sperm contains the *genes* that impart individual personality—so also does the Holy Spirit impart *individual characteristics*.

Spiritual Eggs

Like physical life-giving germs of spermatozoan, God's Holy Spirit unites with our human spirit in our minds upon conversion, beginning the "Born Again" process.

Christians are fed and *nourished* with "spiritual food" from the Church, just as the egg in a mother's womb must be nourished with life-sustaining food via the placenta. The spiritual food of a Christian is the Word of God as Jesus proclaimed: **"The words that I speak unto you, they are spirit, and they are life" (Jn.**

6:63).

Just as the physical life-giving nutrients circulate in the mother's uterus, so must the life of God circulate through our minds. We drink in the life-giving words of God from the Bible through reading and studying and meditating. Then, just as the physical poisons are carried through the umbilicus by the bloodstream away from a fetus in the womb, so must we allow our *sins* to pass from us by asking God for forgiveness through prayer—as the shed blood of Christ *figuratively* bearing our sins away. But this is not all!

Not only must the words of God flow into our minds through Bible study, but spirit must flow into our minds.

Notice that each converted Christian receives a seed—composed of spirit, not matter—which unites with the human spirit in each repentant human mind. That is what begets us! But that "spiritual germ" must spiritually grow like the fetus in a mother's womb. Let **"Christ be formed in you"** said Paul in (Galatians 4:19). And we are to **"grow up into him in all things"**—in spiritual mindedness (Eph. 4:15).

How is that seed, now joined with our human spirit going to grow? By the addition of more Spirit—by the "supply of the Spirit of Jesus Christ" (Phil. 1:19). And how does one receive more and more of God's Holy Spirit—through the spiritual tools God has given us through prayer, Bible study, meditation, fasting and exercising God's way of life!

God's spirit is like the embryonic seed of His character and mind. His spirit, like genes, contains all the characteristics of God. These hereditary traits are "love, joy, peace, longsuffering, kindness, goodness, faithfulness, gentleness, self-control" (Gal. 5:22-23).

A fetus in a mother's womb can only grow through the addition of added physical sustenance from the mother—and a new spiritual egg can only develop through the added nourishment of God's Holy Spirit.

This fantastic begettal and growth process through the Holy Spirit has never been understood by the vast majority of mankind!

Spiritual Babies

Paul declares in (Romans 2:20) that God's ministers are

INSTRUCTOR'S of babies. He says they are as a father (1 Cor. 4:15-16). And like a physical father, God's ministry teaches us God's truth as it is revealed unto babes (Lk. 10:21).

Spiritual babes are mostly carnal minded, and are fed milk, not strong meat (deep spiritual truth). This is because they would not be able to digest it after they have swallowed it (1 Cor. 3:1-3).

Newborn babes [new Christians] should desire the sincere milk of the Word, that they may grow thereby (1 Pet. 2:2). Christians grow spiritually by reading and understanding God's written Word—the Holy Bible! Notice:

> **For everyone that uses milk is *unskillful* in the Word of righteousness: for he is a babe. But strong meat belongeth to them that are of full age, even those who by reason of use have their senses exercised to discern both good and evil (Heb. 5:13-14).**

The Church draws "life" from Jesus Christ by the Holy Spirit of which it is begotten (Jn. 1:18). It is also nourished and sanctified by God's Word (Eph. 5:26; 1 Pet. 2:2). The Church passes on *life* to others by the preaching of the gospel.

We Are what We Eat

If we take in harmful physical food we get sick. Likewise, if we take in wrong spiritual food [worldly ways] we will get sick spiritually! Jesus said, **"It is not what goes into a man's mouth [physical food] that defiles him, but what comes out of him that defiles him"** [evil thoughts, adulteries, murder, etc.] **(Mk. 7:14-23).**

As babes, we should HUNGER and thirst after righteousness (Matt. 5:6). We should grow spiritually in grace and in *knowledge* of our Lord and Savior Jesus Christ (11 Pet. 3:18). Jesus warned: **"Man shall not live by bread alone, but by every word that proceedeth out of the mouth of God"**, the Holy Bible! (Matt. 4:4).

THE FAMILY OF GOD

Understanding Scripture

The prophet Isaiah once asked this valid question:

> **Whom shall he teach knowledge? And whom shall he make to understand doctrine? They that are weaned from the milk, and drawn from the breasts. For precept must be upon precept; line upon line, here a little, and there a little (Isa. 28:9-10).**

Pearls of wisdom can be found in this biblical truth. As Christians, we should not draw a conclusion to a matter based on one scripture? Get all of the facts!

Paul told Timothy for our benefit:

> **All scripture is given by inspiration of God, and is profitable for doctrine, for reproof, for correction, for instruction in righteousness. That the man of God may be perfect, thoroughly furnished into all good works (11 Tim. 3:16-17).**

Peter also gave advice in the understanding of God's Word:

> **Knowing this first, that no prophecy of the scripture is of any private interpretation. For the prophecy came not in old time by the will of man: but holy men of God spoke as they were moved by the Holy Spirit (11 Pet. 1:20).**

King David the Psalmist instructed His son Solomon that, **"A good understanding have all they that do His Commandments" (Ps. 111:10).**

God's Holy Spirit needed

Even though Saul [the apostle Paul before his conversion] read the Bible [the Old Testament] scriptures, he did not believe it, and did things ignorantly. Paul did not yet have God's Holy Spirit!

THE FOOLISHNESS OF GOD

Concerning His ministry, Jesus said He spoke in parables, not to make the meaning clearer, but that it was not for everyone to know of *the mysteries of the Kingdom of God* (Matt. 13:11). God has not called the wise and mighty or noble of this world to understand NOW, but rather, He has called the *foolish* and *weak* of this world (1 Cor. 1:25:27).

Paul writes that the carnal natural mind cannot understand God's deeper truths, as they are foolishness to him (1 Cor. 2:9-16). God's Holy Spirit is what is needed to comprehend God's Word! The proverbs tell us, **"There is a way which seems right unto a man, but the end thereof is the way of death" (Prov. 14:12). "Trust in the Lord with all thine heart: and lean not to thine own understanding" (Prov. 3:5).**

Prove All Things

Words of wisdom in interpreting God's written Word are expounded upon by God's apostle to the Gentiles: **"Prove all things, hold fast that which is good" (1 Thess. 5:21).** "Prove what is acceptable unto the Lord" (Eph. 5:10). "...be ye not unwise, but understanding what the will of God is" (Eph. 5:17). "Study to show thyself approved unto God, a workman that needeth not be ashamed, rightly dividing the Word of God" (11 Tim. 2:15).

Paul continued his exhortation: "For the Word of God is quick, and powerful, and sharper than any two edged sword" (Heb. 4:12). "Wherefore take unto you the whole armour of God, that ye may be able to withstand in the evil day, and having done all to stand...take the sword of the spirit, which is the Word of God" (Eph. 6:13-18). "The Holy scriptures are able to make thee wise unto salvation..." (11 Tim. 3:15). "Thy Word is Truth" (Jn. 17:17). Jesus said to search the scriptures (Jn. 5:39).

"Blessed is he that readeth" (Rev. 1:3). "Be not carried away by every strange doctrine" (Heb. 13:9).

Paul cautioned: "Beware lest any man spoil you through philosophy, and vain deceit, after the rudiments [fundamental concepts] of the world, and not after Christ" (Col. 2:8). Jesus proclaimed of false religious worship: **"In vain do they worship me, teaching for doctrines, the commandments of men" (Mk. 7:7,9,13).** Jesus further said, **"Why call me Lord, Lord, and do not the things which I say?" (Matt. 7:21).** "Learn not the

way of the heathen" (Jer. 10:2).

Spiritually Fat

Solomon, the wisest man who ever lived [unfortunately he didn't apply what he knew] once wrote: **"Those who trust in the Lord shall be made fat"** [spiritually] **(Prov. 28:25).**

Clearly, we see a beautiful *analogy* of a physical baby to a spiritual babe. How physical growth is measured in ounces and pounds, where spiritual growth is measured by our *character.* God wants to see what we will do when thwarted, crossed, contradicted, or deprived of certain things supposed to be desireable. God wants to see how we will handle things in this life and environment, before He ever entrusts us with the entire universe to control!

Finally, after we have received proper understanding of God's ways from the Bible, God wants to see how well we will apply these Godly principles, and that is a measure of our spiritual growth, or CHARACTER!

The Child of Maturity

As a physical fetus in our mother's womb, we have need of proper nourishment supplied by the umbilical cord of our mother. As babies, we are nurtured upon milk and eventually begin eating solid food. As teenagers, we begin to digest meat and eventually leave our parents' household altogether when we become adults. The Bible, in fact, commands us to leave our mother and father and cleave to our wives. All this is the physical growth process!

In the spiritual development of a babe—he or she is nurtured by the Mother Church on the milk of God's Word supplied by God's ministry. As he or she grows to the teenage stage, the spiritual babe begins to grow in KNOWLEDGE as more spiritual food is supplied him. He learns to be *faithful* and *loyal* to God's Church, and to take advice from His spiritual parents (God's ministry).

When he reaches the teenage stage, he begins to ask more and more questions, and no longer accepts things for granted. He begins to "prove all things." He no longer gives "pat answers" to questions he doesn't fully understand, merely mimicking and parroting the ministry. Now he has CONVICTION! He knows his parents have been right all along and *why* they have been right!

Now the spiritual child has reached adulthood and no longer needs his parents to lead him by the hand, so to speak. He can leave his parents' house and come home to roost with his wife. The spiritual adult no longer follows God's way of life because he has been told to—now he follows the teachings of Christ because he knows they are best for his own good!

The adult Christian can stand on his own two spiritual feet and will not fall regardless if his mother is there or not. When Christians come to *spiritual maturity*, they no longer need their mother looking over their shoulder—they will exercise *love* and *law* because they have developed Godly CHARACTER! The mature Christian understands that Godly Character is not something you get from someone else—It has to be developed inherently in us!

As an example, when a mother tells her children to go to bed at a certain hour—they do it because it is a command. But when they reach adulthood, they do it because they know it is a good thing—they have developed a sense of right and wrong—CHARACTER!

Ultimately, this is God's purpose for us—to know right from wrong, and EXERCISE right over wrong because we know it's the ONLY way to live!

Suffering in Marriage produces Perfection

The marriage institution was designed by the All-knowing Creator to produce PERFECTION of CHARACTER in mankind. This may sound strange, but one of the ways God is producing holy and righteous character in mankind is through *suffering in marriage!*

God's Word tells us that Jesus was made "perfect" through suffering in the book of Hebrews (Heb. 2:10). In chapter 2, (verse 9), we read:

> **But we see Jesus, who was made a little lower than the angels for the *suffering* of death, crowned with glory and honour; that he by the grace of God should taste death for every man.**

More of the reason for Christ's suffering is revealed in Hebrews 5:8:

> **Though he were a Son, yet learned he *obedience* by the things which he *suffered*: And being made *perfect* (through sufferings), he became the author of eternal salvation unto all them that obey him.**

Can we believe that? Jesus was not born perfect (Gr. *mature)!* This scripture is not suggesting in any way, shape or form, that Jesus had a sinful nature. Perfection of character has nothing to do with sin. Recall, Adam was created imperfect—yet without sin!

Jesus—an Imperfect Husband?

They say it takes "two to tangle" and two to make an unhappy marriage. Now the fact that Jesus' marriage to ancient Israel went on the rocks (Jer. 3:14) would tend to make one think that the fault was not entirely Israel's. However, the truth of the matter will prove otherwise.

Sure, Jesus had to learn to be a perfect husband—to love His wife even as Himself (Eph. 5:28). Jesus loved His wife and gave Himself [suffered] for His wife (Eph. 5:25).

Jesus learned to be patient, understanding, merciful, compassionate, and kind toward Israel. He was loving toward them, but they were not *giving* toward Him. They were not loyal or *faithful* to their husband! Instead, Israel was REBELLIOUS and sinful committing physical and spiritual adultery!

Jesus had to finally divorce ancient Israel as it became impossible for a believing husband [Jesus] to dwell in peace with His unbelieving mate (1 Cor. 7:12-15).

The Suffering of the Church

Under the New Covenant, Jesus will have a wife that will be a "spotless Bride" (free of sin).

She is NOW *making herself ready* for this heavenly marriage through *suffering* (Rev. 19:7).

The twelfth chapter of the book of Revelation contains a brief synopsis of the history of God's Church. It describes the

THE FOOLISHNESS OF GOD

Church in the wilderness [a *type* of suffering] for 1250 years. It had to *endure* the *persecution* of the satanic system all of these ages!

She is pictured as a woman travailing in birth, and *pained* to be delivered (verse 2). The Church has SUFFERED these many years in a "spiritual wilderness" against the satanic beasts [demons] of this world. The temptation of Jesus in the wilderness was a portrayal of this wilderness experience to the Church in *type*.

Attributes of Marriage

There are five general attributes that marriage produces through adversity that leads us to spiritual perfection. They are as follows:

- **COMMITMENT:** Israel's hardship 40 years in the wilderness was because she was not fully *committed* to her husband. God showed this idolatrous relationship through the analogy of Hosea's marriage. God's prophet Hosea was told to marry a harlot woman (Heb. *unbeliever)* of his people. This wife was *symbolic* of the whoredoms the children of Israel had committed (Hosea 1:2). Israel was committing spiritual adultery by worshipping false gods (Hosea 4:2).

  Hosea's first wife was Gomer, which means "adulteress" in Hebrew (Hosea 1:3). Their first child was Jezreel, which can be translated "illegitimate" or "God sows it" in the Hebrew (vs. 4). The valley of Jezreel is where God broke the bow of Israel (vs. 5).

  Hosea's second child was named Loruhamah (margin, *not pitied,* Heb. "not my people"). The connotation of this name meant, "God would no more have mercy upon the house of Israel" (vs. 6). Through this striking analogy, God was pronouncing Israel's doom for being an unfaithful wife. God was going to send her into captivity at the hand of the Assyrians.

  History reveals the nation of Israel was taken captive by the Assyrian Empire in 721 B.C. and punished for her adulterous sins. Finally, God is going

THE FAMILY OF GOD

to have mercy upon Israel and make her His chosen nation once again. God punishes every son He loves—and He loves Israel! When Israel repents of her heinous sins, the Eternal is going to have mercy upon her. God says of this eventful time:

...I will sow her unto me in the earth; and I will have *mercy* upon her that had not obtained mercy; and I will say to them which were not my people, Thou art my people; and they shall say, Thou art my God (Hosea 2:23).

This is when the New Covenant will be made with the nation of Israel, who will ultimately learn to be *committed* to her husband!

- **FLEXIBILITY:** The second attribute that *distress* creates in marriage is *flexibility*. This is not a compromise of one's principles—but rather an extension or reaching out to one's full potential. Both husband and wife must learn to except change in each other as growth takes place. Growth can only come through change. Israel's marriage did not work because they were *unwilling* to change their ways—REPENT!

- **ANTICIPATION:** Another attribute of *adversity* in marriage is *anticipation*. As people suffer because of sin—they avoid those things that caused the suffering. When Jesus sent His Church in the midst of wolves—He wanted them to *anticipate* or beware of the danger (Matt. 10:16).

- **ADAPTATION:** The fourth asset of *distress* in marriage is that it creates the ability to *adapt*. By adapting to different situations, you learn to live with your mate and hence others. Failure to adapt to changes in doctrine or administration in the Church—could mean our eternal salvation! This is a vital principle to learn.

- **EQUALITY:** Although many have thought the marriage institution to be a 50/50 proposition—in reality it is a 100/100 partnership. However, each mate must fully understand their particular God-given roles. The husband is the head of his wife, even as Christ is the head of the Church. The husband is to love his wife even as his own body—even as Christ loved the Church and gave Himself for it. Wives, on the other hand, are to be faithful to their husbands, unlike ancient Israel (Eph. 5:22-29). Likewise, not only should husbands also be faithful but should not abuse this God-ordained authority and treat their wives like door-mats.

Jesus is our example of how to fulfill the husband's role, and He called His Church (Wife) "friends" and not servants (Jn. 15:15). Husbands should dwell with their wives according to knowledge, and realize they are [in many cases] the weaker vessel [physically] (1 Pet. 3:7). A woman who is dominating over her husband is deadly to their relationship (Prov. 21:19; 25:24). Only when each marriage partner *realizes* and *lives* according to their proper marriage relationships—can their marriage be totally fulfilled and happy! Otherwise, it may not even survive!

The Perfect Man

The Bible tells Christians to "...**come in the unity of the faith, and of the knowledge of the Son of God, unto** *a perfect man,* **unto the measure of the stature of the fullness of Christ" (Eph. 4:13).**

Exactly what is a PERFECT MAN, and then again, what is a "perfect woman?" Is Christ a "perfect man", and will the resurrected Church be the No. 10 "perfect woman?"

Perhaps the answer is contained in the mystery of the creation of Adam and Eve as *prototypes.* There, God said: "**...let us make** *man* **in our image, after our likeness; and let** *them* **have dominion..." (Gen. 1:26).**

The Hebrew word for man is "ish" and the Hebrew word for woman is "isha" which means "a female man." It was Adam who gave the woman this name, but God confirmed Adam's understanding that they were BOTH exactly alike despite the obvious outward differences:

> **In the day that God created man, *in the likeness of God* made he him; male and female created he them; and blessed them, and called THEIR name ADAM, in the day when they were created (Gen. 5:1-2).**

To both God and Adam, it was one creation, "**...in the image of God.**" Once again, God's BISEXUAL NATURE of both man and woman is expressed through the creation of Adam and Eve into one nature! This is God's nature! God has the strength, ability to lead and make decisions, courage, and understanding of a man, yet He also has the tenderness, warmth, gentleness, compassion, and loving nature of a woman.

Christ would be incomplete without the Church, and yet it derives all its completeness, and glory, from Him; as He and the Church form the one "new man" of which Adam and Eve are *prototypes*. Both were separate and distinct from each other—yet each was the compliment of the other. This beauty and distinctness is made evident from the seven branched Candlestick which *shadows* Christ and the Church.

Together, all through eternity, this "perfect man" in Christ, and His Church will perform mighty feats of glory in honor to their Father!

An Allegory of the Two Covenants

There is an allegory of the two Covenants found in (Galatians 4:22-31), notice:

> **For it is written, that Abraham had two sons, the one by a bondmaid, the other by a freewoman. But he who was of the bondwoman [Ishmael born of Hagar] was born after the flesh...**

Notice, the Old Covenant is described as a fleshly Covenant. A carnal Covenant for fleshly, physical carnal people without God's Holy Spirit, and human nature to conquer.

The Old Covenant was based on physical promises (of protection, food, etc.) if they would keep the physical part of the Ten Commandments (the letter of the Law).

It had physical men [the Levites] carrying out the administration to teach them *obedience* to God's Laws. They used physical ritualistic ceremonies (sacrifices, meat and drink offerings)—carnal fleshly ordinances to teach a physical carnal minded nation obedience to God's Laws. They were a schoolmaster—and like any *schoolmaster* they teach people obedience or discipline! The Old Covenant was based on the promise to Abraham [Birthright], purely temporal, physical, and national!

Continuing in Galatians 4:3:

> **...but he of the freewoman was by promise. Which things are an allegory: for these are the two Covenants, the one from the mount Sinae, which gendereth to bondage, which is Hagar. (Vs. 28): Now we, brethren, as Isaac was, are the children of promise.**

Isaac was promised to Abraham when Abraham was 100 years old—and under the New Testament, Christians are promised better promises! (Heb. 8:6-10, 9:15). We are promised God's Holy Spirit that gives Eternal Life! The New Covenant was based on the Septre promise to Abraham, of Grace through Jesus Christ, and the gift of Eternal Life!

Chapter Five

> *Turn, O backsliding children, saith the LORD; for I am married unto you: and I will take you one of a city, and two of a family, and I will bring you to Zion...*
> —Jer. 3:14.

THE O.C MARRIAGE TO ISRAEL

At Mt. Sinai, God set up an organization. At that time God's people—the only people on earth who were the people of God were formed into a nation. As such, they had laws, and government.

They were literally a *kingdom on earth*!

First of all, they formed a civil government. But in this government, God also placed certain church governments, giving them the rituals, ceremonies, and sacrifices of the "law of Moses." Church and state were inseparable. They were a theocratic nation!

This was the start of God's Church, **"The Church in the Wilderness" (Acts 7:38).** A fact that many have failed to notice is that the Old Covenant was also a MARRIAGE COMPACT!

When God first set up an organization on earth, the people who formed this organization were MARRIED to the Lord. It was this marriage that bound Him and His people together! In (Jeremiah 3:14) the Lord warned His wife: **"Turn O backsliding Children, saith the Lord, for I am *Married unto You.*"**

The making of the Old Covenant, as recorded in the 24th chapter of Exodus, was the *marriage ceremony.* If anyone may doubt this, let us merely ask, *when,* if not here, did the Lord ever enter into a marriage ceremony, joining Himself and His people together as Husband and wife? Where else, in all the Bible, can you find any account of a marriage ceremony?

The *marriage ceremony* was the Old Covenant ceremony! They are one and the same! It was this marriage, then, that established *organization* and *government* among God's people!

Israel's marriage was based upon the 10 Commandments, God's statutes and judgments were only the terms and conditions—the basis—of that marriage contract.

The Eternal [Lord] of the Old Covenant, as the Husband, promised to provide for and protect the nation or congregation of Israel. The nation Israel in turn agreed to remain faithful always to Him.

God agreed to perform the duties of a husband, to provide for and bless her. The people of Israel accepted the terms that God gave them. They bound themselves by the Old Covenant to refrain from any adulterous or whorish relations with the false gods of other nations—and to remain chaste and acceptable to their own "husband" (Ex. 34:12-17).

The Lord Divorced His Wife

In the space of at least nine short months after Israel had agreed to the covenant, the people had failed so badly to live by the conditions of the covenant that the Lord, her husband, the One who became Jesus Christ, found it necessary to correct His wife.

The Israelites, being without the Spirit of God, were constantly rebelling—sinning—against their "husband"—and the 10 Commandment Law He had given them (Ezek. 20:13).

The Eternal then added temporary "ritualistic laws" for them to keep because of their rebellion, to impress upon them the weakness of their own inherent *human nature* in respect to keeping God's Law (Lev. 1:1-9).

But ancient Israel continued to be disobedient and

THE O.C. MARRIAGE

UNFAITHFUL to her husband. She broke her part of the marriage contract! She turned from worshipping God, and followed the customs of the heathen—serving other gods! She broke her part of the marriage covenant by committing *spiritual adultery*!

Because God is Holy, He does not "co-exist" with sin! Therefore, He was forced to separate His "wife"—ancient Israel, from Himself (Isa. 50:1; 59:1-2; Jer. 3:6,8).

Even though God had given Israel a bill of divorcement for her sins, God was, however, not free to "marry" again, according to the marriage Law! Adultery is not necessarily a cause for the dissolution of a marriage. That's why the Eternal said, **"I am (still) married unto you" (Jer. 3:14).**

Jesus was Married to Israel

Jesus Christ is the Father's Spokesman—the "Word" of the God family. Realize that Jesus is the "Lord" of the Old Covenant—the One who did the speaking at creation! God the Father planned the universe and Jesus—before His human birth—spoke, and the creation was done by the power of the Spirit of God!

Jesus—the Word—therefore created everything (Jn. 1:3; Col. 1:16). He made the first man and woman and He established the marriage relationship (Gen. 2:21-25).

It was the One who later came as Jesus Christ, the "Lord" who spoke the Ten Commandments on Mount Sinai (Ex. 20:1-2)—for no man has ever seen or heard the Father (Jn. 1:18; 5:37; 6:46; 4:20).

It was the Word that became Jesus Christ that followed Israel (1 Cor. 10:4).

The Lord—the human Jesus Christ of the New Testament, was still bound by His part of the conditions of the marriage contract. That's why Christ never got married when He was in the flesh—for He was already married!

These conditions were, however, limited by death! Only the death of one of the partners of a marriage covenant can sever the marriage relationship—for marriage is binding until death!

Jesus came to His Wife

Jesus' disciples understood that the *Kingdom*, with all authority to govern, whether civil or church government, had been taken away from their people, and turned over to Gentiles. Recall how they asked Him, **"Lord, wilt thou at this time restore again the kingdom to Israel" (Acts 1:6)?**

Jesus came to His own [the nation of Israel] first, or to His wife! (Jn. 1:11). Realize, all the apostles were Jews! The gospel was to go to the Jew first (Rom. 1:16). Jesus said He was sent unto *the house of Israel* (Matt. 15:24). He told His disciples not to go to the Gentiles or the Samaritans—but to *the house of Israel* (Matt. 10:5). The early Church was composed solely of Jews on the day of Pentecost (Acts 2:5). See also (Acts 3:25, 26; 13:36).

The parable of the Vineyard in (Matthew 21) is very graphic in explaining the transfer of the Kingdom to another nation [the Church]. Jesus said to them:

> **Did you never read in the scriptures, The very stone which the builders rejected has become the head of the corner; this was the Lord's doing...Therefore I tell you *the kingdom of God will be taken away from You and given to a nation producing the fruits of it* (Matt. 21:42-43).**

This parable graphically shows that God had given a kingdom to the Israelites (notice vs. 45—the chief priests and Pharisees knew Jesus was talking about them) who had killed God's servants [the prophets He sent them including His Son], and so now God was going to give the kingdom over to a nation that would bring forth fruit [spiritual works]. God sent Moses, Isaiah and many other prophets to Israel (Rom. 10:1821; 11:1-3), but they were still disobedient and killed God's prophets (Matt. 23:37).

When Israel went whoring after the ways of other nations, breaking the Commandments—God DIVORCED Israel, and gave over the government [which included Church government as well as state] to the Gentile kingdom's *symbolized* by Daniel's image and the four "beasts." He gave the government into Gentile hands for 2520 years *until* the second coming of Christ—

THE O.C. MARRIAGE

when the government, church and state, shall be *restored* to Israel!

The Pruning of God's Olive Tree

The expression, "times of the Gentiles," refers to the entire period of Gentile supremacy, dating from Nebuchadnezzar's Babylonian invasion and captivity of Judah in 606 B.C. to the time when a supernatural Stone from heaven [Jesus Christ] smashes the image on its toes. Upon Jesus' second advent, He will restore the government of God to Israel! That process has already begun starting in 1948 when the Jews were allowed to return to their homeland!

The Tribulation period, lasting forty-two months, or three and one half years, will be the most severe period of Gentile rule and treading down of Israel. God's holy city will be invaded by Gentile forces killing thousands of God's people in Jerusalem!

The apostle Paul points out in (Romans 9) that even though God made a promise to Abraham and his seed [the children of Israel]—He could have mercy on Gentiles and make them His people also (vss. 24-26).

In (Romans 11), God shows that the Gentiles can be adopted into His family through the *analogy* of wild olive trees (Gentiles) being grafted into branches that were broken off (Israelites). Furthermore, the branches that were "cut off" (Israelites) can also be "grafted back" into God's Vineyard or Kingdom. And so, all Israel shall some day be saved (vs. 26). Thus, Gentiles can be grafted in or adopted into God's family, through the *acceptance* of Jesus Christ and thereby become the seed of Abraham spiritually (Gal. 3:29).

Gentiles become "spiritual Jews" by having a converted heart (Rom. 2:17-29; Gal. 5:1-12). Paul answers the question, "who are Israelites?" in (Romans 9:4). He says that not all that are of Israel [physical Israelites] are Israel (vs. 6), but the Children of Promise (vs. 8).

Make no mistake, the Church is *Israelitish*! Not just a Gentile Church just *called* "Israel"—it is ISRAEL! It is a spiritual nation, composed of individuals *personally* selected by God the Father!

They have become heirs of the same promises given to the nation of Israel. But those who do not come by faith, and who are disobedient, are *cut off*, [natural born Israelites] while Gentile converts, through Christ, are *adopted* into Israel. Thus, spiritually speaking, Israel is THE CHURCH!

Very few indeed understand this vital truth, and fewer understand the *purpose* for the Church. Basically, there are two reasons *why* Jesus built His Church. The two-fold purpose for the Church can be summarized as follows:

- To preach the Gospel into all nations as a witness, that Jesus Christ is Savior, which is the good news of God's soon coming Kingdom or restored government to the earth (Matt. 24:14). We read in Matthew 28:18-20:

And Jesus came and spake unto them, saying, All power is given unto me in heaven and earth. Go ye therefore, and teach all nations, baptizing them in the name of the Father, and of the Son, and of the Holy Ghost: Teaching them to observe all things whatsoever I have commanded you: and, lo, I am with you alway, *even* unto the end of the world. Amen.

- To prepare individuals to *rule* with and under Christ in God's Kingdom over all the nations of the earth. These individuals will be a chosen people comprising God's *family* who will judge angels as well as those resurrected under the White Throne Judgment (Rev. 2:26-27; 5:10; 19:16; 20:4).

Christ to Marry His Wife

Jesus Christ's death on the stake at Golgotha freed Him from His first marriage contract with ancient Israel. Thus, the Old Covenant was ended and so was the marriage. Israel is free to marry again! Jesus' first coming was to *redeem* Israel, His second advent will be to *rule* it!

Now to *whom* will Christ be married, at the Marriage of the Lamb? Notice it, in your own Bible—Revelation 19:7:

Let us be glad and rejoice, and give honor to him: for the marriage [supper] of the Lamb is come, and his wife hath made herself ready.

THE O.C. MARRIAGE

Who will the New Covenant be made with? We read in Hebrews 8:8 **"...Behold, the days come, saith the Lord, when I will make a *new covenant with the house of Israel and with the house of Judah.*"** Jesus is going to make a new covenant with the same wife He made the first covenant with, but later divorced!

Then He shall *restore* the Kingdom to Israel—both Church government, as well as state! It is the Church which shall be married to the Lamb, establishing God's government on earth, *restoring* the Kingdom to Israel!

So, the Church is God's instrumentally for overcoming the *fault* of the Old Covenant. That fault was *disobedience*. The New Covenant will be made with those in whose minds and hearts God's Law has been written, by His Holy Spirit (Heb. 8:10).

Let's read some New Testament scriptures that prove the New Testament Church will become Christ's Wife. Paul marshals in impressive evidence concerning this subject in Ephesians 5:27:

> **That *he might present it to himself a glorious Church*, not having spot, or wrinkle, or any such thing, but that it should be holy and without blemish.**

Now, let's move to 11 Corinthians 11:2 for more proof:

> **For I am jealous over you with godly jealousy: for *I have espoused you to one husband,* that I may present you as a chaste virgin to Christ.**

Paul pounds the final nail into the coffin on this subject in Romans 7:4:

> **Wherefore, my brethren, ye also are become dead to the law by the body of Christ; *that ye should be married to another, even to him who is raised from the dead,* that we should bring forth fruit unto God.**

The Bride and the Bridegroom

There has been some confusion in recent years as to the identification of "the Body of Christ." The most common belief is that the New Testament Church will become "the Body" and "the Bride" of Christ spiritually. Others believe this would be impossible since "the Body" of Christ (the Bridegroom) is to marry "the Bride."

How then could they represent the same entity?

Still more confusing is the fact that ancient Israel was called "the Bride" of God (Isa. 5:6-8; 62:4-5; Jer. 3:14; Hosea 2:19,26). These and other passages clearly prophesy that *an election of Israel* shall be "the Bride."

We have already seen that had ancient Israel repented and turned to the Lord (Acts 3:18-19), there would have been no need to start the New Testament "Church." All of the Old Testament prophecies concerning the Bride would have been fulfilled in ancient Israel!

Who then is going to be "the Bride" of Christ—Old Testament Israel or the New Testament Israel ? There cannot be TWO BRIDES for this would be spiritual polygamy!

What "ekklesia" means

The Greek word for Church in the New Testament is *ekklesia*. This same Greek word is used 75 times in the *Septuagint* Translation of the Old Testament in describing five different Hebrew words.

However, it is used 70 times in describing the Hebrew word CAHAL, from which we have our English word "call." It simply means "to call together", "to assemble", or "gather together." This Hebrew word CAHAL occurs 123 times and is rendered; "congregation" 86 times; "assembly" 17; "company" 17; and "multitude" 3 times.

Its first occurrence is in (Genesis 28:3) in describing the Nation of Israel as "a called out people." Israel was a people "called out" and assembled from all other peoples.

When Jesus said, **"...upon this rock I will build My Church"** (Greek *ekklesia*). He did not use this word in any "spiritual" sense, but rather that He was "calling out an assembly of people" for Himself.

This same Greek word *ekklesia* is used in (Acts 19:32) to also describe "unbelievers" who assembled together, proving that this word itself has no spiritual connotation. Thus, both ancient Israel and the New Testament Church were "called out peoples."

The Body or Bridegroom

There are many New Testament scriptures which show the New Testament "Church" to be represented spiritually as "the Body of Christ" as well. A case in point is found in 1 Corinthians 12:12-13:

> **For as the *body* is one, and has many members, and all the members of that *one body*, being many, are *one body*: so also is Christ. For by one spirit are we all baptized into *one body*, whether we be Jews or Gentiles, whether we be bond or free: and have been all made to drink into one spirit. For the body is not one member but many. (Vs. 27) *Now we are the body of Christ,* and members in particular. See also (Rom. 12:4-5; Eph. 4:16; Col. 1:24-27).**

Jesus Christ is the invisible head of the Body, notice:

> **...and hath put all things under His feet, and gave Him to be the head over all things to the Church [Greek *ekklesia*], which is *His body*, the fullness of Him that filleth all in all (Eph. 1:22-23—see also Col. 2:19).**

This New Testament Body is *symbolically* described in (Ephesians 4:13) as becoming unto "a perfect man."

The "Mystery" of Christ's Body

Jesus Christ had been promised to come as the Messiah by the Old Testament prophets (Rom. 1:1-2). But the MYSTERY of the Body of Christ had never been revealed, and did not therefore form the subject of Old Testament prophecy. It was the subject of a special revelation to the apostles and New Testament "Church" through the apostle Paul—to whom this MYSTERY was first announced. Paul lets the spiritual genie out of the bottle in regards to this *mystery* in Colossians 1:24-27:

> **Who now rejoice in my sufferings for your sake, and fill up on my part that which is lacking of the afflictions of Christ in my flesh *for His body's sake, which is the Church*; whereof I was made minister according to the dispensation (marg. Stewardship) of God which is given to me to you-ward, to fulfil (A.V. marg. fully preach) the word of God, even the mystery (i.e. the secret) *which hath been hid from all ages and generations*: but now hath been manifested to His saints, to whom God was pleased to make known what is the riches of the glory of this *mystery* (or secret) among the Gentiles, which is Christ in (A.V. marg. Among) you, the hope of glory, whom we proclaim, admonishing every man and teaching every man in all wisdom.**

In chapter 2:2 of Colossians, the apostle Paul further states of this mystery:

> **That they being knit together in love, and unto all riches of the full assurance of understanding that they may know [or have full knowledge of] the mystery [or secret] of God, even Christ, in whom are all the treasures of wisdom and knowledge hidden.**

Here, we learn that this "secret" had *never* before been made known, and that to make it known was to "fully preach the Word of God." Hence, today, the Word of God is not "fully preached" unless the *secret* be proclaimed. Paul makes more flagrant remarks of this *mystery* in Romans 16:25, 26 (R.V.):

> **Now to Him that is able to stablish you according to my gospel and the preaching of**

> **Jesus Christ, according to the revelation of the *mystery* [i.e. the secret] *which had been kept in silence through times eternal*, but now is manifested and by (margin, through) the scriptures of the prophets according to the commandment of the eternal God, is made known unto all nations unto obedience of faith [i.e. on the principle of faith-obedience].**

Here, observe, that the same *secret* is referred to as being made known by a special silent *revelation*, and as having been kept in eternal silence, not a word having been breathed concerning it before!

The great secret of the MYSTERY is revealed by Paul in Ephesians 3:1-7:

> **For this cause, I Paul, the prisoner of Christ Jesus in behalf of you Gentiles—if so, be that ye have heard of the dispensation [marg. stewardship] of that grace of God, which was given me to you-ward; how that by revelation was made known unto me the mystery (i.e. the secret), as I wrote afore in few words, whereby, when ye read, ye can perceive my understanding in the mystery (or secret) of (or concerning) Christ; which in other generations was not made known unto the sons of men, as it hath now been revealed unto His holy apostles and prophets in (or rather 'by', as A.V.) the Spirit; to wit, *that the gentiles should be fellow-heirs, and fellow-partakers of the promise in Christ Jesus*, according to the gift of the grace of God which was given me through the Gospel whereof I was made a minister, according to the working of His power.**
>
> **Unto me, who am less than the least of all saints, was this grace, given, to preach unto the Gentiles the unsearchable (the untractable) riches of Christ; and to make all men see (Greek, to enlighten all as to] what the mystery**

> **[secret) which from all ages hath been hid in God, who created all things, to the intent that now unto the principalities and the powers in the heavenly places might be made known through the Church the manifold wisdom of God, according to the eternal purpose (marg. purpose of the ages) which He purposed in Christ Jesus our Lord.**

The "mystery" that was revealed by the apostle Paul and unknown to the Old Testament prophets, is that: *the Gentiles could now become members of the "Body" of Christ*—His Church (Gr. *ekklesia* or called out ones).

Had Israel obeyed the call in (Acts 3:19-21) and repented when Jesus came, there is not a prophecy in the Old Testament that would not have been fulfilled!

Why was the Secret kept?

But first let us ask, "why was the great doctrine of the *mystery* concerning the grafting in of Gentiles to God's Kingdom ever kept secret at all"? The reason is clear!

Had it not been kept secret, the Jews would have had a reason for their rejection of Christ. They could have pleaded "a stacked deck", and that they were only fulfilling the prophecies—and would have lost at once all their responsibility.

True, the rejection of Christ was foretold, but there was not one word about their rejection of the renewed offer of the King and the Kingdom, which was made authoritatively after Christ's Ascension.

The Wife or Bride

We have already shown the many passages which clearly prophesy Old Testament Israel to be the Bride of the Messiah. But can the New Testament "Church" also be called the "Bride?"

While all the promises to Israel as a nation were *earthly*, there were always those who lived "by faith" and "died in faith", and were "partakers of the heavenly calling" (Heb. 3:1). They looked for no earthly portion, but they looked forward with a heavenly hope to a heavenly blessing.

THE O.C. MARRIAGE

> These all died in faith, not having received the promises, but having seen them afar off, and were persuaded of them, and embraced them, and confessed that they were strangers and pilgrims on the earth. For they that say such things declare plainly that they seek a country...a better country, that is an Heavenly: wherefore God is not ashamed to be called their God; for He hath prepared for them a CITY (Heb. 11:13-16). And of Abraham it is said, 'he looked for a CITY, which hath FOUNDATIONS, whose builder and maker is God' (vs. 10).

Now when we turn to (Revelation 21:9), we read that one of the seven angels said to John: **"Come hither, I will shew thee the BRIDE, the Lamb's wife."**

> (Vs. 27) And he carried me away in the spirit to a great and high mountain, and shewed me that great CITY, the holy Jerusalem descending out of heaven from God, having the glory of God; and her light was like unto a stone most precious.

What are we to understand but that this CITY—which is declared to be the BRIDE, the Lamb's "wife," is the city for which all those who were partakers of the heavenly calling looked; and that these *elect* saints of the Old Testament will form part of this new Bride. This "Holy Jerusalem" also contains the "Church" or Body of Christ. It will also form the Bride, inasmuch as "the Lord God Almighty, and the Lamb, are the Temple of it", and "the Lamb is the Light thereof" (Rev. 21:22).

It will be noted that the names "ON THE GATES of the city" are "the names of the *twelve tribes of the children of Israel*" (Rev. 21:12), while the names "IN THE FOUNDATIONS" are "the names of *the twelve apostles* of the Lamb" (vs. 14).

The apostles form a part of the Body of Christ, [the Church] or the Bridegroom. But the apostles also form a part of the Bride! However, although the Bride and the Bridegroom though in a sense are ONE, they are yet surely distinct!

The "Mystery" solved

Ancient Israel was an *ekklesia* or called out people that formed a *nation* with definite laws and government that was God's *Kingdom* on earth. They had an agreement with God to set the example to other nations that was a covenant which was also a *marriage* agreement. This covenant promised Israel to become a kingdom of *priests*—an holy nation!

But because Israel rebelled against God—her Husband had to divorce her and turned the organization or *government* over to the Gentiles until Christ returns.

When Jesus came in the flesh, He came to give His wife an opportunity to repent—but instead, she crucified Him! It was at this precise time that God called out an *ekklesia,* a different people to become His Bride. The apostle Paul was the first one to understand this MYSTERY—that Gentiles could now become a part of ISRAEL—the WIFE and BRIDE of Christ!

Paul explains how Gentiles could become grafted into Israel. That a Jew or Israelite was a person that had a converted heart inwardly, and no longer was one who was circumcised through heredity. Paul calls this "circumcision of the heart."

Both Old and New Testaments contain an *ekklesia,* (individuals that have been called out) to be a chosen generation, a royal priesthood, an holy nation, a peculiar people (Ex. 19:5,6; 1 Pet. 2:5,9; Rev. 5:10). They will form the spiritual nation of Israel—a holy city—the Bride of Christ!

We cannot apply the *analogy* of the New Testament Church solely becoming the Body of Christ or Bridegroom, anymore than the apostle Paul to be the "father of the Church" (1 Cor. 4:15), and also its "mother" (Gal. 4:19).

To say that all *analogies* must be taken literally is a fallacy. Jesus Himself is called our husband, brother, and friend. The Church is called the "wife of Christ"; yet individual members are "sons of God." God is our Father, yet if Christ were our husband and brother, this would be spiritual incest and a fallacy in the literal sense.

Chapter Six

And when he was demanded of the Pharisees, when the kingdom of God should come, he answered them and said, The kingdom of God cometh not with observation: Neither shall they say, Lo here! or, lo there! for, behold, the kingdom of God is within you.
—*Lk. 17:20-21.*

THE KINGDOM OF GOD

There are many who suppose that the "Kingdom of God" is here right now in a spiritual sense—and that there is no need for a literal future Kingdom from such scriptures as Matthew 12:28: **"The kingdom of God is come unto you"** and Luke 21:31: **"The kingdom of God is nigh (near) at hand"** and Luke 17:21: **"Behold the kingdom of God is within you."**

Many conclude from these scriptures that Jesus was starting the Kingdom of God through His Church while He was still on the earth, and was only speaking of a spiritual Kingdom. But let us notice:

First, to whom was Jesus speaking? Let's read it!

And when he was demanded of the Pharisees, when the kingdom of God should come, he answered them and said, The kingdom of God Cometh not with observation: Neither shall

they say, Lo here! or, lo there! for, behold, the kingdom of God is within you (Lk. 17:20-21).

Jesus was speaking to the non-believing, hypocritical, lying Pharisees. Notice, **"He answered them and said..."** (It was the Pharisees who asked Him the question). Were they in the church? Absolutely not! If one thinks the Kingdom was "within" the Pharisees—was the Church within the Pharisees? Such an assumption is rather ridiculous, now, isn't it?

Notice again precisely what Jesus said. Recall, the CHURCH had not yet been set up. Jesus did not say, **"The Kingdom of God shall be set up in your hearts."** He said none of the things people interpret into this verse. He said to the Pharisees that "the Kingdom of God IS"—present tense, NOW! Whatever He was saying the Kingdom of God is, He made it present tense, not future.

Luke wrote these words originally, in the Greek language. The Greek words he wrote were translated into the English words **"...within you."** But, if you have a Bible with the marginal references, you will notice that this is alternately rendered "in the midst of you" or **"among you."** The context indicates that this indeed is the better translation. If your Bible is a *Moffatt* translation, you will notice that the translation recognized that Jesus was talking of His reign or rule, at the head of government.

This is the *Moffatt* translation of the same verse: **"He answered them, The Reign of God is not coming as you hope to catch sight of it: no one will say, Here it is or There it is, for the Reign of God IS NOW IN YOUR MIDST."**

The *Revised Standard* translation renders it: **"...the kingdom of God is in the midst of you."** All these translations render it present tense.

The Messiah's Reign

Jesus was not talking about a Church soon to be organized. He was not talking about sentiments in the mind or heart. He was talking about His REIGN as the Messiah! The Pharisees were not asking Him about a Church, they knew nothing of any New Testament Church soon to be started.

If Jesus was bringing the Kingdom of God then, why did He tell Christians to pray that thy kingdom come? (Matt. 6:10). Jesus

THE KINGDOM OF GOD

Himself said, **"My kingdom is not of this world"** [age or dispensation] (Jn. 18:36).

Jesus told His apostles that it would be blessed to eat bread in the Kingdom of God (Lk. 14:15). That He would not drink again of the fruit of the vine until the Kingdom of God (Lk. 22:18). Jesus told His apostles that they would eat and drink at Christ's table in His Kingdom, and they would sit on thrones ruling over the 12 tribes of Israel (Lk. 22:30). Jesus said that Abraham, Isaac, and Jacob and all the prophets would be in the Kingdom of God (Lk. 13:28).

Clearly, Jesus was speaking of a literal future Kingdom coming. In (Revelation 11:15) we read when Christ returns again, **"the kingdoms of the earth become the kingdoms of God."** That's when resurrected Christians including Abraham, Isaac, Jacob, all the prophets and the 12 apostles will RULE with Christ on earth (Rev. 5:10,) for 1000 years (Rev. 20:4). Then *after* Jesus gathers the Church to Himself, and *after* He is seated on His throne where resurrected Saints will be ruling with Him, He will gather the nations before Him and say **"Inherit the Kingdom"** (Matt. 25:34). See also (Dan. 2:44).

All of these scriptures indicate that the "Kingdom of God" has not yet been set up and will occur at a FUTURE time when Christ returns. The seemingly contradictory scriptures can be clarified by some of the more modern translations which show that Jesus was merely saying that the Kingdom of God was "among" them. In this sense, He was offering them a chance to be in it in the future.

God put all things under Christ's rule (Eph. 1:20-22, 1 Cor. 15:27, Heb. 1:2, Matt. 28:18). Christ is omnipotent ruler (Rev. 19:16). Angels, and authorities, and powers are subject unto Christ (1 Pet. 3:22).

Here is God's promise to Christians: **"He that overcomes shall inherit all things, and I will be his God, and he shall be my son" (Rev. 21:7). We shall be RULERS over all His goods (Matt. 24:47; Lk. 12:42).**

Many Offices of Rulership

Jesus promised His faithful servants: **"In my Father's house are many mansions...I go to prepare a place for you" (Jn. 14:2-3).** There will be different offices of authority in His

Kingdom (Matt. 5:19). Some will be rulers over more cities than others (Matt.25:14-30).

Speculatively, Abraham will have a high office (Rom. 4:11-13, Gal. 3:7-9, 29). David will rule over Israel and Judah (Ezek. 37:21-24). The 12 apostles will rule over one of each of the 12 tribes of Israel (Matt. 19:27-28).

Resurrected Christians will be Kings and priests (Isa. 61:6, 1 Pet. 2:5,9, Rev. 5:10). Christ is King of Kings! (Rev. 19:16).

The immortal Saints will be reigning, and judging for 1000 years on the earth (Rev. 20:4, Dan. 7:27). As Paul elaborated, **"Know ye not that the saints shall judge the world" (1 Cor. 6:2-3).** Greater or lesser glory, responsibility or authority, will be given to individuals just as the stars of heaven have different glory or brilliance (1 Cor. 15:41-42).

Kings will carry out God's organization of Government. The priest will teach the right way to live during the Millennium. Judges or the Judicial branch will make the judgment matters of the God's laws!

The apostle John was inspired to write God's sentiments: **"To him that overcomes will I grant power over the Nations. And he shall rule them with a rod of iron" (Rev. 2:26-27).**

In summary, Paul writes of our current trials: **"The sufferings of this present time are not worthy to be compared to the glory which shall be revealed in us" (Rom. 8:18).**

The Gospel of the Kingdom of God

God the Father had promised to send a *messenger* into the world from heaven, bearing a *message* from Him for all mankind. This promise is recorded in Malachi 3:1: **"Behold, I will send my messenger and he shall prepare the way before me: and the Lord whom you seek, shall suddenly come to his temple, even the messenger of the covenant..."** That messenger, as explained in Mark 1:2, was John the Baptist, even the messenger of the covenant.

The *message* was that of the New Covenant and this prophecy is recorded in the first chapter of Mark: **"The beginning of the gospel of Jesus Christ, the Son of God."** Then follows the account of John the Baptist preparing the way before Him. Verses 12 and 13 record the *temptation* of Jesus by Satan, wherein Satan sought to destroy Christ spiritually before He proclaimed a word of the message He brought from the Father:

"Now after that John was put in prison, Jesus came into Galilee, preaching the gospel..." What gospel? **"...the gospel of the kingdom of God!"**

The word "gospel" is an old English word for *god spell*, meaning "good news." In other words, Jesus was bringing the "good news" about His coming Kingdom of God!

The Word which God [the Father] sent by Jesus Christ, started at Galilee, after the baptism which John the Baptist preached (Acts 10:36-37).

The Father told Jesus what to say (Jn. 12:49-50; 14:24). Jesus began preaching the gospel of the Kingdom of God and said to **"repent"** and **"believe"** (Mk. 1:14-15; Matt. 4:23, 9:35; Lk. 8:1, 9:11, 4:43). Jesus told His disciples to preach the Kingdom of God (Lk. 9:1-2, 10:1,2,9; Mk. 16:15-16; Matt. 24:14; Mk. 28:19-20). Philip preached "The Kingdom of God" (Acts 8:12). The apostle Paul preached "the Kingdom of God" (Acts 20:25, 28:30-31).

Jesus' entire message, as well as the apostles was about the KINGDOM OF GOD—what it will be like—where it will be—who will be in it—and how to get into it! Let's notice the many scriptures to this effect in which "The Kingdom of Heaven" is synonymous with "The Kingdom of God."

Mk. 4:11 Lk. 8:10	"It is not given to everyone to know of the mysteries of the *kingdom of God*."
Matt. 6:33	"Seek first the *kingdom of God*..."
Matt. 19:24	"It is easier to go through the eye of a needle, than for a rich man to enter the *kingdom of God*."
Acts 14:22	"We must through much tribulation enter the kingdom of God."
Matt. 13:24-26	"Parable of the Tares"—The *kingdom of Heaven* is likened unto a man which sowed good seed in the field.

Matt. 13:31-32	"The *kingdom of Heaven* is likened to a grain of mustard seed..."
Matt. 13:33	"The *kingdom of Heaven* is like unto leaven..."
Matt. 13:44	"The *kingdom of Heaven* is like unto a treasure hid in a field..."
Matt. 13:35	"The *kingdom of Heaven* is like unto a merchant man seeking goodly pearls..."
Matt. 13:47-48	"The *Kingdom of Heaven* is like unto a net that was cast into the sea.."
Matt. 18:23-35	"The *kingdom of Heaven* is like unto a certain King..."
Matt. 20:1-16	"The *kingdom of Heaven* is like unto a man who owns a farm..."
Matt. 22:1-16	"The *kingdom of Heaven* is like unto a certain King which made a marriage for his son..."
Matt. 25:1-13	"The *kingdom of Heaven* is like unto ten virgins..."
Lk. 19:12-27	"The *kingdom of Heaven* is as a man traveling into a far country..."

"Born Again"

Let's understand what is meant by this often misused phrase "Born Again." In this life, a Christian receives God's Holy Spirit when he or she is baptized and begins walking as a new creature in Christ. As long as a Christian remains in a repetitive attitude, he or she will be resurrected from the dead and given a new spiritual body. Being "Born Again" is a process that begins with conversion of the mind.

We have now, as humans, been born of the flesh, and

therefore we are flesh. But God is a Spirit (Jn. 4:24). Human beings are of the earth...earthy...from matter (1 Cor. 15:48-50). The Bible emphatically states that flesh and blood humans cannot inherit the Kingdom of God.

But as we have borne the image of the earthly...mortal...human... we shall, when resurrected of God, bear the image of the Heavenly, that is Spirit (1 Cor. 15:49).

As the apostle Paul declared God's words:

> **Now this I say, brethren, that flesh and blood cannot inherit the kingdom of God: neither doth corruption inherit incorruption. Behold, I show you a mystery: We shall not all sleep, but we shall be changed. In a moment, in the twinkling of an eye, ...we shall be changed. Corruption must put on incorruption, and *this mortal must put on immortality* (1 Cor. 15:50-53).**

Let us realize, before man is to have a changed spiritual body, he is to have a changed mind as Jesus stated to Nicodemus:

> **...Verily, verily, I say unto thee, Except a man be born of water, and of the Spirit, he cannot enter into the Kingdom of God. That which is born of the flesh is flesh, that which is born of the spirit, is spirit. Marvel not that I said unto thee, Ye must be born again (Jn. 3:5-7).**

Christians are NOW the "Sons of God" (11 Cor. 6:17,18; Rev. 21:7). These verses declare that God is our Father NOW—not only at the resurrection from the dead!

Jesus was the first so born of MANY BRETHREN! **"...that He might be the firstborn among many brethren" (Rom. 8:29).**

We were born once with this temporary physical existence, even as Jesus was born physically. We have the glorious POTENTIAL of being changed through the resurrection, even as Jesus. And then we shall be—as Jesus now is—composed of Spirit. No longer with temporary physical existence. Then we shall have life inherent, ETERNAL LIFE!

The Greek verb "gennao"

A great deal of confusion concerning the "Born Again" experience revolves around the interpretation of the Greek verb *gennao*, which can mean either "beget", "bear", (of begetting), or "born" (see *An Expository Dictionary of New Testament Words,* by W.E. Vine).

According to W.E. Vine, the Greek verb *gennao* is used allegorically to contrast Jews under bondage to the Law and spiritual Israel to contrast the natural birth of Ishmael and the supernatural birth of Isaac (Gal. 4:24).

It is used in (Matthew 1:20) for the conception of Christ, as well as the act of God in the Birth of Christ (Acts 13:33; Heb. 1:5; 5:5).

It is used metaphorically in the writings of the Apostle John, of the gracious act of God in conferring upon those who believe the nature and disposition of "children," imparting to them spiritual life (Jn 3:3; 5:7; 1 Jn. 2:29; 3:9; 4:7; 5:1,4,18).

A prime verse that has caused much of the controversy is (1 Jn. 3:9), which reads, **"And whosoever is born of God doth not commit sin."** This verse is more correctly rendered, **"And whosoever is born of God doth not abide in sin."** The *Williams* translation of the New Testament reads: **"No one who is born of God makes a practice of sinning...and so he cannot practice sinning, because he is born of God."**

Once a Christian receives God's Holy Spirit, he or she will still sin occasionally. However, John is explaining in this verse that if God's nature is evident in the Christian, he will not actively pursue a sinful way of life. Thus, this verse pertains to a Christians present state while still a physical human being.

The most controversial verse that uses the identical Greek verb *gennao* is (Jn. 3:3,7), where some have interpreted the "Born Again" experience to apply to the resurrection, rather than the existing state of a Christian. Some have referred to the present state of a Christian as a *begettal*, and the resurrected state as *"Born Again."*

Although the physical analogy of human gestation from conception to birth is a good one, we must be cautious in applying this analogy to the "Born Again" conversion process in order to be biblically accurate.

Biblically, the correct definition of *begotten* as applied in reference to the human father's role always included birth. *Gennao* derives its meaning from the root *genna*, meaning "birth" as applying to both the male and female agent (see Matt. 2:1; 19:12; Lk. 1:13).

When only the female agent is involved in the birth, the Greek verb *tikto* is used (see Matt. 1:21; Lk. 1:57;). This same verb however, can be used in applying to the male agent figuratively (Philemon 10).

We must realize however, that "begettal" is not synonymous with "conception." To put it in modern vernacular, if a man has "begotten" a child, he has literally received (or gotten) the child.

However, this is not necessarily true of the woman. Let's assume the woman had a miscarriage, then the father has not begotten or received the child. The father has played a role in the child's conception, but he has not begotten or received the child. Had the child been actually born, then "begotten" would have been a correct rendition. However, it would have been a wrong translation to substitute *conceived* for *begotten* or *born*. Clearly, there is a difference between *begettal* and *conception*.

"Born from Above"

The apostle Peter applies the term "Born Again" correctly as referring to the conversion process when he says: **"...having been born again, not of corruptible seed but incorruptible, through the word of God which lives and abides forever" (1 Pet. 1:23, NKJ).**

With this background in mind, perhaps we can better understand Jesus' inference of "Born Again" to a converted mind, rather than to a changed body in His statement to Nicodemus, **"Jesus answered and said unto him, Verily, verily, I say unto thee, Except a man be born again, he cannot see the kingdom of God" (Jn. 3:3).**

Nicodemus, as well as all of the descendants of Abraham thought that they could inherit the kingdom of God by virtue of heredity. Jesus was not referring to the composition of a Christians' body in its resurrected state, but rather of the necessity to change one's mind in order to be in God's kingdom and receive a spiritual body. Jesus was explaining to Nicodemus that he could not inherit a spiritual kingdom by virtue of heredity, and that he needed God's Holy Spirit.

Furthermore, the verb *gennao* in (John 3:3), is accompanied by the adverb *anothen*, which can mean "from above." Therefore, the term "Born Again," should really be "Born from Above," meaning a birth from God above, not merely a second birth.

To summarize, the term "Born Again" does not refer to the transition of flesh and blood to spirit. It is referring solely to a converted mind while in a fleshly body. To be "Born Again" speaks of Christian conversion, not our ultimate inheritance.

A Christian is a new creation as soon as he receives the *Spirit* of God, at which time he is "Born from Above." He is considered a spiritual baby requiring the "milk" of God's Word. Eventually this neophyte Christian grows to the fullness of Christ as he grows in grace and knowledge (Eph. 4:13). If he is faithful to God during his lifetime, his or her body will be changed into spiritual essence, just like his elder brother Jesus Christ!

What the Kingdom will be like

There is a prophecy in (Acts 3:21) that declares Jesus will RESTORE *all* things to their pristine state when He returns to the earth as King of Kings, and ushers in the glorious Kingdom of God (Rev. 11:15).

Jesus will bring peace, health, truth and healing (Ps. 72:1-6; Jer. 33:6-12; Isa. 11:9). The nations shall be judged righteously and be governed righteously (Ps. 67:4). Let's read more specifically of what Jesus will *restore* when He sets up the Kingdom of God on earth.

JOY: The Millennium will characterized by the fullness of joy (Isa. 9:3-4; 12:3-6; 14:7-8; 25:8-9; 30:29; 42:1, 10-12; 52:9; 60:15; 61:7, 10; 65:18-19; 66:10-14; Jer. 30:18-19; 31:13-14; Zeph. 3:14-17; Zech. 8:18-19; 10:6-7).

EDUCATION: God shall teach His ways and laws (Micah. 4:1-2; Zech. 8:20-23; Isa. 2:1-4; 30:20-21; 40:40-63; 34:11; 45:18; 33:6). The earth will have a pure language (Zeph. 3:9). The earth will be full of knowledge (Isa. 11:1-2,9; 41:19-20; 54:13; Hab. 2:14) and truth (Jer. 33:6).

DEFENSE: "They shall beat their swords into plowshares and

THE KINGDOM OF GOD

their spears into pruning hooks: nation shall not lift up a sword against nation, neither shall they *learn* war anymore" (Micah 4:3). Peace shall abound (Isa. 32:18; Ps. 72:1-6; Jer. 33:6). "...they shall dwell safely, and none shall make them afraid" (Ezek. 34:28). "Violence shall no more be heard in thy land..." (Isa. 60:18).

WELFARE REFORM: If any will not *work*, they will not eat (11 Thess. 3:10). God will provide assistance to widows and orphans out of His tithing system. He shall save the needy children (Ps. 72:1-6).

HEALTH INSURANCE: There will be an abundance of delicious food and wine (Isa. 25:6). Starvation will no longer exist (Isa. 58:11, 25:6-8; Ezek. 34:12-31). People will be healthy and live to be a hundred (Zech. 8:4-5; Isa. 65:17-25). The blind will see and the deaf will hear (Isa. 35:5).

There will be a complete healing of all deformed (Isa. 29:17:19; 35:3-6; 61:1-2; Jer. 31:8; Mic. 4:6-7; Zeph. 3:19). Jesus healed a blind man in (John 9:1-7), who was physically blind, during the Feast of Tabernacles. This blindness was not due to any fault of the man, and is representative of the *spiritual blindness* that will be healed during the Millennium in which truth will be known to all nations!

LABOR REFORM: Servants (employees) will *obey* their masters [employer] (Col. 3:22). Masters [employers] will give their employees that which is just and equal (Col. 4:1). The labourer will be worthy of his hire (Lk. 10:7). There will no longer be union strikes, or idleness in a fully developed industrial society with Agriculture (Isa. 62:8-9; 65:21-23; Jer. 31:5; Ezek. 48:18-19).

URBAN RENEWAL: A massive clean-up of the cities will transpire after the battle of Armageddon. Oceans will be purified (Ezek. 47:8). Cities will be well planned (Amos. 9:11-15; Ezek. 36:8-11; Micah 4:3; Isa. 61:4; Zech. 8:3-5). There will be a *rebuilding* of the soil and land (Isa. 58:11-12). Deserts will bloom (Isa. 35:1,2,6). Horses will be used instead of cars that pollute (Zech. 14:20). Animals will be tame (Isa. 11:6-8; Ezek. 34:25). The weather will be controlled (Hosea 2:18).

RELIGION: The earth will be *filled* with God's Holy Spirit (Isa. 11:2). The inhabitants will be taught God's *laws* and *statutes* and observe His *Sabbaths* (Ezek. 44:23-24; 46:1). Nations will observe God's feast Days, including the Feast of Tabernacles (Zech. 14:16).

HOLINESS: The Millennial Kingdom will be characterized by *holiness* as the land will be *holy,* the city of Jerusalem *holy,* as the Saints rule from there, the Temple will be *holy,* and the subjects will be *holy* unto the King of Kings (Isa. 1:26-27; 4:3-4; 29:18-23; 31:6-7; 35:8-9; 52:1; 60:21; 61:10; Jer. 31:23; Ezek. 36:24-31; 37:23-24; 43:7-12; 45:1; Joel 3:21; Zeph. 3:11, 13; Zech. 8:3; 13:1-2; 14:20-21).

Generation to Generation

God has set up the family relationship to show us how He will convert the world through a "generation to generation" process!

In (Genesis 18:19) we read how God told Abraham to teach his children His ways through family relationship.

There are many scriptures which tell us to "train up" our children in the way they should go (Prov. 22:6; Deut. 4:9-10, 6:6-7; Joel 1:3).

The earth will be full of the knowledge of God during the Millennial Kingdom of God (Isa. 11:9). It will be by this "generation to generation" process that God's "life style" will produce a God fearing, self-disciplined society. This process will "turn the hearts of the fathers to their children and the children to their fathers" (Mal. 4:5-6).

When God's Kingdom is finally set up on earth, after millenniums of man's rebellion and inhumanity toward man— the Eternal will RESTORE everything that was good and wholesome to what was its original and rightful purpose!

This will take proper EDUCATION!

This process however, will not happen in a presto-chango way—but rather in a slower, more natural way!

THE KINGDOM OF GOD

How to receive Salvation

We have already shown *why* God's Word declares we need a Savior—but *what* must we do now in order to receive salvation? This question was asked by the stirred and repentant jailer in (Acts 16:30). The scriptures in (Acts 16:31), and (Romans 10:9,10,13) say we must *believe in the Lord* Jesus Christ and we will be saved.

But what does that mean?

Jesus thunders loud and clear that it is not enough to say we believe in Him, [call Him Lord, Lord], and not do the things He says (Matt. 7:21; 1 Jn. 2:17).

According to God's Word, salvation is given unto all them that OBEY Him, as stated in (Hebrews 5:9). Here, Jesus defines what He means by *believing on Him.* Believing *On* Him and believing *In* Him are entirely two different things. Believing *in* Him implies we believe Jesus was a great person and said the right things; but believing *on* Him means we are *obedient* and living by the things He said!

The Devil and his demons believe *in* Him (Jas. 2:19). James adds: **"...faith without works is dead" (Jas. 2:19).** Clearly, believing is not enough to receive salvation. We are saved by Christ's life (Rom. 5:10), and by letting Christ live His life *in* us (Gal. 2:20).

Scriptures on Salvation

Here are some dogmatic scriptures on the power of the flesh:

Matt. 7:21	"Not everyone that says Lord, Lord, shall enter the Kingdom of God; but *he who does the will of my Father,* who is in heaven." See also (1 Jn. 2:17).
1 Cor. 11:1-2	"*Keep the ordinances* as followers of Christ."
Matt. 19:17	"If you will enter into life (Salvation) *keep* the Commandments."
Heb. 5:9	"Salvation is given unto all them that *obey*

THE FOOLISHNESS OF GOD

Him."

Heb. 2:3	"How shall we escape, if we *neglect* so great salvation..."
Ps. 24:3	"...who shall stand in his holy place? He that hath clean hands, and a pure heart, who hath not lifted up his soul unto vanity, nor sworn deceitfully."
Ps. 15:1-5	"...who shall abide in thy holy hill? He that walketh uprightly, and worketh righteousness, and speaketh the truth in his heart. He that backbiteth not his tongue, nor doeth evil to his neighbor...He that putteth not out his money to usury (interest), nor taketh reward against the innocent. He that doeth these things shall never be moved."
Rev. 22:14	"Blessed are they that *do His Commandments*, that they may have right to the tree of Life (Eternal Life—Salvation)."
11 Pet. 1:5,10	"Add to your faith, virtue, add to virtue, knowledge, and to knowledge temperance. And to temperance patience, and to patience godliness. And to godliness, brotherly kindness and charity. For *if ye do these things,* ye shall never fall."
1 Pet. 1:22	"Seeing you have purified your souls in *obeying the truth* through the spirit..."
1 Tim. 6:18-19	Good works lay a good foundation for eternal life!

Man to be Changed

Job. 14:14	"If a man die, shall he live again? All the days of my appointed time will I wait, till

THE KINGDOM OF GOD

	my change come."
1 Cor. 15:44	"It is sown a natural body, it is raised a spiritual body."
1 Cor. 15:51	"Behold, I shew you a mystery we shall not all sleep, but we shall be changed." See also (1 Thess. 4:13-15).
1 Cor. 15:52	"In a moment, in the twinkling of an eye at the last trump: we shall be changed."
1 Cor. 15:53	"For this corruptible must put on incorruption, and this mortal must put on immortality."
Rom. 6:23	Eternal Life is a free gift from God.
Phil. 3:21	"Who shall change our vile body, that it may be fashioned like unto his (Christ's) body."

Man to have Christ's Likeness

Ps. 17:15	"Beloved, now are we the sons of God, and it doth not yet appear what we shall be: but we know that when He shall appear, *we shall be like him*, for we shall see Him as He is."
Rom. 6:5; 8:17	"For if we have been planted together in the likeness of His death, [Baptism] *we shall also be in the likeness of His resurrection.*"
1 Cor. 15:23	"But every man in his own order: Christ the firstfruits, afterward, they that are Christ's at His coming."
Rom. 8:29	Christ is the firstborn among many from the dead (resurrection). "He is the head of

THE FOOLISHNESS OF GOD

	the Body of the Church: who is the beginning, *the first-born from the dead"* (Gr. *beginner*). See also (Col. 1:18).
Rev. 3:14	Jesus is only, "The beginning of the Creation of God."
Phil. 3:21	"Who shall change our vile body, that it may be fashioned like unto *his glorious body*."
Matt. 13:43	We shall shine forth as the sun.
1 Cor. 15:49	"As we have borne the image of the earthly (Adam) we shall also bear the image of the Heavenly" (Christ). See also (11 Cor. 3:18).
1 Jn. 3:9	"And whosoever is born (Gr. *gennao*) of God doth not commit (abide in sin)." A Christian will occasionally sin, but his or her life is not characterized by sin.

To have Christ's Mind

1 Cor. 2:16	"For who hath known the mind of the Lord, that he may instruct him?"
1 Cor. 1:10	"But we have the mind of Christ."
1 Pet. 4:1	"Forasmuch then as Christ hath suffered for us in the flesh, arm yourselves likewise with the same mind: for he that hath suffered in the flesh hath ceased from sin." See also (3:8).
Phil. 2:5	"Let this mind be in you, which was also in Christ Jesus." See also (verses 1:27; 2:2; 4:2; 11 Cor. 13:11; Rom. 12:16).
11 Pet. 1:4	We will be partakers of the divine nature of

THE KINGDOM OF GOD

God, not human nature!

Who will be in the Kingdom

Jer. 30:9	King David will be a King over all twelve nations of Israel. See also (Ezek. 34:23-24; 37:24-25).
Matt. 19:28	Each of the original 12 apostles will be King under David, over one of these then super prosperous nations.
Lk. 13:28	Abraham, Issac, Jacob and all the prophets.
Rev. 3:21	To him that overcometh will I grant to sit with me in my throne, and I will give power over the nations.

Who will Not enter the Kingdom

Gal. 5:19-21	"Now the works of the flesh are manifest, which are these; Adultery, fornication, uncleanness, lasciviousness, Idolatry, witchcraft, hatred, variance, emulations, wrath, strife, seditions, heresies, Envyings, murders, drunkenness, revellings, and such like of the which I tell you before, as I have told you in time past, that they which do such things shall not inherit the kingdom of God." See also (1 Tim. 1:10; Eph. 5:3).
1 Cor. 6:9	"Know ye not that the unrighteous shall not inherit the kingdom of God? Be not deceived: neither fornicators, nor idolaters, nor adulterers, nor effeminate, nor abusers of themselves with mankind, nor thieves, nor covetous, nor drunkards, nor revilers, nor extortioners, shall inherit the kingdom of God."

THE FOOLISHNESS OF GOD

Rev. 21:7-8 "He that overcometh shall inherit all things; and I will be his God, and he shall be my son. But the fearful, and unbelieving, and the abominable, and murderers, and whoremongers, and sorcerers, and idolaters, and all liars, shall have their part in the lake which burneth with fire and brimstone: which is the second death."

Man to Become Immortal

The Bible reveals that "immortality" is something that man does NOT YET HAVE but rather will receive at a yet future time. Let's notice some scriptures along these lines.

1 Tim. 6:15-16   Only God has Immortality (Eternal).

1 Tim. 1:17   Jesus Christ is Immortal (Eternal because He always existed).

1 Cor. 15:50-53   We are Mortal, and must put on Immortality.

11 Tim. 1:10   Christ brought the Gospel of how to receive Immortality (Eternal Life).

Rom. 2:7   Immortality is something to be sought for: NOT SOMETHING WE ALREADY HAVE.

1 Cor. 15:22   "For as in Adam all die.." (this disproves the immortality of the soul, for how can you have the first death if the soul is immortal?).

Matt. 22:30   We will neither marry nor die anymore, being the children of the resurrection. See also (Lk. 20:34-36).

Job 4:17   Job knew man was mortal.

Rom. 6:23	"The wages of sin is death: but the gift of God is eternal life through Jesus Christ our Lord." If we already have eternal life, why is it a gift from God?
1 Cor. 15:14-18	If Christ had not risen from the dead, faith in a future life would all be in vain, and them who are in their graves would perish. Perish means "to cease to exist."
Jn. 3:16	"For God so loved the world that He gave His only begotten son, that whosoever believeth on him should not perish, but have everlasting [eternal] life" How could man perish if he already had an immortal soul?"
Lk. 13:3	"...but except ye repent, ye shall all likewise perish."
Matt. 10:28	"Fear not them which kill the body, but are not able to kill the soul: but rather fear him which is able to destroy both soul and body in hell." The Greek word used here for soul is "psuche" which has the same meaning as the Hebrew *(nephesh)*. What Jesus is saying here is that He has the power to destroy Mankind—what We are—body and mind—a SOUL!

Christ Is and Was God

Heb. 1:8	"But unto the Son he saith, thy throne, O God, is for ever and ever..."
Jn. 1:1	"In the beginning was the Word, and the Word was with God, and the Word was God" (Gr. *Logos*—meaning Spokesman).
1 Jn. 1:1	"That which was from the beginning,

THE FOOLISHNESS OF GOD

	which we have heard, which we have seen with our eyes, which we have looked upon, and our hands have handled, of the Word of Life" (Jesus Christ).
Matt. 1:23	Christ to be called Emanuel—which is by interpretation (God with us). See also (Isa. 7:14; 8:8).
Phil. 2:6	Jesus said it was not robbery to be equal with God.
Phil. 2:7	Jesus, was God, and became man—We are men and will become children of God.
Jn. 10:34-35	"Ye are Gods" and the children of the most High! This verse is a direct quote from (Psalm 82:6), and is not referring to men becoming immortal God, for these men shall die (Ps. 82:7). Rather, this verse is a reference to human beings that sat as judges over the poor and oppressed (Ps. 82:2-4). Jesus quoted this Old Testament verse to the Jews who were accusing Him of blasphemy because He said He and His Father were one (vs.30). Jesus equated Himself with God, and would therefore have taken away their authority. This verse refers to men acting as gods in making unjust judgment, rather than teaching that human beings can become equal with God.
Rev. 3:9	In speaking to the ancient Philadelphia Church which contained many Jewish Believers that came out of the Synagogue of Satan we read "Behold, I will make them come and worship before thy feet." Only God is worthy of being worshipped! Not angels or men. The angels said this themselves (Lk.4:33) as well as the apostle Peter (Acts 10:25-26). This scripture

appears to be in reference to O.T. scriptures which indicate that in the Millennium, Gentiles will come and bow down to Israel in recognition that God is with them (Isa. Isa. 45:15; Isa. 49:22-23; Isa. 60:14-16). Zechariah described a time when Gentiles would honor faithful Jews because, "we have heard that God is with you."

Chapter Seven

> *Of the increase of his government and peace there shall be no end, upon the throne of David, and upon his kingdom, to order it, and to establish it with judgment and with justice from henceforth even for ever*
> —Isa. 9:7.

TO RULE THE UNIVERSE

In (Genesis 1) we read that God created the Heavens [Heb. *plural meaning;*] notice (Psalms 8:1,3-4), where the same Hebrew word is used and is plural.

Jesus Christ is now upholding [sustaining] all things [the entire universe] and we are heirs!

The author of the book of Hebrews was inspired to write:

What is man that thou art mindful of him? [Why does God care about man] Thou made him a little lower than angels; Thou hast put all things under his feet. For in that he put all in subjection under him, he left nothing that is not put under him. But now we see not yet all things put under him (Heb. 2: 6-8).

God's Word tells us that Christians will be joint heirs with Christ (Rom. 8:16-17, Gal. 3:29, 4:7, Tit. 3:7, Heb. 1:14, 6:17,

Jas. 2:5, 1 Pet. 3:7).

The entire creation awaits the sons of God! Currently, it is in bondage and decay. But we [resurrected Christians] shall give it life, just as Christ gave the earth life in seven days after Satan's rebellion as we learned in volume one!

Notice, **"Christ is the first of many brethren" (Rom. 8:29).** Of God's Government there is no end (Isa. 9:7).

Our Destiny—The God Family

The fact that the express purpose of every human life is literally to become a member of the God Family astounds many—but as we shall see, it is true!

A God Family into which each individual human being who *qualifies* will have been instantaneously resurrected [if then dead] or changed [if still alive] into a "Son of God," in the broad, rich, full, expansive meaning of this overused and most misunderstood word.

A point of clarification must be made here! Those who will be born into God's Family will never have the same power or authority as the Father or Christ does.

Individuality Not Lost

Yet, with new bodies and changed minds, we will assuredly not be "assembly-line robots" or "diffused love essence in a universal spiritual cloud." Far from it. We will be individuals—as individually distinct from one another as God the Father is individually distinct from Jesus Christ and the Holy Spirit.

Recall, Jesus Christ was eternally God before He was a human being. We, as humans have been created, and although called His brethren—we are not His equals! We will be like Him in that we will be one with him and the Father in love and perfection of character.

As members of the household of God, and immortal children, we will still be subject to the God-head.

Resurrected Saints will be partakers of God's divine nature, and will share the glory and power of God. However, the children of God in their glorified resurrected state will *never* be as exalted or omnipotent as God the Father or Jesus Christ. We will as members of the kingdom of God have immortal spiritual bodies free of pain, God's holy and righteous character—but could not exist without God, or overthrow the government of God!

We will have our own particular personalities, maintain our own special characteristics, generate our own unique ideas, create our own original thoughts, enjoy our own preferential activities, fulfill our own personal responsibilities, and on and on. And we will always be tightly united in the God Family. We will always be ruled by the Father and by Christ, fulfilling God's overall purpose, spreading the love of God throughout the universe, united in the Family of God.

God—A Family

God's prophet Moses was inspired to write when God created the heaven and earth: **"In the beginning God created the heaven and the earth" (Gen. 1:1).** The Hebrew word for God in the English language is "Elohim." That's a uniplural noun. It is like such words as group, church, crowd, family, or organization.

Take, for example, the word church. We read, in (1 Corinthians 12:20), that the Church is ONE CHURCH, the "one body" yet composed of "many members." Even though it takes many members to constitute the Church, it is not many churches—it is only the one Church!

A Family is made up of more than one person, yet only the one family.

God is not merely one Person, but God is a Family. God is a Kingdom—the Supreme divine FAMILY which RULES the UNIVERSE! The whole Gospel Jesus brought to mankind as we read previously, is the Good News of the Kingdom of God!

In one short, most remarkable statement, the God Family sums up the whole purpose of human life—the primary, underlying reason which motivated the God-head to create all physical reality. This declaration gives the all-encompassing reason: **"Let Us make Man in Our Image and after Our Likeness."** This is the very first Biblical reference to man—and with it the God Family announces the firm intention to begin to reproduce "after its kind."

Prior to this verse, the basic life-principle **"after its kind"** (literally from the Hebrew "to, or for, its appointed division"), is repeatedly stressed as God's guiding design for the reproduction and purpose of all life. And so just as God had created the plants and the animals "after their kind," He created man after His own kind—after THE GOD KIND!

Why is the phrase "after its kind" never applied to man, even though it is consistently applied to all other life? The answer is fundamental: **Because the primary purpose of human life is not to physically reproduce after the human kind—but to be spiritually reproduced after the God kind!**

There are three elements in a family—a father, mother, and child or children, **"Of whom the whole Family in Heaven and earth is named" (Eph. 3:15).**

Father

"Elohim" is the divine FAMILY—only ONE family, but more than one divine Person, Jesus Christ spoke many times of, and prayed to His divine Father in Heaven. So, the Eternal Father is a Person, and is God. The Father is Supreme Head of the God Family—the LAWGIVER!

The apostle Paul explains to us that God's Ministry is a kind of "spiritual Father" to the Church membership, and the preaching of the Gospel ultimately led to our begettal. Paul was inspired to write: **"For though you have ten thousand instructors in Christ, yet have ye not many Fathers: for in Christ Jesus I have begotten you through the gospel" (1 Cor. 4:15-16).**

In (11 Corinthians 6:13) Paul refers to his converts as if to his children. See also (Gal. 4:19; 1 Thess. 2:11; and 1 Jn. 2:1) where members of the Church are called "children."

Children

Angels are referred to as Sons of God in (Job 1:6; 38:7). Jesus Christ spoke as the Son of God (as well as the Son of Man). Christians are to follow in their elder brother's footsteps as a Son or Daughter of God (11 Cor. 6:18).

So we have a Father and Son relationship. It is a FAMILY relationship! Humans, in the "likeness" of God, may receive the gift of God's Holy Spirit (Acts 2:38-39). Those thus converted become the *begotten* Sons of God—actually children of God: **"For as many as are led by the spirit of God, they are the sons of God "(Rom. 8:14-17).**

There are no capital letters in the Greek language, but the translators decided to capitalize "Son" when it is referred to Jesus and not capitalize "son" when it referred to Christians. Most reverent and sincere humility no doubt, but it leads to misunderstanding.

Referring to begotten Christians, Paul wrote: **"For ye have not received the spirit of bondage again to fear; but ye have received the Spirit of adoption, whereby we cry, Abba, Father" (Rom. 8:15).** That word "adoption" can just as well be translated "sonship"—or even "Sonship"—but according to the very scriptures the translators were translating, it never entered their minds that we could be the actual "Sons of God." They only took words like "brethren," "sons," "Father" to be metaphors, niceties, condescension from God as it were.

But this scripture clearly declares that we human beings, after receiving God's Holy Spirit, are to call God Abba—which is Aramaic for "father"—and then amplifies and reinforces that by adding "Father" from the Greek. An actual Father, not a pretend Father. Perhaps it was fear of the same charge of "blasphemy" leveled against Jesus by the religious people of His day that caused those men to use the translation "adoption" in the clear light of the context of a double language [Aramaic, Greek] "Father-son" relationship discussed in Romans.

Paul concludes, **"If any man have not the Spirit of God, he is none of His" (Rom. 8:9).** See also (1 Jn. 3:1, Rev. 21:7). Those thus begotten of God are baptized into God's Church (1 Cor. 12:13).

Mother or Wife

The Church is the affianced Bride of Christ, and will RULE with Him at His glorious return to the earth (Eph. 5:25-27; Rev. 19:7).

In one very brief but concise statement, God declares the very purpose for both man and woman in marriage: **"...let them have dominion..." (Gen. 1:26).** Both man and woman were to exercise authority over God's creation!

The Bible also pictures the Church as the Mother of us all (Gal. 4:26). So, we have the Father and Son relationships; and also the Husband—and—Wife—Mother—Relationships—FAMILY RELATIONSHIPS!

The Family of God throughout Eternity

What will it be like once we are resurrected into the family of God? What will we be doing for all Eternity? We cannot be too dogmatic in that we are speculating in part into the realm of possibility. But not the idle, fanciful, and foolish possibilities, but rather those founded on solid biblical principles, and scriptures.

We have already expressed the ultimate purpose for mankind—that the God-head are REPRODUCING THEIR CHARACTER in flesh and blood human beings!

That's the purpose for human life! That's the purpose for the earth. And that very well could be the purpose for the entire universe. But where in the Bible does it indicate that?

In the book of Hebrews we read: **"For unto the angels hath he (God) not put in subjection the world to come, whereof we speak" (Heb. 2:5).** The theme of the context here is "the world to come."

There is but one earth, but the Bible speaks of three worlds, ages, or civilizations on the earth—the "world that then was" (the antediluvian world from Adam to Noah): this "present evil world" (from the Flood until Christ's return, yet future); and "the world to come" (which starts when Christ comes and sets up the Kingdom of God).

This verse speaks of angels as if the world had been put in subjection to angels as we have already shown. Mankind's new vistas are revealed in (Hebrews 2:6) where we read:

> **But one in a certain place testified, saying...Thou madest him a little lower than the angels: thou crownedst him with glory and honour, and didst set him over the works of thy hands. Thou hast put ALL things under his feet. For in that he put ALL in subjection under him, he left nothing that is not put under him. But now we see not yet ALL things put under him.**
>
> **But we see Jesus, who was made a little lower than the angels for suffering of death, crowned with glory and honour; that he by the grace of**

> God should taste death for every man. For it became him, for whom are ALL things, and by whom are ALL things, in bringing many sons unto glory, to make the captain of their salvation perfect through sufferings.

Is it possible God could mean what He says—"ALL THINGS"—nothing excluded?

In the first chapter, the *Moffatt* translation of the Bible renders the Greek word translated "all things" as "the universe."

In other words, it is possible that God has decreed the entire universe—with all its galaxies, its countless suns and planets—everything to be put under man's subjection!

"But now we see not yet all things (the endless universe) put under him" (man). Remember (verse 5), this is speaking of the world or age to come—not today's world.

"But we see Jesus, who was made a little lower than the angels (or, 'for a little while lower') for the suffering of death, crowned with glory and honour." Man, other than Christ, is NOT YET "crowned with glory and honour."

But see how Christ is already crowned with glory and honour:

> **For it became him, for whom are ALL THINGS [the entire universe] and by whom are all things, in bringing many sons unto glory, to make the captain of their salvation perfect through sufferings...for which cause he [Christ] is not ashamed to call them brethren (verse 10-11).**

In other words, Christians having God's Spirit are joint-heirs with Christ to INHERIT all that Christ already has inherited. He is now in glory! He has already inherited the universe. He sustains it by His power. Man, if he is converted, having God's Holy Spirit (Rom. 8:9), is now an HEIR—not yet a possessor.

But see now how Christ already has been crowned with glory and honour—and is already in possession—has already inherited. In Hebrews chapter 1 we read:

> **God...hath in these last days spoken unto us by his Son, whom he hath appointed heir of all things [the entire universe], by whom also he made the worlds; who being the brightness of his glory, and the express image of his person, and upholding (sustaining) all things [the entire universe] by the word of his power...(Heb. 1:1-3).**

Paul presents a clear commentary in (Romans 8:29) of Christ as God's son **"...that he might be the firstborn among many brethren."** Christians, having God's Holy Spirit, are *heirs* of God and joint *heirs* with Christ—who alone as will all Christians, already been changed as God's Son by a resurrection from the dead (Rom. 1:4). He is the FIRST of the human family to be resurrected into the family of God.

To Inherit the Entire Universe

Paul enlightens us further as to our ultimate destiny in Romans 8:19-23:

> **For the creation waits with eager longing for the revealing of the sons of God; for the creation [all the suns, planets, stars, moons,] was subjected to futility; not of its own will but by the will of him who subjected it in hope; because the creation itself will be set free from its bondage to decay and obtain the glorious liberty of the children of God. We know that the whole creation has been groaning in travail together until now; and not only the creation but we ourselves, who have the first fruits of the Spirit groan inwardly as we wait for adoption [Sonship] as sons, the redemption of our bodies (R.S.V).**

But why should the whole universe—the creation—be waiting with eager longing for the appearing of all these resurrected "Sons of God" in the family of God?

The preceding scriptures portray the universe filled with

planets in a state of decay and futility—yet as if subjected now to this dead state in hope. **"Because the creation itself [the universe not now capable of sustaining life] will be set free from its bondage and decay and obtain the glorious liberty of the children of God."**

How did all the planets fall into this bondage and decay? Surely God did not create them in this state, for God's creation was PERFECT!

Decay signifies a state or condition caused by degeneration and decomposition from a previous undecayed state. God's creation was glorious and beautiful.

Perhaps the entire universe was created capable of sustaining life until it became "chaotic" and "confused" in Satan's rebellion. God is not the author of confusion, but Satan is! (1 Cor. 14:33). God is the author of order and continuity (1 Cor. 14:40).

At the end of the book of Revelation, we read about the "new heavens" and "new earth" (Rev. 21:22). There is just the briefest amount of information here to whet our appetites. But under the Father, we, being CHILDREN OF GOD—IMMORTAL, will restore ALL THINGS (Acts 3:21). The whole universe will be put back to its original orderly arrangement.

Present estimates— no doubt underestimates—put the size of the universe at over 20 thousand million light years in diameter. That's about 120,000 million million million miles.

Present estimates—also no doubt underestimates—put the number of galaxies in the known universe at over 1,000,000,000,000. Since each galaxy has roughly 1,000,000,000,000 stars, that means the universe has over 10,000,000,000,000,000,000,000 [ten thousand million million million] individual stars or "suns."

Remember, God is not the author of confusion, but of order and there is a reason why He created such an immense universe.

Once the universe is put back into shape, the God family will begin implementing the next stage in the Father's and Christ's overall plan.

The Increase of His Government

Why has God created the enormity of this universe? The answer may be found in Isaiah 9:7: **"...of the INCREASE of**

His government...there shall be no end..." Perhaps the reason for all the territory of the universe is room for growth—for continuous expansion of the family of God.

What happens when the universe is fully occupied? This question goes far beyond our present meager understanding because we are as yet unable to comprehend it. Suffice it to say that the known universe can be infinite in size. Some astronomers postulate that the physical universe is infinite with space expanding and matter continually coming into existence.

We should recognize that even if the family of God were to continue expanding throughout an infinity of space and an eternity of time—this earth will always remain the headquarters of the universe. All governmental decisions and organization will emanate from the earth as this is where God the Father and Jesus Christ will permanently reside (Rev. 21:23).

The Earth—A Unique Creation

Is there life on other planets as some suppose? Is the earth the first place God has set His hand to reproduce His Character, or has He tried to do it on other planets first? The answer to these perplexing questions can only be determined from our understanding of God's purpose and plan of which we have just disclosed.

It appears God created the vast universe to be governed by angels and the earth was the training ground to see whether they would obey. Lucifer, the great archangel convinced a third of the angels to *rebel* with him and turned the earth into "chaotic confusion" or a state of futility and decay.

This earth, like man himself, is truly unique! And it will most likely be unique as the headquarters of God's government for all Eternity!

Entering the God Family

There are only three ways one can enter any physical family legitimately: 1) by being **BORN** into it, and 2) by **MARRYING** into it, and being **ADOPTED** into it.

Under the New Testament, Christians will be both "born" into it and "marry" into it! Why this divine marital relationship? This marriage within the very FAMILY or Kingdom of God?

First, this gives us additional positive evidence that the Kingdom of God is a family—with Father, Son and His Wife! Those in the Church now, as heirs—are already *now* "children of God", not yet resurrected, who call Him Father! But, then these faithful children of God will be resurrected by God—and also [at the Millennium's conclusion] we [collectively] shall be Christ's WIFE!

Then, many children will be Spirit-born of that divine union—it will greatly enlarge the divine Family—which is the Kingdom of God! During the thousand years beginning from the time of that engagement—God, through Christ and His divine Bride, will set Himself to save the world!

Those who are now called, and who do repent, who do receive Christ as Savior, do follow God's Spirit, not only will eventually be married to Christ—they are to RULE with Him (Matt. 24:45; Lk. 12:42; Rev. 2:26-27; 3:21; 1 Cor. 6:2-3) and they will be priests and kings (Rev. 5:10; 20:6) during the Millennium!

With the Saints made immortal [the collective Bride of Christ]—the human mortals left alive on earth will be ruled by Christ and His Bride. Human mortals will be taught and ruled by *immortals*!

After His return as King over all nations, sitting on the Throne of His Glory, then shall Christ say to His Church: **"Come, ye blessed of my Father, inherit the Kingdom" (Matt. 25:31-34).**

Chapter Eight

> *Then said the LORD unto Moses, Behold, I will rain bread from heaven for you; and the people shall go out and gather a certain rate every day, that I MAY PROVE THEM, WHETHER THEY WILL WALK IN MY LAW, OR NOT*
> —Ex. 16:4.

ISRAEL'S THREE SOJOURNS

Through this fascinating study of the *types*, we have garnered many spiritual jewels from the experiences of ancient Israel. Now, through the three physical sojourns of Israel, we will begin a most incredible study into *our* spiritual sojourn as Christians upon the earth.

By studying Israel's sojourn in Egypt, the Wilderness and Canaan—we will learn more about our Christian calling and *how* to enter the Kingdom of God!

The Egyptian experience under Pharoah's cruel taskmasters was a *type* of spiritual BONDAGE TO SIN, that every Christian must *overcome* in their journey to the spiritual Promised Land!

The Wilderness episode of Israel was a time of TRIAL and *testing* to prove their *obedience* to their God. A Christian must also be *tried* and *tested* by the Almighty God—to PROVE if they will serve God or Satan!

Only after a Christian has relived the Egyptian and Wilderness experience can they enter spiritual Canaan or the

Kingdom of God. Here is where RULERSHIP over the nations is exercised—but only after *obedience* and *faith* have been demonstrated!

In our study of the *types,* we have seen that actual human events of the Old Covenant, involving literal people and physical substances—have had many things in common with spiritual realities that can benefit the Christian experience (1 Cor. 10:11).

Because the spiritual realm is intangible, God has provided a means through the physical senses of which can be seen, touched, smelled, tasted and heard—to perceive spiritual principles governing His Kingdom!

The journey of the nation of Israel from Egyptian bondage through the wilderness into the land of Canaan—is one of the tangible examples through which Christians can better understand their salvation journey upon the earth.

The book of Jude, as well as the 3rd and 4th chapters of the book of Hebrews, brings out this *analogy* loud and clear. These chapters are devoted to Christian admonition, and the writer *graphically* parallels the Christian pilgrimage to that of the wilderness sojourn of Israel, and their entering the land of Canaan flowing with "milk and honey."

Through this beautiful *parallel,* we can comprehend that Canaan is a *type* of the Christian "rest"—that they can enter only after they have been brought through the wilderness wandering.

Canaan is our ultimate goal as a *type* of the Kingdom of God—or God's *rest* pictured by the seventh day! (Heb. 4:4-8).

Let us now take an in depth look at each of these three sojourns of Israel—to better understand our Christian journey as we press towards the possession of the fulness of God's promises!

The Egyptian Experience

The land of Egypt, as we have learned previously, is a *type* of sin, and Pharoah a *type* of Satan holding potential "Sons of God" under BONDAGE to sin.

The process of becoming a Christian is very similar to the events that happened to Israel during the first Passover. The sacrificial blood of Jesus Christ, *symbolic* of the Lamb's blood on the Israelite doorposts—must be *accepted* as the payment for our sins. Then we can receive the Passover *protection* through the *atoning blood* of Jesus Christ!

This is what separates us from the world of sin (Egypt) around us! But Satan's hordes of hell, like the Egyptian army, will not leave us alone! They pursue after us even after we have left the world's ways (Egypt).

The "lords of darkness" continue to badger and tempt us through the lures of *human nature*—the "lust of the flesh", the "lust of the eyes," and the "pride of life!"

However, we can conquer our human nature by burying ourselves with Christ, just as the Israelites were baptized in the Red Sea as Pharoah's armies chased after them in hot pursuit!

Once we receive the gift of God's Holy Spirit—His very life begins to come inside of us. God's "seed of life" gives us a *new heart* or mind and we can then harness our human nature—even in Satan's world (Egypt)!

But we must be vigilant, realizing being redeemed from sin (Egypt) does not mean we are taken out of the world held captive by Satan's cruel taskmasters! Satan's minions no longer have power over us as he does over the nonbelieving! (11 Tim. 2:26; 1 Jn. 5:18).

The Egyptian experience of Israel teaches us that it is possible to live in an imprisoned world of sin and bondage. But once we prove that we have conquered this environment—it is time to move on! During Israel's Egyptian slavery—they proved to God, they would still choose Him over the gods of Egypt!

As we begin our Christian journey out of sin, the gods of our Egyptian experience such as gluttony, alcoholism, lust, sex, addiction, resistance to authority, must be squelched!

Neophyte Christians must CONQUER the "wicked impulses" of the flesh before they can experience the next phase of their growth sojourn. Every pull of the flesh must be subdued including *rebellion* toward God, government and authority!

The carnal mind is against law and government and therefore must have the mind of God to help it do what is not natural! God's holy Spirit is the "comforter" and helpmate that we need to govern our fleshly appetites!

Non-believers have to muster up their own strength or willpower to conquer the flesh—but this "pull yourself up by your own bootstraps" philosophy is doomed to fail without God's added power! The one vital difference between the Egyptian experience of Israel and the Christian, and in fact the difference between the Old Covenant and the New Testament—is that Christians have been given the POWER of God's Holy Spirit within them as a help-mate to contain the flesh!

The first stage in our Christian sojourn is *conquering* our human nature of rebellion, gossiping, envying, witchcraft, covetousness, greed, hatred, murder, idolatry, adultery, immorality, fighting, incest, whoredom, drunkenness, gluttony, etc.—all that is natural to our human nature and unnatural to a godlike nature! (Gal. 5:19-21; Heb. 13;4; Eph. 5:18; Col. 3:5-9; 1 Cor. 5: 1-5, 6:18; 1Thess. 4:3-5; Rom. 1:26-27).

Conquering the Flesh

Those who have not yet received God's Holy Spirit to help them break the shackles of sin—are still held *prisoner* to the Egypt of this world! They are Satan's captives, and held ransom as slaves to sin!

Before we are fit to RULE with God over His Creation and restore that which was lost in Eden—we must be able to conquer the bondage to "Pharoah" by allowing God's Holy Spirit to *rule* in our lives, and by being subject to God's will and not our own!

Putting the apostle Paul's words in modern vernacular:

If we choose to live after the ways of human nature [our fleshly appetites], we shall die— but if we choose to live according to God's will, we shall live [eternally] (Rom. 8:13,14).

How then do we draw close to God and *conquer* the indulgences of the flesh? By praying, studying and meditating upon God's Word, fasting periodically, exercising God's Holy Spirit, and by fellowshipping with other Christians! This takes *daily* effort on our part! It takes organization, time, discipline— SACRIFICE!

But realize also! God will never coerce, force or bribe anyone to live a godly way of life! However, He stands ready to offer His Holy Spirit to those who *willingly* choose to have Him enter and guide their lives!

Like Joshua who led God's army against the cities of the Philistines—our Commander-in-Chief sends His Holy Spirit as our spiritual warrior to fight the Philistines of sin! When we do our part—God will do His! These stories are for our admonition!

God's Word admonishes us to confess our sins and set aside time to study God's Word, and fellowship with other Christians instead of the world.

Once *we* do our part in fighting the battle of the flesh—God will fight alongside of us as He fought for Joshua and Gideon! God slew the Egyptians—but Israel fought in Canaan (showing that *we* must do our share of the fighting).

Israel had to demonstrate that they were absolutely serious about overcoming their obstacle. They had to go to war against it! Then, like a withering, consuming fire before them, God intervened and gave them victory.

Undoubtedly, Israel would have found it much more comfortable had God chosen to step in while the enemy was still way off in the distance. But that would have required little faith or commitment on the part of Israel.

That's why God didn't do it like that—and still doesn't! Overcoming is really a joint venture—God supplies the *power,* but only after we first supply the *initiative.* The resulting success is a joint achievement!

Here are some dogmatic scriptures on the power of the flesh:

Gal. 5:19-21   "Now the *works of the flesh* are manifest [clear or obvious], which are these; Adultery, fornication, uncleanness, lasciviousness, Idolatry, witchcraft, hatred, variance, emulations, wrath, strife, seditions, heresies, Envyings, murders, drunkenness, revellings, and such like: of the which I tell you before, as I have also told you in time past, that they which do such things *shall not inherit the kingdom of God."*

Rom. 8:13   "For if ye live after the flesh, ye shall die; but if ye through the Spirit do mortify the deeds of the body, ye shall live."

Rom. 13:14	"But put ye on the Lord Jesus Christ, and make not provision for the flesh, to fulfil the lust thereof."
Gal. 5:16	"This I say then, Walk in the Spirit, and ye shall not fulfil the lust of the flesh."
1 Jn. 2:16	"For all that is in the world, the lust of the flesh, and the lust of the eyes, and the pride of life, is not of the Father, but is of the world."
1 Cor. 9:27	"But I keep under my body, and bring it into subjection: lest that by any means, when I have preached to others, I myself should be a castaway."
Rom. 6:12	"Let not sin therefore reign in your mortal body, that ye should obey it in the lusts thereof."
Lk. 8:14	"And they which fell among thorns are they, which, when they have heard, go forth, and are choked with *cares and riches and pleasures of this life,* and bring no fruit to perfection."
Gal. 6:8	"For he that soweth to his flesh shall of the flesh reap corruption; but he that soweth to the Spirit shall of the Spirit reap life everlasting."
1 Pet. 4:1,2	"Forasmuch then as Christ hath suffered for us in the flesh, arm yourselves likewise with the same mind: for *he that hath suffered in the flesh has ceased from sin;* that he no longer should live the rest of his time in the flesh to the lusts of men, but to the will of God."
Eph. 2:2,3	"Wherein in time past ye walked according

to the course of this world, according to the prince of the power of air, the spirit that now worketh in the children of disobedience; Among whom also We all had our Conversation in times past *in the lusts of our flesh, fulfilling the desires of the flesh and of the mind*; and were by nature the children of wrath, even as others."

The Bitter Waters of Marah

After the children of Israel had been delivered from Egyptian bondage, and after they had been *baptized* in the Red Sea after being chased by Pharaoh—a strange but highly significant event happened to them while groping in the wilderness.

Soon after leaving Egypt, the Israelites began to rejoice and sing a triumphant song as God *guided* them in the wilderness (Ex. 15:1,13). But then, they began losing *faith* in their Deliverer as they didn't have any water to drink for three whole days (vs. 22).

Then the Israelites stumbled upon the **"bitter waters of Marah" (vs. 23).** Again, they became frustrated and disillusioned with life.

Are there any "bitter waters" in our life? Can we identify with these disillusioned Israelites? Oftentimes life becomes "bitter" or intolerable when we don't do things God's way!

Indeed, life has "bitter moments"—but we needn't let them last! Sometimes we may feel as though "life is against us" (Gen. 42:36)—but this is a time to have *faith* and confidence that God will *guide* and *deliver* us!

What did the Eternal do to rectify this terminal situation? He told Moses to cast a tree into the bitter water to make it sweet! (vs. 25).

What significance was this "sweet tree"? What do trees represent in the Word of God?

Recall how there were two trees in the Garden of Eden and one *symbolized* "eternal life." Servants of God become trees of righteousness (Isa. 61:3) when they are faithful to God (Ex. 15:26). Then they have the right to eternal life!

Notice also during this episode, how there were 12 wells of

water that healed *disease* surrounded by 40 palm trees (Ex. 15:26:27). Compare (Revelation 22:1) where a "tree of life" will produce 12 manner of fruit for the *healing* of nations during the Millennium!

"Healing waters" *symbolic* of God's Holy Spirit flow spiritually out of the belly of Christ and into the tree of life that will change the "bitter waters" of Marah into sweet!

Jesus is the "living water" that we need in our daily lives to change our bitter experiences into sweet (Jn. 4:10). Christians need the full supply of the spirit of Jesus Christ (Phil. 1:19). Our loving God promises to supply all of our needs (Phil. 4:19).

Just as the ancient Israelites sang the song of Moses after their deliverance in Egypt—resurrected Christians will also sing the victory song as they overcome the end-time Pharaoh [Beast Power] (Rev. 15:3). Victory will be proclaimed over the Beast (Rev. 15:2) as he will have power to make war with the Saints (Rev. 13:17).

Then, like ancient Israel, Christians who endure to the end and overcome the "bitter waters in our lives" will be able to say, the Eternal, **"My soul, my strength, my salvation" (Ex. 15:1-2).**

The Wilderness Experience

After the Israelites had made their exodus from Egypt [a *type* of sin] and were baptised in the "Red Sea"—they were ready to be *tried* and TESTED by the hot desert sun in the wilderness.

This is a beautiful *parallel* to the Christian redemptive experience. For after we come out of the Egypt of this world [sin] we are *baptised* into the death and resurrection of Jesus Christ!

When the Israelites reached Mt. Sinai, they were fed manna from heaven and were *healed* by the brazen serpent. This entire sequence of events was to teach Israel to have FAITH and *trust* in their benevolent God for their daily needs!

The "spiritual manna" of a Christian is Jesus Christ, and we must eat Him spiritually as *pictured* by the New Testament *symbols* of the bread and wine given at Christ's last Passover. The Passover bread stood for Christ's beaten body that *heals* us in times of sickness [*symbolized* by the brazen serpent], and His shed blood cleanses us from all sin.

When Christians live by their Savior's words and have Him in their daily lives—they are following God just like Israel that followed Him in the cloud. When the cloud moved during the day, Israel followed. When the fiery cloud stopped at night—Israel pitched their tents! Likewise, Christians who are following Christ must learn to have faith, patience, wisdom, strength; etc. as they look to their spiritual leader Jesus Christ!

It was at Mt. Sinai in the Egyptian wilderness that the nation of Israel was married to God and received His 10 Commandments—to see if they would be *faithful* to their husband! During the Christian wilderness trek, we are also *tried* and *tested* daily to see if we will be faithful to God.

There are always spiritual "Ox in the ditch" situations that tend to trouble us and *prove* our Christianity! We are constantly faced with sickness, marital problems, government regulations [Church & State], financial difficulties, child rearing traumas—all kinds of doubts, pressures and decisions! Sometimes we are perplexed, even persecuted—but God promises He will never forsake us (Heb. 13:5).

Why has a loving God led us into this confused and barren spiritual wilderness? Here is the reason He gave to the ancient Israelites:

Then said the LORD unto Moses, Behold, I will rain bread from heaven for you; and the people shall go out and gather a certain rate every day, *that I may prove them, whether they will walk in my law, or no* **(Ex. 16:4).**

Notice! It was to PROVE if the nation of Israel would be faithful to Him! If we were to *never* have had to experience trial, and therefore *never* had to learn to depend on God for anything, we would be filled with vanity and self-righteousness! Our human nature would get the best of us, and we would tend to think we can achieve our goals through our own talents and abilities!

Therefore, our all-wise God HUMBLES us through sickness, financial despair, persecution, etc. to help us realize our inherent weakness without Him in our lives!

It is during *trial* that the most self-righteous of individuals get on their knees, fast, read their Bibles and confess their sins! It is through the "school of the wilderness" that we learn to overcome our environment through *faith* and *obedience* to Christ!

Developing the Character to Rule

Recall, our ultimate destiny is not a heaven where Christians are strumming harps, or floating on a cloud, but rather RULERSHIP in God's Kingdom with Jesus Christ! To be wisked off to heaven to float around in a never never land all day long is one thing—but to be *qualifying* to be a ruler as a "king" or "priest" in God's government on earth is quite mind blowing and awesome!

If we are to be *rulers*—we must first learn to be *ruled!* The first place to start is by bringing our own little microcosm [including ourself] under *subjection* to the perfect will of God Almighty!

Coming out of the land of Egypt was a *type* of our Christian journey coming out from under Satan's domain and under God's divine government! But being *under* God's government and ruling *over* God's government are two entirely different concepts!

Our journey has begun, we have a new monarch on the throne—we are marching towards the Promised Land! We have a changed heart, but we are still dubious about certain things and there is a great deal of mayhem and fear in our lives!

The "desert school" in the wilderness on this earth is where God will teach us the three R's of His divine laws—and we will learn to OBEY them through the power of His Holy Spirit! It is here that we will also learn about our enemies who will try and prevent us from reaching our ultimate goal. It is on earth that we will learn to be faithful to God—as we make the transition from flesh and blood to spirit!

Should we miss this painful and sometimes agonizing experience and proceed directly to the Promised Land—we would never have learned godly CHARACTER! Can you imagine how ungrateful the Israelites would have been if they were handed the land of "milk and honey" immediately after leaving Egypt? It would have been like being born with a silver spoon in their mouth!

Can we begin to comprehend the necessity of the

"wilderness experience"?

Do we have a diabolical Creator that takes delight in our pain and suffering? Assuredly not! However, every tear and doubt is absolutely essential in our spiritual growth to conquer the Promised Land!

When we will have graduated from our school in the wilderness, we will have received a diploma in *faith*—but faith through trial! We will have learned *obedience* to God's government—but through trial! We will have been taught *brotherly love*—but through trial! Only through hardship, doubt, perplexity and persecution can we develop godly CHARACTER!

Another purpose of the Israelite wilderness wandering was to develop a strong belief in God in order to conquer their enemies. Recall how Israel was a configuration of disoriented Hebrew slaves when they left Egypt—but God molded them into a strong and audacious army by the time they were ready to invade the Promised Land!

Similarly, if Christians are to RULE with Jesus Christ in His Kingdom—we must learn to rule over our little kingdom (job, body, household, etc.). If we cannot overcome these by faith, and rule this miniature kingdom of ours—how are we ever going to be entrusted to govern with Christ over all His possessions?

As Jesus stated in Matthew 25:21:

...Well done, thou good and faithful servant: thou hast been faithful over a few things, I will make thee ruler over many things: enter thou into the joy of thy Lord.

If we are to press towards the mark of *rulership* over the nations—we must be an *overcomer!* That means we will have to overcome the daily trials and tests God puts us through with great joy—realizing they are more precious than gold refined in a fire! (1 Pet. 1:7).

Each new trial or burden signals thoughts of discouragement, and triggers our human nature to give up and quit! But God wants us to press forward as a Christian soldier and *fight* for our Christian inheritance! Instead of throwing in the towel—God desires that we prayerfully come before Him and *humbly* seek His will!

The only individuals who will cross over "spiritual Jordan" are those who have spent time in the wilderness of this world, and developed Godly character!

Jordan—A Type of Passover

The "crossing over" the river Jordan to inherit the promised land—was but a *type* of the "passing over" of the Passover in Egypt.

After being in the wilderness for 40 years, the second generation Israelites crossed the Jordan on the 10th day of the 1st month (Josh. 4:19), on dry ground (vs. 22).

Anciently, this was the day in which the preparation of the Passover lamb began (Ex. 12:3).

This momentous occasion was similar to the "passing over" of the Red Sea, which was a *type* of water baptism (Josh. 4:23; 1 Cor. 10:20).

Water Baptism, of course, is the next step one takes after *accepting* the sacrifice of Jesus Christ—the Christian *deliverer* and Passover!

The significance of the Passover in relationship to Israel's timely entrance into Canaan is observed in their being circumcised after crossing over Jordan dry-shod during Passover (Josh. 5:10). Passover and circumcision are related in that circumcision *pictures* the putting off of the old sinful way of life, once *accepting* the perfect sacrificial Lamb of Jesus Christ!

The walls of Jericho kept the physical Israelites from inheriting the promised land. Likewise, the "walls of sin" in our lives will keep us out of God's eternal Kingdom unless we knock them down!

What a beautiful Christian analogy?

The Canaan Experience

Finally, we come to the end of our journey! It has been a long and agonizing journey to spiritual Canaan—but we have made it!

Alas, we have come out of spiritual Egypt [conquered human nature and our environment] *paralleling* the Israelite experience of SLAVERY or bondage to Pharoah (Satan). We have made our pilgrimage through TRIALS [doubts, fears, sufferings, confusion] of the hot barren desert of this world. At last we are ready to inherit "the land of milk and honey."

But *what* and *where* is the Christian Promised Land where we will receive our spiritual "milk and honey"? Is it Heaven, Paradise or New Jerusalem? Is it being changed through the resurrection? What exactly is the *mark* or *goal* we are pressing towards to complete our spiritual journey? (Phil. 3:14).

Surely this question is imperative to answer, for if we do not know *what* goal we are pressing towards—we will not struggle with all diligence to attain it!

Could this *confusion* be partly responsible for Israel's disloyalty in the wilderness?

What then does the Bible promise as the Christian's reward? It is RULERSHIP with Christ on the earth! See (Dan. 7:18; Isa. 60:12; Rev. 20:6; Matt. 5:5, 6:10; Rev. 5:10; Ps. 37:9, 11, 22, 34).

Jesus' entire commission was to preach the gospel [good news] about His Father's coming Kingdom to the earth! Christians are a colony of citizens whose citizenship is in heaven (Phil. 3:20).

The entire salvation process of atonement, receiving the gift of the Holy Spirit, developing our talents and human potential, being changed through the resurrection, receiving a spiritual body and eternal life, becoming a king or a priest—is for the sole purpose of RULING with God over His creation for all eternity!

Canaan was a *type* of that far city [God's Kingdom] that all the Saints of old looked to but were unable to inherit (Heb. 11:13-16).

Canaan was where the patriarchs Abraham, Isaac and Jacob wandered. It was into Canaan that father Abraham was called by God—out of the bondage of the sin-filled idol worshipping Chaldean city of Ur (Gen. 12:5).

Later, Abraham's grandchildren, through Jacob, sojourned in Egypt for 430 years (Ex. 12:40; Gen. 15:16) until God had forgiven them their sins. Then the Eternal forgave them of their iniquities as *typical* of the Passover lamb's blood—and prepared them for their sojourn back to their rightful inheritance.

The events of Israel's trek from Egypt and sin [including forgiveness by atonement] to trial by wandering in the wilderness, to INHERITANCE by blessing in Canaan, is a beautiful *replica* of a Christian's life on the earth.

Like the nation of Israel, the Church has begun it's sojourn in bondage and are miraculously delivered from slavery by the *atoning blood* of Jesus Christ. Then, both physical and spiritual Israel begin to march towards a *land of promise*.

But before they reach this land of milk and honey, they are both *tried* and *tested* to prove their faithfulness, dedication, loyalty, faith, courage and obedience to their Deliverer! And in both instances, only those who are OVERCOMERS, or true *fighters*, will inherit God's promises!

What a beautiful *parallel* between Israel's past history and God's Church today?

Spiritual Warfare

The Canaan experience of Israel portrays our RULING with Jesus Christ over the earth during the Millennium! This is a time picturing 1000 years of love, joy, peace, patience, gentleness, goodness, faith, meekness, temperance [self-control], etc., as all of the fruits of God's Holy Spirit start to bloom (Gal. 5:22-23).

The training and activity the Israelites went through in Canaan was a *prototype* of millennial life that all Christians will one day encounter.

During Israel's stay in the wilderness, they did not experience the abundance of fruits and vegetables or "milk and honey" as they did in the promised land. That's why the Feast of Tabernacles envisions the abundance of choice edibles—only to be experienced in Canaan! While in the wilderness, Israel *never* experienced such abundance in quality foods!

The Canaan experience is yet another Christian parallel to the Feast of Tabernacles *picturing* millennial life? The *fruits of God's Holy Spirit* will flourish like never before during this time!

Before any Christian can taste of this spiritual Promised Land—they must *overcome* the world, human nature and Satan! Through the dynamic and inspired apostle Paul, God's Word tells us, **"...we wrestle not against flesh and blood, but against...the rulers of the darkness of this world, against spiritual wickedness [literally wicked spirits] in high places" (Eph. 6:12).**

Make no mistake about it—Christians are in a spiritual

battle! In order to be a Christian soldier who can do battle against our spiritual adversaries—our Commander-in-Chief has given us the example of Israel to know how to arm ourselves. As the saying goes, "to be *forewarned* is to be *forearmed!*"

It is a highly significant fact that when God brought the Israelites out of Egyptian slavery—He fought for them! Starting with the plagues in Egypt, swallowing up of the Egyptian army in the Red Sea following the exodus, to the giving of the Law at Mt. Sinai—God fought for His people!

This is also true of Christians—for Jesus fought for our redemption by withstanding the temptations of Satan in the wilderness! But as soon as Israel received the Law at Mt. Sinai in the wilderness [their boot camp]—God began organizing them into a disciplined army to inherit Canaan (Num. 10:1,2). Upon entering Canaan, the Israelites were expected to *fight* for their inheritance—and so will Christians!

Any Christian who doesn't think they are in a SPIRITUAL WAR against the deceptions of the world, human nature and wicked spirits—is only kidding himself!

While in the school of the wilderness, Israel was being taught *faith* and *obedience* while God was forming them into a marching army to conquer their enemies!

When God felt His troops were ready to do battle, He told them to send twelve captains [one from each tribe] to search out the land of Canaan (Num. 13).

Upon observation of Canaan, the 12 spies gazed upon the clusters of grapes, pomegranates and figs (Num. 13:23). Truly it was a land flowing with milk and honey, they said (vs. 27). But the spies *feared* the Amalekites, Hittites, Jebusites, and Amorites that dwelt in the land (vss. 28-33).

Even though the Eternal had brought them out of the land of Egypt through miracle after miracle, the *faith* of these Israelite spies wavered when they saw the giants of the sons of Anak in the land (vs. 33).

Then all the congregation chimed with a loud voice, **"...Let us make a captain, and let us return into Egypt" (Num. 14:4).** Israel's faith wavered!

After witnessing the miracles of God Almighty in Egypt and in the wilderness [except for Joshua and Caleb—Num. 14:6]— this faithless congregation preferred going back to the brutal taskmasters in Egypt, rather than trust God and FIGHT their enemies!

Christian Bootcamp

Hopefully, we can learn from the Christian counterpart in these unbelieving and complaining Israelites? Christians must ask ourselves whether we identify with spiritual Joshua or Caleb, desiring to face our spiritual enemies—or prefer Satan's captivity to sin?

For their rebellion and incitement of the Eternal—God wanted to smite every last one of them with pestilence, and disinherit them— and then start another nation through the seed of Moses (Num. 14:12-13).

However, Moses convinced God that destroying the disbelieving Israelites would only prove to the world that God could not fulfill His promise of bringing His people into the land of Canaan (Num. 14:14-17).

Therefore, the Eternal extinguished His wrath and ordered the Israelites to return into the bootcamp of the wilderness, to be taught additional *faith* and *obedience* for another thirty-eight years!

Christian soldiers, like the Israelites of old, are being taught by the school of the Holy Spirit to have *faith* and TRUST in their God—and He will help them fight their spiritual enemies! Christ's army is being formed now to invade the spiritual forces of evil who now occupy our Promised Land! Now is the time to be a Christian sheep—but there appears to be a coming time when Christian soldiers will follow their Commander-in-Chief on white horses to do battle against Satan's hordes of hell (Rev. 19).

Finally, when the Israelites developed a deep abiding faith to cross over the river Jordan to inherit the land God promised them—the Ark of the covenant [symbolic of Jesus Christ] went before them and was placed in the middle of the Jordan river until every last Israelite crossed over!

Similarly, Jesus Christ who is the captain of our salvation, was the First-Fruit from the dead and awaits the resurrection of the rest of His army before attacking the infidel forces of Satan!

The events that happened to Israel also show us that God does not expect us to fight our battles alone—rather He fights alongside of us! Joshua did not bring down the walls of Jericho single handedly—he had help from God's holy angels (Josh. 5:13; 6:20).

The "long day of Joshua", when the sun stood still for "about a whole day" during a crucial battle, as well as the hailstones that destroyed the armies of the Amorites (Josh. 10:11-13)—were all *miracles* provided by God to ensure the decisive edge and enhance victory!

Of course, our VICTORY must be won over carnal nature, the lust of the world and the temptations of the Devil! But we must realize that we have a General who helps us fight our physical and spiritual battles!

Once we gain victory over *our* physical habitat, God will resurrect us to conquer the spiritual world of Satan and drive him out of the earth (our Canaan). As resurrected Christian Sons of God, and as Christ's Bride—we can then proceed to gain total victory over the earth!

Through Jesus Christ and His resurrected Bride, God is going to completely invade and annihilate the entire kingdom of "unclean beasts" that now roam in and occupy our Promised Land! A big part of the Messiah's commission is to "break the bonds" of Satan by setting his hostages free (1 Jn. 3:8).

There are many scriptural references to the destruction of these *spiritual* Hittites, Amorites, Canaanites, Hivites, [Satan's legions] in our land (see Deuteronomy 7:1,2) where God said of them: **"...thou shalt smite them, and utterly destroy them; thou shalt make no covenant with them, nor show mercy unto them."**

Can we see the *duality* between these ancient mercenaries who possessed Israel's land, and Satan's demons who now roam and control the earth? They must be totally destroyed without mercy!

Counterparts between the war Israel had with these heathen nations and our spiritual battle with Satan are found in the following verses (1 Jn. 3:8; Rom. 16:20; Lk. 10:18,19; Mk. 16:17; Rev. 12:7,8; 19:14,15).

Inheriting the Promised Land

The "rulers of darkness" of this age are insidious, crafty and RUTHLESS—they have nothing to lose or fear! Their goal is to devour Christians—and we are powerless against their multifarious schemes without God's help!

But if we develop the godly faith and character to be an "overcomer" in the wilderness—we shall drive these enemies of the cross out of our land as did the ancient Israelites!

The Devil and his cohorts of fallen angels are cunning warriors—and they relentlessly shoot fiery darts at us trying to put a crack in our spiritual armor! But this is where we must do our part in drawing close to God through the spiritual armor He provides.

The nation of Israel *feared* the Giants who possessed their land—and except for Joshua and Caleb, all those who left Egypt under Moses never reached Canaan!

Could *fear* be our achiles heel that destroys our faith—and robs us of our inheritance as it did the *disobedient* of Israel? Notice the admonition given to Christians in Hebrews 3:16-19:

> **For some, when they had heard, did provoke: howbeit not all that came out of Egypt by Moses. But with whom was he grieved forty years? was it not with them that had *sinned*, whose carcasses fell in the wilderness? And to whom sware he that they should not enter into his rest (the Kingdom of God), but to them that believed not? So we see that they could not enter in because of *unbelief*.**

Joshua, as we have seen, was a *type* of Christ leading his people into the physical promised land. Realize that FEAR and UNBELIEF, or a lack of faith, is classified with all of the sinful works of the flesh that will prevent individuals from attaining salvation (Rev. 21:8).

Only those "overcoming Saints" who develop a tenacious faith and trust in God [without bickering or complaining], will be found worthy to inherit God's eternal rest! The *overcomer* must never give in or give up—but instead he must pursue the Land of Promise as a relentless soldier!

Prior to coming out of Egypt, the Eternal deliberately took the Israelites the long route to the land of Canaan by avoiding the country occupied by the Philistines. God did this because He knew the Israelites did not yet have enough *faith*, and would return to Egypt rather than fight (Ex. 13:17). However, once Israel was trained in the boot camp of the wilderness—God accepted no excuses!

Like the ancient Israelites, God gives us time to develop *faith* and to *overcome* our human nature, the world and Satan! If we do, the last enemy to be destroyed will be death! (1 Cor. 15:26). Then, as qualified OVERCOMERS inheriting the earth—we can proceed to conquer the universe!

Three Spiritual Burials and Resurrections

There are *three* spiritual *deaths* and *resurrections* that all Christians must experience before they can enter the family of God. These symbolic *deaths* and *resurrections* are pictured very graphically through the *types!*

In the "first spiritual death and resurrection" experience, we are CALLED by God out of this evil world, then we are CHOSEN in the "second spiritual death and resurrection" experience. If we are FAITHFUL during the "third spiritual death and resurrection" experience in our calling—we will experience the fourth spiritual death and resurrection experience!

These are the words of our Commander in Chief regarding the final battle for the earth: **"These shall make war with the Lamb, and the Lamb shall overcome them: for he is Lord of lords, and King of kings: and they that are with him are** *called,* **and** *chosen,* **and** *faithful"* **(Rev. 17:14).**

The 1st Spiritual Death and Resurrection "Water Baptism"

The "first spiritual death and resurrection" all Christians *must* experience before entering the family of God—is that of *crucifying* the fleshly desires of human nature!

The ceremony of WATER BAPTISM *symbolically* depicts *the* burying of our "old man" or old way of life that is hostile towards God's loving way of life. We are saying *symbolically*, that we are willing to quench our "fleshly" appetites of lust, pride, vanity, sex, self-seeking, greed, lying, gossiping, jealousy; etc; etc.

We must *overcome* our human nature, the world around us, and Satan's influence over these—by *crucifying* ourselves spiritually as Paul put it so very beautifully in Galatians 2:20:

> **I am crucified with Christ: nevertheless I live, yet not I, but Christ liveth in me: and the life which I now live in the flesh, I live by the faith of the Son of God, who loved me, and gave himself for me.**

God's holy Word tells us that "sin is pleasurable" for a period of time (Heb. 11:25), but we must not let this *temporary* gratification destroy our eternal lives! Instead, we must mortify [destroy, subdue, discipline] our fleshly desires by pounding the nails into our own flesh [spiritually speaking] and arising a new person in Christ to conquer our human nature!

Again, Paul admonishes us: **"For if ye live after the flesh [human nature], ye shall die: but if ye through the spirit do mortify [crucify] the deeds (desires) of the body, ye shall live" (Rom. 8:13).**

When we accept Jesus as our personal Savior—a part of us must *die*—in order that the rest of us can live eternally!

The 2nd Spiritual Death and Resurrection "Trials"

Trial and testing bring forth fruitfulness as witnessed by many biblical examples. Only after Abraham was willing to sacrifice his only legitimate son Isaac—did he receive God's blessing!

Abraham *died inside* as he raised the knife to kill his son born by promise. At that precise moment, every joy, hope and dream he had for Isaac perished within him as he raised his knife in anguish to kill his son. Abraham didn't even question God as to how he could justify breaking the 6th Commandment, **"Thou Shalt Not Kill"**—he just did God's will without question!

Here again, death and resurrection produce fruitfulness of life! Joseph in prison, Job and his boils, Jonah in the belly of the great fish, Jacob subservient to Laban, and wrestling with God—all depict spiritual death to their own ambitions and desires through TRIALS!

It was through these servants' trials and sufferings that *death in Jesus* [spiritual death to the conscience] occurred and their lives were changed for the better! Only when they surrendered their will to God was spiritual fruit born in their lives!

Jesus, our ultimate teacher and example, learned character development through the many trials He underwent, notice:

> **For it became him, for whom are all things, and by whom are all things, in bringing many sons unto glory, to make the captain of their salvation perfect [mature] *through sufferings* (Heb. 2:10). Though he were a Son, yet learned he *obedience* by the things which he *suffered*; And being made perfect (mature), he became the author of eternal salvation unto all them that obey him (Heb. 5:8,9).**

The Christian, suffering in like manner of Christ, will also benefit from suffering as he can have empathy towards others:

> **Who comforteth us *in all our tribulation* (trials), that we may be able to comfort them which are in any trouble, by the comfort wherewith we ourselves are comforted of God. For as *the sufferings of Christ abound in us*, so our consolation also aboundeth by Christ (11 Cor. 1:4,5).**

Paul continues to expound upon the passing from spiritual death to spiritual life through trial:

> **We are hard pressed on every side, yet not crushed; we are perplexed, but not in despair; persecuted, but not forsaken; struck down, but not destroyed— always carrying about in the body the dying of the Lord Jesus, that the life of Jesus also may be manifested in our body. For we who live are always delivered to death for Jesus' sake, that the life of Jesus also may**

be manifested in our mortal flesh (11 Cor. 4:8-11 NKJV).

Trials and tribulation produce spiritual FRUIT in our lives as we die in Christ, as Jesus said in John 12:24: **"...except a corn of wheat fall unto the ground and die, it abideth alone: but if it die, it bringeth forth *much fruit.*"**

Our leader in human suffering once said of His Church: **"Ye have not chosen me, but I have chosen you, and ordained you, that ye should go and bring forth fruit" (Jn. 15:16).**

Through suffering and persecution [even unjustly] in society, at work, or at home—God will never leave us or forsake us, and will eventually exhonerate us! But only when we die within, can we be raised to help others with the greatest of comfort!

Like the ancient Israelites in Egypt, sometimes we have to make bricks without straw—and it all boils down to proper attitude during trials!

The 3rd Spiritual Death and Resurrection "Self-Denial"

Going across the river Jordan by the *faithful* Israelites is a beautiful portrait drawn by the majestic hand of God, *picturing* the third spiritual death of *redemption,* and rising into the land of promise on the other side *symbolizes* the third resurrection.

This is the resurrection of CONQUEST, when the Christian can deny himself as Paul said to the Corinthians: **"For which cause we faint not, but though our *outward man perish* [is crucified], yet the inward man is renewed day by day" (11 Cor. 4:16).**

Reaching the "third spiritual death" means we have conquered our own personal pursuits of life without "self-gratification," and are willing to do things for others—even though this is not our natural tendency! It means we are willing to voluntarily give up our life's ambitions without bickering or complaining to please our Creator!

Here, we are offering our *bodies* in service as "living sacrifices!" Notice Paul's wording, **"...that ye present your *bodies* a living sacrifice" (Rom. 12:1).** It is our *body* that must be offered up! Sometimes it is a *tired* lifeless body—but we must continue to give it towards God's service even when it is not convenient!

How many of us relish to go visit friends or loved ones in a hospital? Or how many look forward to doing the dishes after inviting brethren over for dinner? How many are willing to fast and give their bodies in prayer to God when a loved one is suffering?

What did Paul mean by presenting our *body* as a living sacrifice to God? It means doing things that are not pleasant or natural! It means going places at times that are not convenient or accommodating!

This is SELF-DENIAL of our own pleasure seeking—and doing God's will instead! Luke, the beloved Physician, wrote Christ's prophetic words concerning self-denial:

> **...if any man will come after me, let him *deny himself*, and take up his cross daily, and follow me. For whosoever will save his life shall lose it: but whosoever will lose his life for my sake, the same shall save it... (Lk. 9:23-24).**

As Christ Himself said, we must deny ourself (crucify ourself) and take up His cross and follow Him (after His example). Paul related these same thoughts to us: **"Always bearing about *in the body the dying of the Lord Jesus*, that the life also of Jesus might be made manifest *in our body*" (11 Cor. 4:10).**

When the Israelites entered the Promised Land, they met some initial resistance by hostile enemies—but destroyed them all in battle! However, when they encountered the fierce warriors of the Philistines—their faith began to waiver!

Unlike the weak-kneed Israelites, Christian soldiers must face their spiritual enemies eye-ball to eye-ball and believe they are invincible with Christ on their side! They must never show *weakness* or *mercy* in destroying the enemies of the cross—and must CONQUER every last "spiritual Philistine" in their lives that would prevent them from entering God's eternal promised land!

There are times that Christian soldiers must cross the river Jordan spiritually and go to war!

Christian soldiers must press towards righteousness with

their shield of faith, their sword of righteousness and helmet of salvation—as they quench the fiery darts of the devil!

Make no mistake about it—we are engaged in spiritual warfare!

Chapter Nine

THE 7 STEPS OF SALVATION

Bit by bit, piece by piece, God has REVEALED His MASTER PLAN for mankind so that it can be assembled into a beautiful mosaic!

Through duality, types, symbolism, numbers, the creation week, parables, the Temple analogy, the tabernacle furniture, the offerings, the days of Noah, Israel's journey to the promised land, and God's Feast days—God's GRAND DESIGN for human salvation has been clearly brought into focus!

Furthermore, each of these areas contribute to the general sequence of God's plan, namely, 1) the personal redemptive work of Jesus Christ, 2) the perfecting of the Saints to form His Church, and 3) the setting up of the Church to restore the government of God to this earth.

Through the *types,* the *character* of Jesus Christ in wisdom, knowledge, compassion, empathy, authority, power, and holiness rings out loud and clear. All the major *types* in God's Word define God's unbounded love for His creation by sending His only begotten Son as ATONEMENT for a lost world, only to have hope through the RESURRECTION!

Throughout the *types,* we have seen that much *symbolism* applies to the life of Christ. However, we must also realize that the same *symbolism* refers to those who are walking in His footsteps. Therefore, the more we understand about Christ's redemptive work, the more we will comprehend our own spiritual existence!

Though the outworking of salvation has definite dimensions, this may not be experienced in a precise step by step manner in each Christian. The order may vary in each individual. However, each Christian should experience a *personal* as well as *historical* relationship to each of God's feast days.

In other words, there is a *personal* passover, atonement, trumpets, tabernacles etc. as well as a *historical* event to be experienced. There is a *personal* repentance and national repentance. There is a *personal* inner peace [millennium] as well as a national millennium etc.

Actually, each Christian experiences all of the facets of God's feast days to a certain degree at the moment of accepting Jesus as our personal Savior. Immediately, He becomes under the Passover blood's protection, and the leavening of sin depicted by the days of Unleavened Bread begins to be *removed* from his life after REPENTANCE and the symbolic meaning of water baptism.

As the fruit of God's Holy Spirit grows in each Christian's life, *pictured* by Pentecost, inner peace or REST, envisioned by the Feast of Tabernacles, enters his or her life. Atonement is relived *daily* as our debt of guilt is cancelled because of Christ's spotless sacrifice.

Trumpets is experienced *daily,* as we blow the trumpet of war against the *daily* battles, we encounter such as fleshly desires of lust, greed, vanity, hatred, lying, gossip, jealousy, etc.

Although God's feast days portray seven dimensions of salvation, it should be noted that salvation does not necessarily occur to each human being in a set pattern.

In studying the *types,* the first rule of thumb is to realize that every *type* breaks down eventually, and we should therefore look for the *main* truth God is presenting to us through it.

When we begin to focus on every last detail, we become disillusioned and miss the point God is trying to make. For example, the Bible speaks of the Church as the Bride of Christ. But to carry the meaning to where a Bride is feminine in nature [not the characteristics of tenderness, warmth, etc.] is misinterpreting the meaning.

The Bible also calls members of God's Church "Sons of

God." This would be a clear contradiction from a feminine Bride if we attempted to apply every detail of each *type*.

With this rule of thumb in mind, let us look deeper into the general orderly sequence of God's MASTER PLAN and assemble the *final* pieces together. We will now amalgamate the numerical sequence of the creation week, the tabernacle furniture, Israel's journey to the promised land, and God's feast days together!

Repentance, the First Step of Salvation

SANCTIFICATION, REDEMPTION, REPENTANCE: Passover and the 1st day of Unleavened Bread picture the death of our Lord, acceptance of our Lord by repenting, and protection from the judgments to come.

Number: The number *one* denotes UNITY, as the evening and morning became the first day. A Christian must struggle constantly with his human nature, and *repent* in order to become AT ONE with God! This nature is characteristic of fleshly Adam—and overcome by the nature of the second Adam—the spiritual Jesus Christ!

The Creation Week: The dividing of the *light* from *darkness* on the first day is a *picture* of REPENTANCE, as we divide the darkness of sin from the light of truth in our lives.

Jesus is the true "light" of truth that helps us divide the human nature in our lives and allows God's spirit of light and truth to guide us in this world of darkness! See (Ps. 43:3, 119:105; Rom. 2:19-20; Eph. 5:7-10; Jn. 1:4-9, 8:12; 1 Jn. 1:5) where the Bible equates *light* with *truth!*

Consider something very significant! Although God allowed the darkness to coexist on the earth with light, He did not call darkness "good." This is *dual* to Satan and his rulers of "darkness."

Tabernacle Furniture: The *bronze altar* for the burnt offerings stood in the courtyard, and is where the sacrifices were consumed by the altar's blazing heat. The many different offerings [Sin, Burnt, Meat and Peace] represented the different stages of the ATONING WORK of our Savior.

Each kind of offering contained in *symbol,* God's blueprint design for establishing conversion of the soul and ultimately world peace! Each offering is a *graphic* representation of Jesus Christ and characteristic of a *finer* point or *detail* to Christ's *atoning work.*

The Sin-offering was not a "sweet-savour" offering because it was the embodiment of sin. It was completely consumed and only the priests ate of it. It graphically portrayed a *repentant sinner* awaiting God's judgment.

In the Burnt-offering—the individual came as a *worshipper,* being *accepted* of God. Christians have washed their mind with the Word of God and start to live a godly life pictured by *baptism.* This is pleasing to God—but they must *continuously* prove their devotedness to God by being a "living sacrifice." Therefore, like the ancient Israelite's offering that was completely consumed upon the altar as a **"sweet-savour"**—so Christians show that they are *pleasing* to God and desire *nothing* for themselves.

The big difference between the Meat-offering is that it was a "sweet-savour" offering and the priests *could* eat of it! It *pictured* the sending forth of God's Holy Spirit to start His New Testament Church as the nucleus for saving mankind. But the *individual* could not yet eat of it!

Thus far, only God and the priests [*symbolic* of the Church] had anything to eat. These offerings were *symbolic* of one's relationship with other people.

The Peace-offering was *symbolic* of peace coming to us only after the person doing the giving learned to LOVE God and his neighbor—without receiving anything back! In the Peace-offering, the person giving the Peace-offering *could* eat it along with the Levite priests.

Thus, the individual *finally* received *satisfaction* from GIVING! In the Peace-offering, God was fed because our self-sacrificing is pleasing to Him. The one giving the offering was also fed, because love, which is giving, is satisfying! When we *give* something to someone else—we as well as the person receiving can rejoice!

What a beautiful plan and way of life!

Israel's Journey: The events that happened to the nation of Israel are examples of spiritual realities. Many of their occurrences are *dual*, and are prophetic happenings of the future,

SEVEN STEPS OF SALVATION

both in the spiritual and physical world.

The blood of the Passover lamb was for a *sign* upon the houses of the Israelites. At midnight the death angel *passed over* those houses that had been SEALED by the blood of the Passover Lamb.

The judgment upon the Egyptians, the Passover and the exodus were *types* of future events that will happen once again. It was on the 1st day of Unleavened Bread that the Israelites left Egypt. This was a day of great rejoicing and happiness, as they were set free from the slavery in Egypt!

Before leaving on their journey into the wilderness, Israel was commanded to remove all leaven from their homes for seven days. The separation of leaven from the camp of Israel is *symbolic* of the separation from Egypt, a *type* of sin. This division is *symbolic* between "light" and "darkness" of the 1st day of creation!

Feast Day: THE PASSOVER and 1st DAY OF UNLEAVENED BREAD

Past: On the tenth day of the first month of God's sacred calendar, a Lamb without blemish was selected to be killed as the Passover Lamb. The *symbolism* to our Lord is obvious, as He was without sin [spotless] and was examined under scrutiny by the religious leaders of Israel—yet they could not find any fault in Him!

The entire lamb was to be roasted with fire, *symbolic* of the fiery *trials* our Lord was to go through to develop character! Jesus had to endure many afflictions in order to qualify as the REDEEMER of the human race. Because He overcame human nature, the world and Satan, He fully *qualifies* to be the **"firstfruit"** to lead many sons unto glory!

The **"bitter herbs"** eaten during the days of Unleavened Bread *symbolized* the hard and difficult life that had engulfed the Israelites under the cruel taskmasters of Pharaoh. This season reminds Christians of the *suffering* our Savior endured as a man who was despised and rejected of men, a man of sorrow and acquainted with grief. *Bitter herbs* also remind us of our own trials as we follow in our elder brother's example.

The world hated Jesus and will also persecute those who acknowledge Him as their personal Savior. Christians must through much tribulation enter the kingdom of God!

The Eternal killed the firstborn of Egypt because Pharaoh [a type of Satan] was holding God's *firstborn* in captivity. There is a *duality* here to the Christian, as Satan holds them captive, being God's firstborn spiritually, until they are DELIVERED by the shed blood of Jesus Christ.

The entire land of Egypt was to mourn their dead, except for the children of God. God's people were SANCTIFIED or *"set apart"* from the terrible judgments to befall the Egyptians.

God executed judgment upon those worshipping false gods, but spared those who worshipped only the true God! The blood of the Passover lamb "separated" the homes of those who feared and obeyed God from those that worshiped idols! False religion was "separated" from true religion, just as God separated the light from darkness on the 1st day of creation.

This is the basic meaning of the Passover—past, present, and future! God "passed over" His people, but sent plagues of judgment on the wicked about them!

Present: Passover envisions REDEMPTION of erring sinning mankind by Jesus Christ. This is God's plan for restoring mankind to His throne of grace, which was otherwise forfeited through deceit and rebellion.

To be redeemed means to restore a person to the rightful or lawful owner—in this case Jesus Christ paid the debt of Believers and thereby became their Savior by providing the corresponding ransom for their sins.

Christians believe they were like a person who was kidnapped, and needed someone to pay the ransom money. They have now been legally restored back to God's grace according to His penal code of justice!

The Passover observance, and the communion service to a Christian today is a solemn occasion, *symbolizing* the death of Jesus Christ—the Savior of the world! The blood of the Passover lamb saved ancient Israel from physical destruction, and the blood of Jesus Christ, cleanses Christians of all sin so they can now be spiritually saved!

The Passover lamb delivered ancient Israel out of the clutches of Pharaoh, and Jesus Christ, the *antitype* and Christian Passover, is our deliverer from Pharaoh's antitype—Satan the devil!

SEVEN STEPS OF SALVATION

The children of Israel started out of Egypt the night of the 15th on the 1st Day of Unleavened Bread on their own. Christians must do the same thing once they accept the blood of Christ. Israel started out on their own strength, and Christians must follow their example—then God will *intervene* and help them in time of need!

Egypt is a *type* of sin, and soon after Israel left Egypt, Pharaoh's army went after them in hot pursuit. This is a *type* of Satan's legions of demons pursuing neophyte Christians, as soon as they accept the sacrifice of Christ and want to come out of sin. Then they come out of *spiritual* Egypt under the mighty hand of God!

While in Egypt, Israel was subject to Pharaoh's cruel taskmasters—they were helpless, powerless! They were vulnerable, just as a sinner is to the power of Satan without God's help. However, after Israel took the blood of the lamb God acted and as a result—freed Israel from sin just as God acts to release the devil from Christians!

Thus, accepting the blood of Christ and coming out of sin is a *picture* of the 1st Day of Unleavened Bread.

Future: God is going to judge the entire earth in a future Passover, which will have *similarities* to the first Passover in Egypt. Just as God sent devastating plagues upon the nation of Egypt, [*symbolic* of this sin filled world], God is once again going to send plagues of JUDGMENT upon this hell-bent world in a future Passover—just before Jesus returns to the earth visibly with *power* and glory!

The nation of Israel will be a captive people at that time, but God will once again have *mercy* on them, and DELIVER them out of the hand of their enemies in a future Passover! This miraculous deliverance will *parallel* the second exodus!

Fulfillment in Jesus: *Jesus* is our Passover Lamb, who without spot [sinless] was killed for our behalf! It was Jesus' blood that was *symbolically* taken into the Tabernacle in heaven, and sprinkled upon the Mercy-Seat before the Father. Thus, by His perfect sacrifice of love, we can now be saved from eternal death!

Baptism, the Second Step of Salvation

HUMAN NATURE SEPARATED BY BAPTISM: The 7th Day of Unleavened Bread *pictures* overcoming human nature through water *baptism* or **"spiritual death"** to the world, crucifixion and resurrection with Christ in a new way of life.

Number: The number *two* denotes *difference* or DIVISION and *pictures* the divisive human nature within our flesh that is at war with God's Holy Spirit. The lives of Cain and Abel are *reminiscent* of these two *natures* or **"attitudes of life"** struggling within us. The lives of Abraham and Lot, Isaac and Ishmael, Jacob and Esau, *pattern* the contention of the flesh striving against the Spirit.

The Creation Week: The dividing of the *waters* by means of the firmament of heaven on the second day is a *picture* of WATER BAPTISM, which comes after *repentance*. Once a Christian accepts the sacrifice of Jesus Christ for their sins, repents and if possible, baptized—they still must battle "human nature" which is at constant war with the Spirit of God.

Spiritually speaking, God separates our human nature from His Holy Spirit by placing a *firmament* within us. Our human nature is ceaselessly battling God's Spirit as the apostle Paul declares in (Romans 7:23), but our **"spiritual nature"** can *conquer* our **"fleshly nature"** with God's help. God *separates* our physical lusts from our spiritual desires, just as He *divided* the waters on the 2nd day of creation by a *firmament!*

Tabernacle Furniture: The *bronze laver* of the Tabernacle speaks to us of the **"washing of regeneration in the Word of God."** This brass pot contained *water* in which the priests *washed* their hands and feet before ministering to the people.

This *typified* the Church's CLEANSING OF SIN through water baptism, and our regeneration through God's Holy Spirit.

Israel's Journey: The First Day of Unleavened Bread was a day of great merry making and celebration, instituted when Israel was set *free* from being bondslaves in Egypt. Seven days later, on the last day of Unleavened Bread, the Israelites crossed the Red Sea.

SEVEN STEPS OF SALVATION

Crossing the *Red Sea* was a portrait of WATER BAPTISM as Paul recorded in (1 Corinthians 10:2). After coming out of Egypt, *typical* of sin, the Israelites had to cross two bodies of water before their freedom was secured in the land of promise. Thus, *water* stood between Egypt [sin] and the promised land [eternal life], as the Red Sea and the Jordan river BOTH had to be crossed. The Red Sea stood for *baptism* and the Jordan for FAITH, spiritually speaking!

Thus, the baptismal bridge between a Christian and eternal life is characterized by baptism [repentance] and faith! Just as God separated the waters during the creation week, *symbolic* of dividing our human nature from our spiritual nature—He now spiritually parts the waters for us to walk from Egypt to the promised land. But we must do the walking—in *obedience* and *faith*!

God delivered, or saved Israel twice when He brought them forth from Egypt. Once, during the Passover when they were spared God's judgment, and set free from slavery to the Egyptians. God saved Israel the second time shortly thereafter, when He saved them from the pursuing Egyptian army. God *miraculously* prepared a way for Israel to cross the Red Sea, but drowned the attacking Egyptian army.

What a thought provoking *parallel* to a Christian's deliverance?

Feast Day: THE 7th DAY OF UNLEAVENED BREAD.

Past: The saving of the Israelites through crossing of the Red Sea, and the destruction of the Egyptian army in the Red Sea makes an exact picture of *resurrection*. The passing of Israel through the Red Sea is a like *figure* of BAPTISM, and *baptism* is a mirror of **"spiritual death"** followed by resurrection!

The *symbolism* here to a Christian experience, is God's people Israel going through spiritual death—through the watery grave of baptism—to be resurrected on the other side of the grave! The enemies of the cross destroyed in the grave!

God made a pillar of cloud come *between* Israel and the Egyptian army during the night so that Israel received light, but the Egyptians were in "darkness" and couldn't see what Israel was doing. This parallels the creation week, even as the firmament of air *divided the waters* on the second day.

Again, we are reminded of the firmament that "divided the waters" on the second day of creation to Israel's deliverance. Moses stretched out his hand over the Red Sea and the Lord caused the sea to go back by a strong east wind, and made the sea dry land as the waters were divided!

What remarkable consistency in God's plan!

It wasn't long after Israel left Egypt [sin] that Pharaoh began chasing after them with his militia in 600 chariots of fire. This event is *typical* of Satan's minions who immediately pursue after the newly born child of God. Oftentimes, we, like Israel, become fearful and discouraged. But then we realize we are *powerless* without God's help and intervention in our lives.

Then God does intervene and fight for us to *conquer* the wiles of the devil! The waters became a "wall" unto the Israelites as the Eternal *parted* them for their safe journey on dry land. This event is *dual* to a Christians's *protection* from the bombardment of Satan's fiery missiles!

These waters were a *symbol* of God's Holy Spirit as *the living waters of God* are a "wall" to each Christian, and a FORTRESS against the pounding waves of the devil's onslaught.

Therefore, the Last Day of Unleavened Bread is a beautiful *Rembrandt* of a Christian repenting of sin, being baptized, and receiving the gift of the Holy Spirit to *fight* the powers of darkness!

Present: God gave stern instructions to the Israelites not to eat bread with leavening in it for seven days. The spiritual implication to a Christian is to put sin out of their lives completely! Leavening is a *type* of sin and the number seven *pictures* completness!

Christians must *separate* the leaven of the world [the sins of malice and wickedness] with diligence in their exodus to God's promised Kingdom. Christians are admonished to eat only of the bread of **"sincerity and truth"** which is the bread of life! (1 Cor. 5:8).

The Passover *pictured* the death of our Savior for remission of sins. However, the acceptance of Christ's blood does not forgive unrepentant sins. God's Word tells Christians to press towards perfection, as they keep God's royal law of love in their hearts.

SEVEN STEPS OF SALVATION

Unleavened bread is what SANCTIFIED or *"separated"* the Israelites from the rest of the world. The commandment given to Israel to eat unleavened bread, and "bitter herbs" [a *type* of purging agent] *typified* the purging of sin out of our lives spiritually!

The ceremony of water baptism dramatizes a person's sincere desire to CRUCIFY their old self, or old way of life and rise a new person in Christ! The neophyte Christian then begins to walk in **"newness of life" (Rom. 6:3,4).** That's why Paul associates the "old way of life" to old leavening that must be cast out, that we may be a *new lump* or have a "new life" in Christ—a *resurrected* spiritual life!

Once we have accepted Jesus as our Savior and the way of life He stressed, every Egyptian, *figuratively* speaking will be destroyed in the Red Sea!

Future: Christians have been purchased by the precious blood of Jesus Christ, which *redeemed them,* and "sanctified" them from the Egypt of this world. God's Word indicates those living in the end-time will escape the coming plagues and judgments to be poured out undiluted upon this evil world.

You will recall the reason God brought the plagues upon Egypt was because of their false religious beliefs and the worshipping of idols! The great *future* Passover of God will be a judgment upon all the ungodly who partake in the IDOLATRY of false religion—when this world's satanic inspired system will fall down like a house of cards!

God's judgment has not yet "passed over" the world and spared His "elect." His wrath and fury is yet to be unleashed, from which Believers can only escape through the "mark" of the Passover Lamb—*if* they have been faithful to the end!

Fulfillment in Jesus: Jesus Christ is the Christian's *Unleavened Bread* of "sincerity and truth." Each Christian is to walk in the HOLY and righteous example of Jesus Christ in conquering and rooting out sin!

During the Millennium, all sin will be stamped out as this "spiritual leavening" is removed from God's holy creation. Finally, at the Millennium's conclusion, absolute perfection—free of sin, will only exist.

Interestingly, one cannot find any mention of silver in God's spiritual city of perfection "New Jerusalem." The reason, of course, is that *silver* personifies *redemption,* and there will no longer be any need for redemption—because all sin will have been removed from God's utopia and pristine world.

All the leaven of Satan's rebellion will have been removed by Jesus Christ! What a wonderful world to look forward to!

Receiving the Holy Spirit, the Third Step of Salvation

THE RECEIVING OF THE HOLY SPIRIT: The Feast of Pentecost *shadows* the sending of the Holy Spirit, and Christ as the *firstborn* from the dead through *resurrection.* It *pictures* the small grain harvest of souls.

Number: The number three denotes *finality* or *completeness* in DIVINE PERFECTION or resurrection, in that one produces spiritual fruit through a resurrected spiritual life after accepting Jesus. Noah's life is a *model* of the embryo Christian who is called out of the world of sin to become *righteous.*

After one has their conscience awakened to their sinful human nature—they must *repent* and come out of the world of sin in *faith.* Then, if possible be *baptized* to receive God's Holy Spirit, which is His *power* and *mind,* which enables them to live a righteous life and produce spiritual fruit in a *regenerated* life!

The Creation Week: The gathering together of the waters under the firmament, the appearing of the land, and the vegetation on the third day is a *picture* of the fruit of GOD'S HOLY SPIRIT working in our lives. When the Holy Spirit grows in our lives, love, joy, peace, longsuffering, gentleness, goodness, faith, meekness, temperance, etc. begin to blossom.

It is interesting to note that "dry land" appeared on the third day of creation, *typical* of Jesus' *resurrection* after three days as the first *sign* of a **"new life."** Thus, a Christian *parallels* the life of Christ spiritually by producing good fruit in their resurrected life in Jesus!

Tabernacle Furniture: The *golden lampstand* in the holy place *typifies* Pentecost in that both contain the common denominator of LIGHT. Recall also on the day of Pentecost, the HOLY SPIRIT came like cloven tongues of fire [light] and sat upon the early church (Acts 2:3). Also, the *light* of the *shekenah* shown through into the Holy of Holies acknowledging God's Holy presence.

It is *light* that subdues darkness!

The oil in the golden lampstand *symbolizes* Jesus as He gives light to His Church through the Holy Spirit! (Rev. 1:20). Each church member individually is a child of light (Eph. 5:8). Jesus said His Church was to be the **"light of the world" (Matt. 5:14).**

Israel's Journey: The wilderness experience of the Israelites is very *picturesque* of the Christian experience. While in the desert waiting patiently to inherit the promised land, Israel had God's feast days outlined to them—but they had no crops to fulfill them.

Pentecost and Tabernacles envision the FIRSTFRUITS of the barley wheat and fruit harvests respectively of their land. But Israel could not observe these feast days properly until they were actually in their land.

Israel's beginning pilgrimage through the wilderness is *typical* of our beginning journey of attaining the life of Christ in us. The giving of the Ten Commandments, statutes, judgments, Tabernacle and priesthood—all *typified* the beginning of the New Testament Church, beginning on Pentecost.

Feast Day: PENTECOST.

Past: Pentecost is a *memorial* of Israel entering into the covenant relationship with God, and is a memorial of Christians entering into the New Covenant relationship with God through Jesus Christ.

The Christian Day of Pentecost, when Jesus poured out the HOLY SPIRIT, can only be understood by understanding the original Pentecost that God established when bringing Israel out of Egypt.

Jesus Christ was the Spokesman who made the first covenant for God. It was this same personage who received the long promised New covenant from God the Father, and poured it out on his Church on the same day which memorialized the "Israel" of the first covenant.

Thus, Pentecost always falls on Sunday, the same day of the week that Israel entered into the first covenant, as they arrived at Mt. Sinai.

In our study of the *types,* we have come to realize that there is but ONE Israel of God in both Old Covenant and New Testament. Both *picture* a called out group of people to perform God's work in preparation for a future greater work.

Both are God's early rain harvest in preparation for the millennial fruit harvest.

Present: The physical CIRCUMCISION of Israel was but a portrait of the spiritual *circumcision of the heart*—that God's Holy Spirit gives to Christians. God's HOLY SPIRIT cuts away our old fleshly foreskin of human nature, and renews our minds to walk in the spirit!

A Christian today enters into Israel's covenant promises by accepting the same conditions—that includes keeping God's laws, and commandments!

Pentecost pictures the early grain [wheat] harvest of Christ's Church, being **"a kind of firstfruits"** of His creation. This feast envisions the beginning of God's great harvest, and is a technicolor of those individuals called *now* to be the future kings and priests ruling in God's kingdom.

The New Testament Church began on the Day of Pentecost or Firstfruits, and *pictures* the entire Church age of the New Testament from its beginning in A.D. 31 to the time of Jesus' return to the earth. During the course of this time, only a small number [firstfruits] have been called, chosen, and faithful (Rev. 17:14).

Christians are **"firstfruits"** and therefore have only an earnest or down payment of the Holy Spirit—a first installment as it were at the present time. Later, at the resurrection, they will reap the remainder of the harvest as they become Spirit beings, and the Holy Spirit permeates their very body!

Currently, Christians have been "waved" as firstfruits before the Father and have been ACCEPTED—however, they must remain *faithful* to the end to receive the remainder of God's installment!

Future: In the latter days, God will bring the physical nation of Israel back out of captivity, and CIRCUMCISE THEIR

SEVEN STEPS OF SALVATION

HEART so that they will truly love God and enter into His New Testament. Then they will receive the blessings that God had promised to them under the covenant, when He brought them out of Egypt.

One of the principal tasks God has given to the Messiah is to bring the descendants of Jacob back to the land, and give them the New Testament as He promised their forefathers. This task is yet for the future, and will be done in the time described as the time of Jacob's trouble. Then God will POUR out His spirit upon all of Israel!

In the latter days, Jesus Christ will bring Israel out of tribulation, and circumcise their heart so they will truly love God with all their heart and soul! At this time, they will enter into the New Testament and be a blessed and leading nation upon the earth!

The pouring out of the Holy Spirit on Pentecost was only a *type* of what is to occur to the entire nation of Israel—just prior to our Lord's return.

God will begin His conversion or **"circumcision of the hearts of Israel"** by sending them a man with the spirit and power of the prophet Elijah! He will convert many of them to Christianity in a similar feat as witnessed on the Day of Pentecost, when the apostle Peter began preaching with power and authority! This modern-day Elijah will turn the hearts of Israel back to their spiritual Father!

The Day of Pentecost will have its "kingdom-wide fulfillment" when Jesus returns. Then a wide river will flow out from Jerusalem to the inhabitants of the earth (Ezek. 47:1-12).

The convocation of Pentecost will have its "eternal fulfillment" as God's Holy Spirit will be a **"pure river of life"** proceeding out of God's throne to all those who would drink of it freely (Rev. 23:1). God's Spirit of power and creativity will flow freely in full measure throughout eternity!

Remember, the Law given to Moses on tables of stone was a *type* of God giving His Law of Love to His Church by His Holy Spirit written in their hearts. Thus, God's Holy Spirit will give them God's Law of Love, God's Law of Life for all eternity!

Fulfillment in Jesus: Jesus is the FIRSTFRUIT (1 Cor. 15:20-23) of the dead and therefore takes preeminence in all things Christians will eventually do. He is the "beginning" (Rev.

1:8); "the firstborn" (Col. 1:15,18); "the first-begotten" (Heb. 1:6; Rev. 1:5); of the Church of "the firstborn" (Heb. 12:23).

Faith, the Fourth Step of Salvation

FAITH, RESURRECTION, WARFARE: The Feast of Trumpets *pictures* the resurrection and return of the Saints with our Lord and Savior, to vanquish the nations under Satan's rule through *warfare.* They will then inherit the promised Kingdom Land, and reign with Christ over the nations.

Number: The number *four* denotes RULERSHIP over *nature* or *creation* and pertains to the things in the heavens and the earth.

Abraham's life is a pattern of FAITH that eventually every child of God must endeavor to have in order to please our great God! Christians who have a deep abiding *faith,* even as Abraham, will inherit the same promises of Abraham—which includes *rulership* with Christ over God's creation of the universe!

The Creation Week: The creating of the sun, moon and stars in the firmament on the fourth day, was accomplished by our Creator to tell the seasons and times of the earth!

The two great lights chosen to RULE were the sun (day) and the moon (night) were *mirrors* of the Father (Sun) and Jesus (moon) *ruling* over His Church (the stars). Recall the vision given Joseph as well as the prophecy in Revelation 12 speaking of the woman clothed with the sun, and the moon under her feet, and upon her head a crown of twelve stars.

The Church being in the express "image of Jesus," is a direct *reflection* of Him, even as Jesus is the reflection of the Father, and must let their **"light shine"** before all men to see.

The Church of the living God, being now the spiritual organism of the body of Christ on the earth, is sounding forth the *trumpet* warning of alarm as did Jesus to a world in darkness and gloom. They are bringing "light" to the world, just as the sun brought the light of day from the darkness of night on the fourth day of creation!

SEVEN STEPS OF SALVATION

Tabernacle Furniture: Inside the *Ark* was the 10 Commandments written on two tables of stone, along with Aaron's rod that budded and the pot of manna.

Here in *emblem,* we not only have a picture of mercy and forgiveness, but also power, AUTHORITY, wisdom and healing! In essence, we have everything needed to mold us into the perfect stature of Christ!

The moral law of God is witnessed by the 10 Commandments. The pot of manna was *emblematic* of the body and blood of Christ—His very substance that comes inside of us. Aaron's rod that budded is a *symbol* of the RESURRECTION, and the power of God's Holy Spirit. Here we have the three basic ingredients every person needs for salvation!

Spiritually speaking, when Christians have been molded into the *Ark of the Covenant,* that is to say, when they have become what the Ark of the Covenant personifies—they will have had the *fullness* of God settle down to rest in them! The Ark of the Covenant must be built up within Believers!

The Ark of the Covenant also represents the Lord Jesus Christ as the Commander-in-Chief of the hosts of heaven. It signifies WAR! When the Israelites prepared for *battle* against their enemies—the Ark went before them, and God scattered their enemies! The Ark led Israel across the Jordan into the promised land!

Israel's Journey: The organization of Israel into an ARMY pictures a time of WAR, prior to our Savior setting up the Kingdom of God.

After leaving Egypt, Israel had to endure the hardship of the wilderness, overcoming every obstacle that came into their path, including the enemies that occupied their rightful land. Palestine had been promised them as soon as they left Egypt, but now they had to conquer their land by means of force!

Similarly, Christians have the spiritual promises given them now, but must overcome the spiritual war they are engaged in with Satan and his demons. Christians wrestle not with flesh and blood Philistines and Canaanites, but with wicked spirits in high places.

Eventually, the battle will be won, and the Promised spiritual land secured as all heavenly rebellion is put down! Then, Jesus Christ as spiritual Joshua, will give all faithful

Believers eternal rest as He brings God's Kingdom to the earth!

Feast Day: TRUMPETS.

Past: The Feast of Trumpets begins the fall feast days and it is called Rosh Hashanah by the Jews. This day starts the Jewish civil New Year and marks ten days of repentance and prayer.

On the Day of Trumpets, a trumpet [Heb. *shofar*] was blown throughout the land of Israel. The *shofar* was a ram's horn that signaled impending WAR, and a time to gather the people for warfare!

Present: The trumpet has a *dual* meaning to Israel and the Church. Scripture indicates that at the sound of the last trumpet, Christians of all ages will be **changed to spirit** as they are RESURRECTED into the air to meet their King, elder Brother and Bridegroom (1Cor.15:51; 1Thess. 4:14-17). This seems to be indicative of the "two silver trumpets" our Lord instructed Moses to make for the assembling of the people.

Then those "elect" of the nation of Israel that have been held captive by the "Beast system" under Satan's dominion will be gathered out of all nations and brought back to their homeland "one by one."

The Feast of Firstfruits *pictured* the gathering of the Church. The Feast of Trumpets *pictures* the coming of Jesus Christ with His Bride—to set up the Tabernacle of David and to RESTORE again the Kingdom to Israel.

Figuratively, the pillar of cloud has rested just before the promised land. When the last trumpet of God is blown, Christians will meet their Lord in the air and help conquer the rebels who control their land.

Individually, Christians are engaged in spiritual WARFARE daily against the works of the flesh, Satan and the world. When the trumpet of God blows in our lives, we must *conquer* our promised land unflinchingly. Christians must not allow the enemies of the flesh to destroy everything God has tried to accomplish in their lives!

As the Feast of Trumpets is fulfilled in each Christian personally, they begin to experience a feeling of tranquility or "rest." This is the beginning of their spiritual CONQUEST of the promised land, that will eventually culminate in *rulership* with

SEVEN STEPS OF SALVATION

Jesus Christ forever!

Spiritually speaking, Christians receive inner peace and rest now, when they successfully **"overcome"** the spiritual dragons in their lives. They enter their own personal Canaan by winning their personal war now—and later enter into the eternal spiritual Canaan of God's Kingdom!

Future: The Feast of Trumpets *pictures* the time when God is going to call upon all men, particularly the nation of Israel, to repent and turn to obey Him!

Those who will refuse to turn from their evil ways will suffer the consequences of the Great Tribulation, and the impending plagues. Unlike the time when their forefathers were protected and **"set apart"** by the Passover Lamb's blood in Egypt—these plagues will be poured out on Israel with full intensity!

This will be a time of WAR and the beginning of "Jacob's trouble", including famine, pestilence and national captivity!

The Feast of Trumpets will have its "kingdom-wide" and "eternal-wide" fulfillment as Jesus Christ makes every enemy His footstool. Then, He will give the reigns of the kingdom back to His Father. At that time, the family of God may expand to all the planets, without the fear of any dissenting spirit beings!

Fulfillment in Jesus: The Ark of the Covenant represents Jesus Christ *symbolically* as strong and MIGHTY in battle! When the Ark was carried in battle, Israel followed and was VICTORIOUS over their enemies!

When Jesus walked the earth proclaiming the **"good news"** of God's soon coming Kingdom and casting out demons—He was a *trumpet* for His Father. He declared war against "unclean spirits" and as Commander-in-Chief of the armies of heaven—will lead His angels and Church against them in the final battle for the earth!

Jesus is now preparing for the battle of Armageddon in which Satan and his hordes will be disposed of for 1000 years. Then, after that he will be allowed to be unchained for a brief period of time, only to be eventually destroyed permanently!

The earth will only be conquered through war at Jesus Christ's second coming—then all the enemies of the cross will be made our Lord's footstool!

THE FOOLISHNESS OF GOD

Like the ancient Israelites, Christians must have a deep abiding *faith* in their Commander-in-Chief, and follow Him into our Promised Land—as He *destroys* every last ENEMY for us!

Grace, the Fifth Step of Salvation

PURIFICATION OF ALL GUILT, GRACE, SONSHIP: The Day of Atonement is a shadow of our spiritual *cleansing of sin* or "covering" of sin, the binding of Satan, and the time the Church will be at-one with God through marriage. The fulfillment of this event will take place *after* the Millennium, when Satan is destroyed forever and "New Jerusalem" is perfected as Christ's Bride.

Number: Five is the number associated with GRACE and that of God adding His gifts and blessings to His creation. Five is the leading number in the Tabernacle measurement, and the Church is the spiritual fulfillment of the Tabernacle. At the Millenniums conclusion, when every adversary of salvation has been overcome, when the Bride of Christ, God's spiritual Temple, has been perfected—God will *add* innumerable BLESSINGS to His Bride throughout all eternity!

The life of Isaac *pictures* the REWARDS of being a Son of God. After one *repents* of human nature, has been *baptized* in the blood of Christ for sins, has received the *Holy Spirit* of God, has grown in *faith* as a result of exercising God's Holy Spirit—they are now a true SON of God!

As one grows towards spiritual maturity, God increases their blessings upon that individual. Like Isaac, who was a *type* of Christ, every Christian must be willing to give up his life in service to God.

The price of SONSHIP has been the precious blood of our Savior Jesus Christ—and Christians must now lay down their lives as *living sacrifices*.

Isaac's mother Sara received *grace* from God only after she began living God's way through the crucible of time! It took the casting out of the bondwoman Hagai from Abraham's camp—before Sara, who was barren, could receive God's GRACE.

Sara had encouraged her husband Abraham to conceive a child through his handmaid when she was without child. But Isaac, the "fruit of grace", could only be born after repentance.

Likewise, Sarah's counterpart in the Church is superficially barren, but soon she is to receive God's *grace* and begin to be "fruitful" and "multiply."

The Creation Week: The creation of fish and birds on the *fifth* day of the creation week, the Day of Atonement and "Mercy-Seat" all contain the common denominator of **"newness of life."**

It was on the 5th day of creation that all the animals "clean" and "unclean" were created. These "unclean" animals *symbolize* unrepentant sinners, including Satan and his legions of demons, who will be separated from the "clean" or holy of God's creation.

After the Millennium, as every unrepentant "unclean" thing is destroyed in the Lake of Fire—God will create a new heaven and earth for His spotless Bride to live in ONENESS forever!

Tabernacle Furniture: The term "Mercy Seat" is a misnomer and could just as well have been translated "the Propitiatory Cover" or "Lid of Atonement." It was the lid or cover of the Ark of the Covenant. It *pictures* the COVERING of sin, but far more than mercy is imputed by the Mercy Seat.

The Mercy-Seat pointed to the Eternal's "throne of grace" where the meeting place of the Law and Mercy transpires. Only on the Day of Atonement could the high priest enter within the Veil with the blood of the Sin-offering, and sprinkle it's blood *seven* times on the Mercy-Seat. Thus, the Mercy-Seat was *emblematic* of the perfect atoning sacrifice of Jesus Christ, and God's heavenly throne of GRACE and rulership.

Israel's Journey: The Day of Atonement is very similar to Passover in that both require the shed blood of Jesus Christ. The Passover blood on their doorposts in Egypt *covered* the Israelites in their homes while the death angel "passed over" them.

Similarly, the ANTONEMENT blood of Jesus, *symbolic* of the high priest sprinkling it on the Day of Atonement, will cover Israel in a *future* Passover deliverance when they are again in captivity.

Feast Day: ATONEMENT.

Past: The Day of Atonement, called *Yom Kippur* by the

Jews, is the most solemn holy day of God's feast days, and *foreshadows* the time when *all* of Israel's sins will be COVERED.

On this most solemn day, the Israelites were to **"afflict their souls"** or fast without food or drink. The reason for this self affliction, was to teach them through the physical, their reliance upon God who fed them (mana) in the wilderness—and by depriving their bodies of food, they would draw closer to their God expressing their sorrow for their sins.

Yom Kippur is derived from the Hebrew words meaning "atonement" or "covering", and is *reminiscent* of the time the Eternal will *cover* the sins of Israel!

Once a year on the Day of Atonement, the high priest was to enter into the Holy of Holies with the BLOOD of the goat chosen by lot to represent our Savior. The two goats to be sacrificed in the ceremony the high priest performed, most likely *symbolized* Christ and Satan.

The high priest would take the golden censer full of burning coals from off the altar of incense which stood before the Veil, then he placed some *finely* beaten incense upon the coals as he entered behind the Veil into the Most Holy Place. This caused a **"sweet fragrance"** and cloud to cover the Mercy Seat (Lev. 16:12, 13).

The blood of the goat designated to *represent* Christ was then sprinkled *seven* times, indicative of the *perfect* sacrifice of Christ, although His blood was not sprinkled but shed in reality.

Only on the Day of Atonement was the high priest to put off the beautiful glittering ephod and wear the white linen garments with linen miter, *symbolic* of the *holy* and *righteous* character of Jesus Christ (Lev. 16:3, 4).

It was the high priest taking the blood within the Veil [representing God's throne], to the Mercy Seat, that *typified* the risen Christ *figuratively* taking His blood, once and for all, within the Veil to the very throne of God in heaven. There, He would intercede for us as our High Priest.

The Azazel goat representing Satan was let go into the wilderness by a **"fit man,"** picturing Satan being restrained from deceiving the inhabitants of the world. Upon the return of Jesus Christ, Satan will be bound by a "fit man" (most likely Michael the archangel) for 1000 years in uninhabited wilderness. This entire reconciliation period may extend 1000 years later to the final day of Atonement!

The driving away of the second live goat shows final ATONEMENT, by placing the sins on their true perpetrator, Satan the devil. It depicts the complete removal of sins and their author [Satan] from the presence of God and His people—thus the *complete* deliverance of the people from the power of Satan!

Present: Character is produced by TRIAL and test, and finally coupled with rejoicing. This is also *pictured* by God's feast days. Passover was to be eaten with **"bitter herbs"** followed by seven days of unleavened bread. Pentecost, Trumpets and Tabernacles were Feasts of great rejoicing! But on the Day of Atonement Israelites were to "afflict their soul"or "fast."

Fasting characterizes the Christian experience of loving and serving God with humiliation and repentance during good times and times of dire straits. This life is full of "sweet and sour," "milk and honey," and "bitter herbs." There are *blessings,* but there are also *trials*! It takes rain and sun to produce delicious fruit. And it takes the summer sunshine and the winter's snow to produce seasonal beauty.

Jesus explained that the Bride should *fast* when He departed, for that personal closeness would be missing. This is the bond that draws us near to God!

Each individual Christian has the Day of Atonement fulfilled in their lives daily, as they confess their sins. Through the precious blood of Jesus Christ, Christians are daily WASHED of the sins they commit as long as they are in a remorseful attitude (1 Jn. 1:7-9). God's word tells Christians that they must "resist" the devil and he will flee from them (Jas. 4:7), just like the Azazel goat *fled* into the wilderness.

God has "covered" each individual Christian's sins just as He *covered* the nakedness of Adam and Eve with coats of animal skins (Gen. 3:21). This covering of our first parents *symbolizes* the spiritual covering of sin [our nakedness] through the blood of Jesus!

Future: As already demonstrated, there are many prophecies that declare the national captivity of the descendants of Jacob, followed by a time of *sorrow* and repentance. God will punish them for their insubordination to His government, then

THE FOOLISHNESS OF GOD

there will come a time that God will hear their crys, and FORGIVE their sins and remove the defilement of their land.

Israel will be a captive people when Christ returns to the earth with His Bride. His primary function at that time will be to gather Israel *one by one* out of all nations where they have been held captive, and bring them back into their own land.

A trumpet blast will be blown signaling this glorious event. This was *foreshadowed* by the ceremony on the Day of Atonement, in the Jubilee year!

God will then give them the New Testament as He begins writing His laws in their hearts and minds! Israel will be *washed clean* of their past sins, and those surviving Jacob's trouble will be given a new Spirit to walk in all of God's intended ways!

Israel will then become a BLESSED people above all nations of the earth, as she becomes abundant and fruitful. Her sins will have been *covered* and the sins that defiled her land removed. This is the basic meaning of the Day of Atonement for Israel, and the year of Jubilee which *typified* the great day of deliverance for the earth by Jesus Christ!

Fulfillment in Jesus: God's plan of salvation for the world is revealed in the mysterious ceremony the high priest of Israel performed on the Day of Atonement. Of course, everything he did upon that day, *typified* what our real High Priest of God, Jesus Christ was to do!

Jesus was the only being allowed to enter beyond the Veil into heaven. There, He appeared on behalf of His house [the Church] to RECONCILE them back to the Father, and then He appeared to reconcile the nation of Israel back to the Father as their long awaited Messiah!

Jesus fulfilled the Day of Atonement as our great High Priest by offering His blood, and spiritually entering the Holy of Holies with His blood for Himself and His household, and for the sins of the people.

Unlike the high priest of Israel, Christ entered heaven itself to PURIFY the holy furnishings of the true Tabernacle of God. Christ's blood has now been sprinkled before the Father and ACCEPTED—atonement has been made for all of mankind.

Jesus is our personal Day of Atonement being a propitiation or **"covering"** for our daily sins. On the Day of Atonement, the trumpet announcing the year of Jubilee was blown—this *typifying* our total release from the bondage of this world through Jesus Christ!

Jesus has first reconciled the Church, then He will reconcile the nation of Israel back to the Father—later through them, He will reconcile the entire earth back to the Father!

The future Day of Atonement will find its complete Kingdom-wide fulfillment during the 1000 year reign of Christ with His Bride, as He restores back to the Father what Satan has stolen! The Millennial Jubilee will be the restoration of all possessions to their rightful inheritors!

The future Day of Atonement will be the act of uniting the Bride and Bridegroom, while the Feast of Tabernacles will be the Kingdom-wide fulfillment of that courtship—consummating in marriage as "New Jerusalem" is presented to the Bridegroom!

Service, the Sixth Step of Salvation

SERVICE, RULERSHIP, MILLENNIAL REST: The Feast of Tabernacles *pictures* the millennial rest upon the earth, as Jesus *dwells* with His faithful servants as King of Kings and Lord of Lords.

Number: The number *six* denotes MANKIND and everything related to mankind. It was on the sixth day that man was created in God's **"image"** and **"likeness."** The Feast of Tabernacles is God's sixth feast and is a "dress rehearsal" of the time man, then resurrected, will finally RULE the earth in the fullness of God's "image" and "likeness" for one thousand years!

Jacob's life is a *replica* of the resurrected Christian serving in the family of God throughout the Millennium. Faith and sonship were necessary prerequisites for SERVICE or bodily acts of performance. Jacob's life of untiring service in his lengthy toil for Rachel, is but a *foretaste* of a Christian's dedication throughout the Millennium.

The Creation Week: The creation of animals and of mankind in God's "image" on the sixth day is a prelude of the Feast of Tabernacles, God's sixth festival. To create man in God's "image" and "likeness" means to create divine holy and righteous character.

The work of God on the sixth day of creation expresses

God's plan for making humans in His "image" and "likeness!" First comes the earthly "animal" or *human nature*, followed by the creation of mankind in God's "heavenly image."

Only after the human race has developed character through trial and test, and are able to discern **"good from evil,"** and reject the evil and adhere to the good—can they become a part of the body of Christ.

Deep spiritual implications are found in the words: **"God created them *male* and *female* in His image..."** "Male" and "female" expresses more than the physical—it depicts the spiritual organism of CHRIST and THE CHURCH as the perfect specimen of "Male" and "Female" in God's image. Oneness of "Male" and "Female" will not be complete until the Church as Christ's Bride has been perfected into the "image of God."

Christ's Bride is being constructed not of physical bone, but of spiritual composition from His body! Thus, it is Christ's Bride that is the *antitype* of God's proclamation, **"Let us make mankind in our image, after our likeness."** In a spiritual sense, Jesus Christ will not be complete until His Bride has been fashioned in God's "image" and "likeness."

Adam was created from physical substance, and Eve was fashioned out of him. Eve was made for Adam to be a help mate, and together were called "man" who God made after His *image* and *likeness* (Gen. 5:2).

Christ, the spiritual Adam, is *fashioning* His Church out of His spiritual substance, and the individual members are being fashioned in the **"image of God."**

Tabernacle Furniture: The *Altar of Incense* was *symbolic* of offering SWEET PRAYER to our loving Father, and was burned daily in the holy place. Jesus Christ *typified* this "sweet fragrance" by submitting to the perfect will of God, as do Christians who follow in His footsteps!

At the moment of His death, our Lord rent the Veil in the Temple in two, as Christ became the fulfillment of *sweet* incense to the Father.

The Veil separated the holy from the Most Holy—or the throne of God, from man's waiting room. The Veil represented *Christ's flesh* and when the Veil was rent in two upon Christ's death—the door to God's throne was now freely accessible to mankind once again!

SEVEN STEPS OF SALVATION

Spiritually speaking, in *type* Moses has led us through the wilderness to the River Jordan. The holy Veil stands for the River Jordan, and now Joshua must lead us across to the other side or into the Holy of Holies through the Veil spiritually!

The Veil separated the wilderness from the promised land spiritually. Both the Veil and Jordan *symbolize* death followed by resurrection! The death of our Savior allowed us to have free access to God's throne, entering now as a priest into fellowship with the Father.

In fellowship with the Father and His Son as a priest in full service, Christians participate in the true Sabbath *rest* of God!

Israel's Journey: Moses led the children of Israel out of Egyptian bondage, and instituted God's law and His feast days while sojourning in the wilderness for forty years. Yet they could not celebrate certain feast days until they were actually in their land.

Because of this, the Feast of Tabernacles was never once celebrated under Moses, but rather under Joshua who led them into the promised land!

It will be Christ, not in the form of Moses the Law giver, but rather spiritual Joshua, who will lead His people into the promised land.

Like the Israelites of old, Christians must keep on eating the spiritual manna while they are in the hot desert sun in anticipation of the Promised Land. Christians, like them, must press on in FAITH to receive the better promises of the spiritual Promised Land. Then, and only then, will we be able to feast during His Kingdom on all the good and delicious FRUITS God has in store for us.

Crossing over the river Jordan and the attack upon Canaan *symbolize* our deliverance from this world into God's spiritual Promised Land.

Feast Day: TABERNACLES.

Past: The Feast of Tabernacles began an eight day festival of REJOICING with food and drink! To the Israelites, the Feast of Tabernacles is a *memorial* of the time they left Egypt and dwelt in *tents* or booths on their journey to the promised land. These transportable homes were *temporary dwellings* till they would settle down in their permanent residence.

The booths that Israel was commanded to dwell in *typified* the *dwelling* of God in His people, and their abiding in Him!

Present: Today, many Christians observe the Feast of Tabernacles as a time of *great rejoicing*, anticipating the ABUNDANCE of food and drink which is a *foretaste* of the abundance of good things during the 1000 year reign with Christ.

This jubilant festival reminds us of God's past redemptive work, and teaches us His *future* plans for restoring His chosen people. Many Christians observe this festival with the understanding of the events it memorializes, and the prophetic events they foreshadow.

The Passover *pictured* the intervention of God to save Israel by devastating plagues on Israel's oppressors. Christians can reflect upon the past Passover, and the future Passover and second exodus at this time. The prophecies of the future deliverance of Israel, along with her repentance and covering of sin *pictured* by the Day of Atonement, should also be meditated upon during this occasion.

This is a feast that Christian's can really become ecstatic about, because of the knowledge God has given concerning His promise to save all of Israel! This is a festival that calls for special food and rejoicing!

The Feast of Tabernacles pictures dwelling in temporary dwellings physically [our bodies and homes], in anticipation of the RESURRECTION and the Kingdom of God. While in the flesh, Believers are merely *temporarily* residing in a physical body, awaiting the time when they will be resurrected and inhabit a permanent spiritual body!

The temporary dwellings ancient Israel built depicted our temporary sojourn upon the earth, before Believers, as ancient Israel enter the promised land. The Promised Land Christians will inherit will not be physical or temporary, but rather spiritual and ETERNAL!

Tabernacles presents the fullness of the indwelling of God in us. It is God's purpose to *dwell* in the individual and collectively to dwell [tabernacle] among His people in a new earth. Currently, God is building His Church out of the body of Christ for that very purpose. When the "female" part of Christ is complete—God the Father will abide among the nations of the earth!

Christ is the *sanctuary* of the Father, as the Father dwells in Him, and He in the Father (Jn. 10:37,38; 14:20). Christians are to become a part of God's sanctuary as Christ dwells in them—then they may also be ONE with them (Jn. 17:20,21).

The fullness of the tabernacles experience personally for Christians will be when they are clothed over with a **"spiritual house"** or body at the resurrection. But let us reflect upon the many scriptures and parables that remind us that a resurrected body, will only house a resurrected mind—that has developed godly character!

***Future*:** The Feast of Tabernacles reminded Israel of their supernatural deliverance from Egypt, and today reminds us of a future deliverance of Israel.

The Feast is for the purpose of reminding God's people that He once saved Israel from Egypt, and it is also a testimony to them that He will perform a similar work in the last days.

Once again God will make Israel dwell in tents as in the time their forefathers journeyed from Egypt to the land of promise. Modern-day Israelites are once again going to dwell in tents as they are led out of captivity on their journey to the land God has set aside for His people.

The nation of Israel will march through the Red Sea dry-shod and dwell in tents for the *second* and final time! This is the basic meaning of the Feast of Tabernacles [tents] for the nation of Israel!

The connection between rain and the pouring out of God's HOLY SPIRIT during the Millennium is clearly indicated from Zechariah 14:16-17:

> **And it shall come to pass, that every one that is left of all the nations which came against Jerusalem shall even go up from year to year to worship the King, the LORD of hosts, and to keep the feast of tabernacles. And it shall be that whoso will not come up of all the families of the earth unto Jerusalem to worship the King, the Lord of hosts, even upon them *shall be no rain*.**

To portray His plan, God took the yearly material harvest

seasons in Palestine as the *picture* of the spiritual harvest of souls. In Palestine there are two main annual harvests. The first, produced by the early rain, is the spring grain harvest, and is *typical* of Pentecost and the "firstfruits" of the Church age. The second, produced by the "latter rain" produces the main harvest of souls, *picturing* the Millennium!

The Feast of Tabernacles is held in the 7th month for 7 days. The number 7 pictures *completion*, and as the Feast of Tabernacles comes to completion after 1000 years under Christ's rule—God's plan will be coming closer to PERFECTION. The Feast of Tabernacles is held on the 15th day of the 7th month (Lev. 23:34). Using God's day for a year principle, it may very well be 15 years before the Millennium actually starts after Christ's return—since not all the nations will willingly accept Christ (Zech. 14:16).

Paul makes God's Word ring out loud and clear in regards to keeping the Feast of Tabernacles: **"By all means must I keep this Feast that comes in Jerusalem" (Acts 18:21).** This verse is left out of the many versions, but appears in the original manuscripts. It appears that Paul was keeping this feast as both an Israelite and a Christian.

Solomon's Temple with all its glory was dedicated to God in the Feast of the seventh month [Tabernacles] (11 Chron. 5:1-4,11). But God's spiritual house, which is far more glorious than Solomon's (Haggai 2:6-9), will be dedicated to God during the Millennium!

The "Kingdom fulfillment" of the Feast of Tabernacles will be when the Lamb's wife will be created in God's **"image and likeness."** At this time, God's work for 7,000 years will have been completed as the Lamb and His Wife become the holy city "NEW JERUSALEM."

The "consummation fulfillment" of the Feast of Tabernacles will be when Jesus Christ and God the Father *tabernacle* together with their creation, notice: **"Behold, the tabernacle of God is with men, and he will *dwell* with them, and they shall be his people, and God himself shall be with them, and be their God..." (Rev. 21:3).**

Fulfillment in Jesus: The Father dwells or *tabernacles* in Jesus and Jesus *dwells* in Believers as He relieves His life in us through God's Holy Spirit.

SEVEN STEPS OF SALVATION

As "inner peace" is established within Christians through God's Holy Spirit *dwelling* in them—they can rejoice as the Feast of Tabernacles is fulfilled in them personally.

Rulership, the Seventh Step of Salvation

ETERNAL REST, RULERSHIP: The last feast day that God gave the nation of Israel is The Last Great Day, which speculatively pictures eternity, the consummation of salvation, when "New Jerusalem" dwells with the Father and Son forevermore!

Number: Seven is God's number for *completeness* in SPIRITUAL PERFECTION and the Last Great Day is the seventh festival of God, *picturing* the spiritual perfection of God's plan. The number seven denotes *spiritual perfection,* even as God rested from all His labor on the seventh day of creation.

Joseph's life *epitomizes* a Christian's reward. After a life of suffering and trial—he is richly rewarded by given power to RULE! Joseph's life *parallels* that of Jesus Christ.

Joseph was hated by his own family who conspired to kill him. Both Joseph and Jesus were judged and persecuted unjustly! Many Christians have been cast off by family and friends—but the day is fast approaching when Christians, like Christ and Joseph, will be *exalted* above measure, and have RULERSHIP over the nations!

The Creation Week: The resting of God on the seventh day of creation *symbolizes* the 7th festival of God, or the eighth day following the seven-day festival of Tabernacles.

The 7th day of creation is related to the Last Great Day in that *all* the family of God will finally rest *after* all His work is completed! God's work will be completed on earth after the Millennium, when every enemy of the cross has been made Christ's footstool, and every human being has been given the opportunity to drink of the river of life!

Then God can say with complete joy as He did during the creation week, **"It is finished, and it is very good."**

Tabernacle Furniture: The 12 loaves of *shewbread* made of fine flour, portrayed the spotless character of the body and blood of Jesus Christ. Like fine flour, which is without coarse particles, the life of Christ was *pure* and *fine*. It is because of Christ's body, our heavenly manna, that we will be sustained for all ETERNITY!

The 12 loaves *symbolized* God's perfect governmental organization of "New Jerusalem" with each of the 12 apostles RULING over one of the 12 tribes of Israel. Here we have the unbroken fellowship between Christ, the eternal **"staff of life"** and His consummated Bride!

The shewbread in the holy place was *emblematic* of the communion or "fellowship" Christians will have with Christ and the Father throughout all eternity! The Father is preparing His table so His children can share their common goals and interests with the head of the family. These goals will be carried out throughout all the universe!

Israel's Journey: Finally, *rest* in the Promised Land for all Christians comes after trial and test and warfare. God's Millennial *rest* is *pictured* in (Hebrews 3 and 4) as a *type* of the *rest* Israel received after they entered the promised land under Joshua.

But God's ETERNAL REST far exceeds anything imaginable in this life or that has been revealed in the *types*. Truly, as Paul said, **"...we see through a glass darkly"**—but note this, whatever God has in store for us in eternity—it will be insatiably satisfying!

Feast Day: THE LAST GREAT DAY.

Past: The *eighth day* is a separate feast from, but immediately follows the Feast of Tabernacles. During the last feast of Tabernacles Jesus was to keep on earth, He healed a blind man and said, **"If any man thirst, let him come unto me and drink. He that believeth on me...out of his belly shall flow rivers of *living water*."** These rivers represent the flowing of God's Holy Spirit!

It is not coincidental that the Last Great Day in which Jesus *healed* the blind man, and offered His Holy Spirit was a weekly Sabbath! (Jn. 9:1-7). Furthermore, it was not accidental that the Last Great Day is the 7th annual Sabbath, even as the weekly Sabbath is the 7th day of the creation week *picturing* the

SEVEN STEPS OF SALVATION

MILLENNIUM.

Both days are *abstracts* of the Kingdom of God, when God's Holy Spirit will be poured out abundantly to all peoples of the earth.

On this day, Jesus healed a blind man who was *physically* blind and said his blindness was not due to any fault of the man. This physical blindness is representative of the *spiritual blindness* that will be healed during the Millennium in which truth will be known to all nations!

***Present*:** The N.T. Church began receiving the Holy Spirit upon Pentecost Day, and all Israel will begin receiving it upon the coming fulfillment of the Last Great Day—when they come to Jesus Christ in deep repentance!

Future: The eighth day pictures a "new beginning" and *typifies* the first day of the new week of ETERNITY, the beginning of a "New Heaven" and a "New Earth" with a "New Jerusalem."

The Church commences as a relatively *disorganized* spiritual organism of Christ. It concludes as "New Jerusalem", the Bride of the Lord.

The Church eventually becomes the **"mature body"** of Christ, capable of judging and overseeing God's creation throughout the universe, as the Lamb's Wife!

The earth will still be the focal point or headquarters for the universe throughout ETERNITY. It will be the *eternal* home of Christ and His Wife, and the Father all "tabernacling" or *dwelling* together in peace!

"New Jerusalem," the city of perfect beauty and holiness, will be the *consummation* of God's glorious plan. Every enemy of God will have been conquered and every tear will have been wiped away as God's harvest of the earth is completed!

But notice also, there is no silver mentioned in the holy city! There is gold and precious jewels—but no silver!

Why? Because *silver* is a *symbol* of REDEMPTION—and there will no longer be any need for redemption in the remainder of God's plan!

God may indeed continue to expand His family throughout the other planets. How He will do this remains a mystery—but one thing is for sure—there will no longer be a need for a Savior!

Fulfillment in Jesus: The story of redemption is a love story of a man winning his bride. It is a Cinderella story in which an ugly woman is turned into a beautiful woman after she receives a golden slipper. The analogy here of course, is God's people becoming beautiful in His sight, after He gives them the golden slipper of His Holy Spirit!

Jesus is our millennium of PEACE as He relives His life in us. When one grows in the fruits of the Holy Spirit, it may be said that the millennium of "inner peace" has been established within us.

On the sixth day of creation, God made man in His image, and on the seventh day He rested. Reflecting back on His handy work of the previous six days, God said **"it was very good."** Christ is the "millennial rest" of God, and His work is very good! As the fruit of the Holy Spirit of God is established in Christians, they have *inner peace* and enter into God's rest!

Salvation is not a thing—it is the person of Jesus Christ! Jesus IS eternal life, peace, power, healing, government, wisdom, joy, redemption—Jesus is EVERYTHING!

Jesus is the alpha and omega or **"the beginning"** and **"the end"** of God's creation. Thus, salvation has a definite beginning and a definite end!

Once the Bride is formed as the mature body of Christ, and the "New Heavens" and "New Earth" are created—ETERNITY waits for the Lamb and His Wife to expand the family of God with all kinds of possibilities!

Chapter Ten

"THE NEW HEAVENS" AND "EARTH"

Imagine if you can, 1000 years from now into eternity—what will you be doing?

With the passing of time, Christians have journeyed like Israel in *type* from Egypt to the Promised Land. They have fulfilled the feast days of God spiritually, as they have experienced Passover to Tabernacles.

Spiritually, they have come from the outer courtyard of the Temple, into its gates, cleansed themselves in the laver, entered the holy place—and are now ready to enter the Holy of Holies forever! Those faithful to God are ready to experience eternity, *symbolized* by the Last Great Day—as they start a "new beginning" in eternity!

Now we come to the grand finale of God's plan, the crescendo— the crème' de'la creme if you will! God has been waiting for this incredible moment for 7,000 agonizing years! If you thought that salvation, spirit bodies, marriage feast, Millennium, was all there is to look forward to—you are in for a surprise!

Here we shall expand our minds to explore "the mysteries of the universe" in eternity!

The Marriage of the Church

At this point, the reader is encouraged to review (Vol. 2, p.

161) the Parable of the Royal Marriage Feast, in which the basic wedding pattern between Christ and His Church will transpire.

Recall the three stages of the Hebrew wedding pattern that *parallel* the Church, namely: 1) the *betrothal period* in which the Bride is chosen by the groom's parents (God the Father has chosen us), without the groom's prior knowledge. A formal contract (the New Testament) is then written up, 2) the *wedding feast* begins lasting anywhere between a day to a week (the Millennial Feast), and 3) finally, the *marriage is consummated* when the groom takes the bride to his home (at the end of the Millennium).

Currently, the Church is in the *betrothal* stage. After Christ returns with His *resurrected* Bride, the 1000 year "marriage feast" will take place. Then the marriage will be *consummated* between Christ and His Bride (New Jerusalem), beginning the "New Heavens" and "New Earth!"

By understanding the Hebrew custom of marriage in *type*, and also God's numerical system—it makes sense that the spiritual *consummation* of the Church would come, not after 6000 years of human history, but after 7000 years leading to perfection! The number 7 being indicative of "spiritual perfection" when Christ would present His spotless Bride to Himself!

The Overcomers comprise "New Jerusalem"

Granted, that the Bride of Christ, "New Jerusalem" will be presented to Christ as a spotless Bride *after* the Millennium when the *marriage* will be consummated—WHO will comprise the Lamb's Wife?

Will Christ's Wife be comprised of the nation of Israel, the New Testament Church, the 144,000 Tribulation Saints, or Millennial Saints?

Reflecting back to (Revelation 21:1-7) in regards to *whom* comprises "New Jerusalem" after the Millennium we read:

> **And I saw a new heaven and a new earth...And I saw the holy city *New Jerusalem*, coming down from God out of heaven, *prepared as a bride adorned for her husband* [notice she is prepared**

> **to get married].. And I heard a great voice out of heaven saying, Behold, the tabernacle of God is with men, and he will dwell with them, and they shall be his people, and God himself shall be with them, and be their God...He that OVERCOMETH shall inherit all things, and I will be his God, and he shall be my son.**

What can we learn from this scripture?

God says the *overcomers* shall inherit New Jerusalem! Lest there be any doubt that the "overcomers" will inherit *all things,* including "New Jerusalem"—read the following verses in Revelation concerning Christ's promises to His seven Churches (Rev. 2:7,11,17,26; 3:5,12,21).

Here we find that only *overcomers* will "eat of the tree of life" (2:7), "not be hurt by the second death" (2:11), "will be given hidden manna" (2:17), "will be given a new name" (2:17), "will be given authority over the nations" (2:26), "shall rule the nations with a rod of iron" (2:27), "shall be clothed in white garments, and shall not have his name erased from the book of life" (3:5), "will be made a pillar in the Temple of God, and will not go out of the Temple, and Christ will write the name of the city of His God [New Jerusalem] and His [Christ's] new name" (3:12), "will be granted to sit with Christ in His throne" (3:21).

Another point in hammering down the final nail on this subject is that the first Adam and his wife Eve were a *type* of the second Adam [Christ] and His Bride.

Did you ever wonder *why* God created Eve out of one of Adam's ribs instead of making her out of the dust of the ground like Adam? It was because He wanted to form Adam's bride out of a part of Adam's body!

Likewise, Christ's Bride comprising all *overcomers* will be fashioned out of His body or the very substance, or essence of which He was made—SPIRIT!

Conclusively, the foundation for the future holy city is built upon Jesus Christ, the Church and Israel! The Bride of Christ is comprised of *overcomers* of the Church and Israel! Both are built into the heavenly Jerusalem by the heavenly Architect!

Tabernacles and God's Eternal Dwelling House

God's *resting* after the 7th day of the creation week is *typical* of His eternal resting with His creation! The main theme of the Bible is that of God abiding and *dwelling* with His people—and we with Him!

This is the central issue of the concept of the "New Jerusalem" of God—that of God *tabernacling* with His creation FOREVER! "New Jerusalem" is the Father's house that is being fashioned out of "spiritual jewels." It will be the Lamb's Wife and the eternal dwelling place of God among His people. Notice the many scriptural references that make this concept abundantly clear:

Jn. 14:23   "Jesus answered and said unto him, if a man love me, he will keep my words: and my Father will love him, and we will come to him, and make *our abode with him.*"

Jn. 17:21   "That they all may be one; as thou, Father art in me, and *I in thee,* that they also may be *one in us...*"

Jn. 6:56   "He that eateth my flesh, and drinketh my blood, *dwelleth in me, and I in him.*"

Jn. 15:4   "*Abide in me, and I in you.* As the branch cannot bear fruit of itself, except it abide in the vine; no more can ye, *except ye abide in me.*"

Gal. 2:20   "I am crucified with Christ: nevertheless I live; yet not I, but *Christ liveth in me...*"

Col. 2:9   "For in him dwelleth all the fulness of the *Godhead* bodily."

Eph. 3:17   "That Christ may *dwell in your hearts* by faith..."

Rev. 3:20   "Behold, I stand at the door, and knock: if any man hear My voice, and open the door, *I will come in to him,* and will sup with him, and he with

NEW HEAVENS AND EARTH

me."

Hide and Seek

Ever since the Garden of Eden, it was God's intended purpose to *dwell* among His creation. But Adam and Eve disobeyed their Creator by eating of the tree of the knowledge of good and evil, and then hid themselves from God's face!

Mankind has been doing precisely the same thing for the past 6,000 years—that is, *hiding* from God's ways while He is *seeking* to make us realize that His way of life is the only way for lasting happiness!

God showed Himself to His people once again upon Mt. Sinai—but God's awesome presence accompanied by thunder and smoking, terrified the fearful Israelites! They showed their discontent by making a "golden calf" to worship instead!

Again, God tried to *dwell* among His people as Jesus came to His own—but the Jewish people chose to kill Him! In fact, one of Jesus' names "Emanuel" means "God with us!" God tried earnestly to *dwell* among His people in Eden, Sinai and Galilee—but mankind would not have it and rebelled!

In His wisdom, God chose another way to *dwell* among His people—by creating a "spiritual house" composed of "spiritual stones", with Jesus Christ at the apex, being the Chief Corner Stone. God will yet *dwell* among His creation in a great SPIRITUAL TEMPLE that He is now molding together through the mortar of His Holy Spirit!

Notice the many scriptures to this effect:

Ex. 25:8	"And let them make me a sanctuary; *that I may dwell among them."*
Ps. 132:13	"For the LORD hath chosen Zion; *he hath desired it for his habitation."*
Ps. 132:14 have	"This is my rest for ever: *here will I dwell:* for I desired it."
Acts 7:49	"Heaven is my throne, and earth is my footstool: what house will ye build me? saith the LORD: or *what is the place of my rest?"*

THE FOOLISHNESS OF GOD

Eph. 2:22   "In whom ye also are builded together for *an habitation of God through the Spirit."*

1 Jn. 4:13   "Hereby know we that *we dwell in him, and he in us, because he hath given us of his Spirit."*

11 Cor. 6:16   "...ye are the temple of the living God; as God hath said, *I will dwell in them,* and walk in them; and I will be their God, and they shall be my people."

Never again will God dwell in a Temple made with hands (Acts 7:48). Presently, God is in a tabernacle [temporary dwelling] but He will finally *dwell* with His children at the end of the Millennium for ever more!

God is now *perfecting* His Church, the Bride of Christ to be joined in perfect holy matrimony! This perfect union between Christ and His Church will make them ONE in Christ, as they become **"bone of His bone, and flesh of His flesh"**—just as Jesus is ONE with the Father! Then, the Bride and Groom can bear children, as the nations of the earth can be brought into this beautiful fruitful union!

The Eternal Tabernacle of God

When we read of the description of the "New Jerusalem" of God, there is no Temple or light there—for the city itself is the eternal Temple of God, as God the Father and God the Son are the light of it!

The *overcoming Saints* will be the pillars of the Temple structure who carry out God's government to the nations. The River of Life [God's Holy Spirit] will flow freely to all nations to drink abundantly of the Tree of Life which is Jesus Christ, who will provide healing for the nations of the earth in this eternal spiritual city!

Solomon's Temple, in all its glory, was a *type* of the spiritual Temple of God. Each stone of this magnificent edifice was prepared and shaped at their quarries, rather than at the Temple location. These beautiful stones were made so precisely, that, **"...there was neither hammer nor axe nor any tool or iron**

heard in the house, while it was in building" (1 Kings 6:7). Likewise, God's "spiritual stones" are being fashioned in advance of their placement, notice:

Jn. 14:2   "In my Father's house are *many mansions:* if it were not so, I would have told you, I go to prepare a place for you..."

Eph. 2:20   "And are *built upon the foundation of the apostles and prophets,* Jesus Christ himself being the chief corner stone; In whom *all the building fitly framed together groweth unto an holy temple in the Lord:* In whom ye also are builded together for an habitation of God through the Spirit."

Eph. 4:16   "From whom *the whole body fitly joined together* and compacted by that which every joint supplieth, according to the effectual working in the measure of every part, maketh increase of the body unto the edifying of itself in love."

1 Pet. 2:5   "Ye also, as lively [living] stones, are built up a *spiritual house,* an holy priesthood, to offer up spiritual sacrifices, acceptable to God by Jesus Christ."

1 Cor. 3:9   "For we are labourers together with God: ye are God's husbandry, *ye are God's building."*

1 Cor. 3:16   "Know ye not that *ye are the temple of God,* and that the Spirit of God *dwelleth* in you?"

Heb. 3:6   "But Christ as a son over his own house; *whose house are we,* if we hold fast the confidence and the rejoicing of the hope firm unto the end."

1 Tim. 3:15   "...*the house of God, which is the church of the living God,* the pillar and ground of the truth."

The Church is the affianced Bride or the Holy City of "New Jerusalem" that is the Body of Christ. But the Body of Christ is the Father's gift to His Son, as every member of that Body is "hand picked" by the Father (Jn. 6:37), just like every stone of Solomon's Temple was chosen in advance!

Here is another *mystery* revealed by Christ's names. Did you notice that the Bride in (Revelation 19:7) is called the "Lamb's Wife," instead of "Christ's Wife," or "Jesus' Wife," or the "Word's Wife," or the "Wife of the Son of God?"

Remember, names have deep spiritual significance in the Word of God, and this particular terminology has specific connotation. The reason the Church is called "the Lamb's Wife" is because it was Christ coming as a *lamb* to be slaughtered for the sins of His Bride. The Church composed of both Jew and Gentile eats His body and drinks His blood *symbolically* during the communion service commemoration—and therefore the Church will be *married* to the Passover Lamb!

God desires to Dwell with His Creation

Most definitely, the Eternal desires to *dwell* with His people. This is a major lesson of the Feast of Tabernacles.

Numerous Bible passages point to the fact that God wants to be with the people through whom He is working.

For example, God moved the great cloud between the host of Israel and the warriors of Egypt to protect the Israelites (Ex. 14:19-20). When the Tabernacle in the wilderness was finished, the presence of God filled it (Ex. 40:34-35). The glory of God filled the Temple in Jerusalem (11 Chron. 7:1-2). The apostle John said that the hope of all those who purify themselves spiritually is to see God "as He is" (1 Jn. 3:2-3).

God's instruction to the nation of Israel was to keep the Feast of Tabernacles" in the place which he shall choose" (Deut. 14:23, 16:15). It was to remind Israel of God's desire to *dwell* with them. Today, New Testament Christians renew their hope of dwelling with God in the "New Earth."

Ezekiel's Message

Ezekiel, whose name meant "God strengthens," was a prophet in exile. From a priestly family (Ezek. 1:3), he grew up in Judea during the last years of Judah's independence. He was deported to Babylon with King Jehoiachin in 597 B.C.

NEW HEAVENS AND EARTH

A main message of the book of Ezekiel vividly illustrates God's desire to be with His people.

Ezekiel lived with the Jewish exiles by the River Chebar (Ezek. 1:1, 3:15). He was called to be a prophet in the fifth year of his captivity. The last date mentioned in the book of Ezekiel is the 27th year (Ezek. 29:17). We may deduce that Ezekiel's work lasted 22 years, from about 593 to 571 B.C.

Ezekiel began his prophecies at a time when the nation of Israel was at the lowest ebb of its history, spiritually and nationally.

On the day the final siege of Jerusalem began, Ezekiel's wife suddenly became sick and died. In this, Ezekiel became a *sign* to the people of greater sorrow coming as he wasn't allowed to mourn.

Ezekiel's last prophecies were uttered after Jerusalem had fallen and the Temple had been destroyed. Only a pitiful *remnant* was left in the land. Israel's spirit was broken.

But a prophecy, centuries before had detailed what would happen if Israel broke the covenant with God. God predicted that the Israelites would say, **"Are not these evils come upon us, because our God is not among us?" (Deut. 31:17).**

God warned, **"And I will surely hide my face in that day for all the evils which they shall have wrought" (verse 18).**

Ezekiel recorded God's departure from the Temple and the midst of the people (Ezek. 10:4, 18-19, 11:22-24). Only a few brief centuries after God entered the Temple, He reluctantly left *dwelling* with His chosen nation. The destruction of the city and deportation of the remaining tribes was imminent.

But Ezekiel received and delivered prophecies that pointed toward the Kingdom of God and the return of the presence of God to earth! These were prophecies of hope and consolation on a grand scope. The close relationship between God and His creation will yet be restored!

The book of Ezekiel concludes with a name of God given only in the book of Ezekiel. This appears to be the last name by which God reveals Himself and His character in the Old Testament. The last words of Ezekiel are *Yahweh-shammah*, meaning **"God is there" (Ezek. 48:35).** It is a fitting name!

This name represents God's promise that He will finish His plan for mankind. God is going to once again dwell among His people. This is the fabulous time we look forward to!

God and Man Reconciled

Jesus Christ is coming back to earth, as King of kings, to rule the entire earth and set up the Kingdom of God (Rev. 19:16). He is going to replace this world's present evil governments and establish an everlasting kingdom. God's presence will never again be removed from that Kingdom.

When God again dwells among His chosen people, what will it be like? As nations begin to see the positive results of the righteous and living rule of God's government, they will seek Christ and ask for instruction in God's way of life (Isa. 61:1). The prophet Micah wrote that people will flow to the government of God to be educated in the art of peace (Micah 4:1-3).

Isaiah wrote, **"Cry out and shout, thou inhabitant of Zion: for great is the Holy One of Israel in the midst of thee" (Isa. 12:6).**

Jeremiah says, **"At that time they shall call Jerusalem the throne of the Lord" (Jer. 3:7).** This hope stirred the minds of the prophets and patriarchs (Ps. 140:13).

Ezekiel prophesied about God's return to His spiritual Temple:

> **And behold, the glory of the God of Israel came from the way of the east: and his voice was like a noise of many waters: and the earth shined with his glory...and, behold, the glory of the Lord filled the house (Ezek. 43:2,5). Neither will I hide my face any more from them (Ezek. 39:29). I will dwell in the midst of the children of Israel for ever (Ezek. 43:7,9).**

Ezekiel put the crowning touch on this subject of God's presence when he spoke of the time we shall see God "as he is": **"And the name of the city from that day shall be, The Lord is there" (Ezek. 48:35).**

The Eighth Day and Eternity

As already demonstrated, the spiritual significance of the

number *eight* is that of "a new beginning"—and therefore it is highly probable that the eighth day of the Feast of Tabernacles also *pictures* the first day of the new week of eternity!

After the Millennium, when the "New Heavens" and "New Earth" with a "New Jerusalem" are created—the eighth day of the Feast of Tabernacles will most likely find its fulfillment in the eternal week which has no end!

The first seven days of the Feast of Tabernacles *pictures* the Millennium and the first seven days of the creation week, after which God will finally *rest* with His people! Thus, redemption will have been completed in mankind as God now *dwells* with His people, as they enter into His eternal rest! Then the "first day" of eternity will begin as *symbolized* by the eighth day of the Feast of Tabernacles!

Recall how earthly marriage is a *type* of the heavenly between the Lamb and His Wife. Also realize that the Hebrew nuptial custom *parallels* the marriage of Christ to the Church. Therefore, the possible reason God the Father does not come to *dwell* with His people until after the Millennium—is because the Lamb's Bride, even though resurrected, will not be spiritually mature until *after* the Millennium!

Just like any human courtship—it takes time to become mentally adjusted for marriage! Throughout the 1000 years of priestly service, undoubtedly the Bride will become increasingly refined!

Similarly, the Feast of Tabernacles *pictures* the maturing of the Lamb's Bride, even as the fruits and vegetables harvested during this time have come to full succulant maturity! *Figuratively,* that is why the Feast of Tabernacles was to be observed in the Land of Promise! It was there that the harvest [picturing the Church] would grow to full "spiritual maturity!"

Perhaps that is why "New Jerusalem" does not descend as the Lamb's Wife as a sparkling diadem until after the Millennial Jubilee has been completed?

Entering the "Holy of Holies"

The Old Covenant Tabernacle and Temple, with their various offerings, were merely *types* of the progression to "spiritual maturity" in the life of a Christian as we have seen. The spiritual concept of Christians progressing from the outer court to the Holy of Holies will now be discussed.

Recall how the outer court was where the people brought their animals to be sacrificed. Inside the Tabernacle was the holy place where only the ordinary priests could go, but not the rest of the people. The holy place was separated by the Holy of Holies, where God *dwelt* and where only the high priest could only enter once a year on the Day of Atonement.

Spiritually speaking, the Holy of Holies could only be entered by Christian priests through Christ—the door [Veil] that leads us to God's throne. All those outside the perimeters of the Tabernacle's sanctuary were in the "court of the Gentiles." Spiritually speaking, this stood for all those unrepentant sinners who were not even allowed in the inner courtyard to offer up sacrifices.

The golden altar in the holy place, where only the priests could enter, pointed to the *holiness* in the New Testament Church. The brazen altar in the *courtyard* outside the Tabernacle was for the sacrifices of the people.

Between the door of the Tabernacle and the altar in the courtyard stood a brass laver or pot of water. Before administering to the people, the priests had to wash in it, *personifying* the "cleansing" or purifying of sin through water baptism!

The anointed priests stood for the New Testament Church, as they must **"come out of the world"** by repenting of sin (*symbolic* of those sacrifices in the courtyard). Thus, spiritually speaking, only those who have accepted Jesus as their personal Savior, and are filled with God's Holy Spirit can enter the door of the Tabernacle, and move from the holy place into the Holy of Holies!

However, before Christians can enter the Holy of Holies as priests, they must utilize God's Holy Spirit in full and dedicated service to Him. To be baptized, and allow God's Holy Spirit to remain dormant without exercising it in service—is to stop at the holy place spiritually!

But there is a great giant step that must be taken before one can enter the Holy of Holies—and that is in becoming an *overcomer* or a bond-servant for Christ!

To begin our spiritual life at the Passover, after accepting the precious blood of Jesus Christ, and end spiritually at Pentecost, would mean to miss out on the Feast of Tabernacles and the Last Great Day spiritually!

It would be like the nation of Israel coming out of Egypt and remaining in the wilderness forever! It would only have been a half way point in our spiritual journey, and spiritually like remaining at the feast of Pentecost forever!

After Israel was delivered from Egypt, God led them through the wilderness and fought their battles for them. He fed them and clothed them and protected them as their husband! Likewise, when one becomes a Christian, God does most of our fighting for us!

The wilderness was a training experience to see if the Israelites would be faithful to God's laws and government. Israel's wilderness training spiritually *parallels* the Christian Pentecost experience in that after they receive the Holy Spirit they must walk in *obedience* to God—before they can proceed to the Feast of Trumpets and spiritually *conquer* the Promised Land!

The next phase of God's plan is the Feast of Trumpets *picturing* our "conquering" and fighting for victory in becoming an *overcomer!* Only when we become an overcomer can we enter the Promised Land or the Holy of Holies in the Tabernacle!

"New Jerusalem" is the *consummation* of God's *spiritual building*, and all *overcomers* will comprise Jesus' Bride and become this spiritual jewel of a city! Then this entire spiritual city will become ONE GREAT HOLY OF HOLIES! The apostle Paul put it so very succinctly in 11 Corinthians 5:1, when he said: **"For we know that if our earthly house of this tabernacle were dissolved, we have a building of God, an house not made with hands, *eternal in the heavens.*"**

"Spiritual Firstfruits"

Let's stop and analyze these deep concepts and expand our minds a little more into enternity. Consider the fact that "firstfruits" or "overcomers" are going to have **"better promises"** being in the first resurrection (Heb. 8:6).

But what were these promises?

To better understand what are the *better promises* that the writer of the book of Hebrews was referencing—who was addressing newly converted Jewish believers—the reader is encouraged to read Vol. 3 p. 73, regarding the Old Covenant.

THE FOOLISHNESS OF GOD

Recall, the Old Covenant was also a *marriage ceremony* between God [Jesus] and the nation of Israel. The marriage Covenant and the Old Covenant was one and the same! It was this marriage, then, that established *organization* and *government* among God's people!

The 10 Commandments, God's statutes and judgments were the terms and conditions—the basis—of that marriage contract. The Eternal [Lord] of the Old Covenant, as the Husband, promised to provide for and protect the nation or congregation of Israel. The nation of Israel in turn agreed to remain faithful always to Him.

God agreed to perform the duties of a husband, to provide for and bless her. The people of Israel accepted the terms that God gave them. They bound themselves by the Old Covenant to refrain from any adulterous or whorish relations with the false gods of other nations—and to remain chaste and acceptable to their own "husband" (Ex. 34:12-17).

The Israelites, being without the Spirit of God, were constantly rebelling—sinning—against their "husband"—and the 10 Commandment Law He had given them (Ezek. 20:13), and so the Eternal then added temporary "ritualistic laws" for them to keep because of their rebellion, to impress upon them the weakness of their own inherent *human nature* in respect to keeping God's Law (Lev. 1:1-9).

But ancient Israel continued to be disobedient and UNFAITHFUL to her husband and turned from worshipping God, and followed the customs of the heathen—serving other gods! She broke her part of the marriage covenant by committing *spiritual adultery*!

Jesus' disciples understood that the *Kingdom*, with all authority to govern, whether civil or church government, had been taken away from their people, and turned over to Gentiles. You'll remember how they asked Him, **"Lord, wilt thou at this time restore again the kingdom to Israel?" (Acts 1:6).**

Jesus came to His own [the nation of Israel] first, or to His wife! (Jn. 1:11). Realize, all the apostles were Jews! The gospel was to go to the Jew first (Rom. 1:16). Jesus said He was sent unto *the house of Israel*! (Matt. 15:24). He told His disciples not to go to the Gentiles or the Samaritans—but to *the house of Israel*! (Matt. 10:5). The early Church was composed solely of Jews on the day of Pentecost! (Acts 2:5). See also (Acts 3:25, 26;

13:36). The parable of the Vineyard in (Matthew 21) is very graphic in explaining the transfer of the Kingdom to another nation [the Church].

The promises of all spiritual blessings, and of eternal life, revealed in the gospel, and made sure through Christ, are of infinitely greater value, better promises. The Old Covenant promises were mainly of earthly, temporal promises, contrary to the heavenly blessings of the New Testament. The Old Covenant's original design of a ritual system was, a schoolmaster leading and preparing us for our true High Priest, Jesus, the Christ.

The book of Hebrews explains that there was a fault with the Old Covenant, otherwise there wouldn't have been a need for the new. What was the fault? Hebrews 8:7-8 helps us understand why Israel failed and what was the fault of the Old Covenant, notice: **"For if that first covenant had been faultless, then no place would have been sought for a second. Because *finding fault with them.*"** God determined to make a new covenant. In this crucial indictment, God says plainly where He found fault: not with the law, not with the Ten Commandments, not with the statutes and judgments, but *with the people themselves.*

Although the book of Hebrews says that God found fault "with them [Israelites]," the apostle Paul readily recognized the problem was not with just the nation of Israel, but Sin. Paul states a universal problem for all humanity—Jews and gentiles are all under sin (Romans 3; Galatians 3:22). This was Israel's dilemma under the Old Covenant, and it is the dilemma of all human beings. Sin is easy. It is a way of life that comes naturally to us (Romans 7:13-23).

The solution God revealed to Jeremiah for the problem of sin was the same one proclaimed hundreds of years later in the book of Hebrews: **"Behold, the days are coming says the Lord, when I will make a new covenant with the house of Israel and with the house of Judah—not according to the covenant that I made with their fathers in the day that I took them by the hand to bring them out of the land of Egypt, My covenant which *they broke*, though I was a husband to them, says the Lord" (Heb.8:8-10; Jeremiah 31:31-32).**

God inspired Jeremiah to proclaim that a New Covenant would be established that would have a better outcome than the Old Covenant established at Mount Sinai. **"But this is the**

covenant that I will make with the house of Israel after those days, says the Lord: I will *put My law in their minds and write it on their hearts;* **and I will be their God, and they shall be my people. No more shall every man teach his neighbor and every man his brother, saying, 'Know the Lord,'** *for they all shall know Me* **from the least of them to the greatest of them, says the Lord.** *For I will forgive their iniquity, and their sin I will remember no more"* **(verses 33-34)**. This New Covenant would have an additional dimension, an extra ingredient. The Holy Spirit would make the difference.

The New Covenant is a better covenant because God's way of life, reflected in the Ten Commandments, *becomes a part of our very being.* People in whose lives the work of writing the law upon their hearts and minds is completed are given a promise— not just physical blessings as with the Old Covenant, but *eternal life.* Then, throughout eternity, they will reflect God's way of life, summarized by love, in everything they think, say and do.

The promises in the first covenant as outlined in Exodus 20-24 pertained mainly to the present life. They were promises of length of days; of increase of numbers; of seed time and harvest; of national privileges, and of extraordinary peace, abundance, and prosperity, etc. But looking for the promise of eternal life, one cannot find it! In the New Testament, however, the promise of spiritual blessings becomes the principal objective. The mind is directed toward heavenly things!

But what else are going to be the better promises of those "firstfruits" in God's Kingdom? God had promised the Israelites that they would be "a kingdom of priests" and a "holy nation" if they would be faithful to Him (Ex. 19d:6). But they were not faithful and so God called a spiritual people to be "kings and priests" *ruling* over His Kingdom during the Millennium.

To Rule over Nations

Those who are "firstfruits" will be rulers over the nations during the Millennial reign of Jesus Christ, and forever! (Rev. 2:26,27).

True, the word translated "forever" in the Bible can refer to the time period designated to fulfill a particular dispensation— but realize also there are going to be nations on the newly created earth (Rev. 21:24,26; 22:2; Isa. 65:17-25; 66:22).

NEW HEAVENS AND EARTH

These nations do not dwell in Jerusalem, but their kings may visit it (Rev. 21:24). *Who* then are these nations existing on the newly created earth, and *who* are the kings ruling over them?

Recall the promise Christ made to the *overcomers* in (Revelation 22:5) was to reign for ever and ever. Those qualifying as *overcomers* will rule from Jerusalem, the headquarters for eternity and their eternal residence where the Father and Son comprising the Temple *dwell* (Rev. 3:12; 21:22).

Over *what* nations of the earth will the overcomers reign? Whoever these nations are, they will need healing of sickness, for the leaves of the tree of life are for their healing (Rev. 22:2). Therefore, these nations that need healing cannot be those qualified as "overcomers," for "overcomers" will never be in need of healing again (Rev. 21:4).

Chapter Eleven

> *Of the increase of his government and peace there shall be no end, upon the throne of David, and upon his kingdom, to order it, and to establish it with judgment and with justice from henceforth even for ever. The zeal of the LORD of hosts will perform this.*
> — Isa. 9:7

GOD'S PLAN BEYOND THE MILLENNIUM

As we look up into the sky at night cluttered with twinkling lights, surely one has to ponder if our earth is just one tiny planet circling one tiny star in a vast universe? The Bible has given names to a few constellations of stars such as Arcturus (the Bear), Orion and Pleiades (Job 9:9). Who hasn't heard of the Big Dipper, but have you ever wondered why there are countless more in the universe?

Images from the Hubble Space Telescope suggest there are 10 times more galaxies in the universe than originally thought. Some estimate there are more than 100 billion galaxies within our universe, and approximately 100 million stars inhabit the average galaxy.

Multiplying the number of galaxies, which is about 2 trillion, by 100 million stars in the galaxy suggests there could be about 10 raised to the 20th power stars in the universe.

This is the awesome potential for resurrected Christians—

the glorious DESTINY God has in store for those who seek to do His will and follow His way. God's Word has stated that Christians were born to RULE the universe with Jesus Christ!

H.A. Ironside provokes our imagination as to God's future Kingdom:

> **To be a priest, one must be a priest to someone. To 'reign' presupposes one must have subjects over which to rule or teach. To 'have judgment' means these individuals must make decisions about situations that affect others. Where and over whom do the saints carry out these functions?** (*Lectures on the Revelation*, p. 31).

Although it is not an easy supposition to prove, the expansion of the Family of God throughout the Universe should not be considered unlikely. If we are correct in our previous contention that the God Family will indeed expand throughout the Universe, it makes a profound difference in our understanding of the plan of God as to *how* this will be accomplished! It is a fundamental, yet *key* question and deserves our careful attention within the spectrum of possibilities.

Who will God's family rule over, and *what* laws will they implement? Here, we must ask some very pertinent questions—yet their answers are imperative in order for us to comprehend this mind-boggling concept. How is God going to expand his family throughout the universe into eternity?

Will this be done through sexual copulation on a physical or spiritual plateau as was done on planet earth, and will children therefore be born? Why did God create sex anyway, and where is its *antitype* in the spirit world? Will a reproductive system be necessary for all eternity?

The inspired apostle Paul wrote in (11 Corinthians 6:18) that God, **"...will be a Father unto you, and ye shall be my *sons* and *daughters,* saith the Lord Almighty."** Will these spiritual "Sons" and "Daughters" be spirit beings with vestigial organs—or look like God the Father? Is God male or bisexual?

BEYOND THE MILLENNIUM

An imaginable glimpse into the future

It is difficult to comprehend our future regardless as to which view one takes without speculating. At best we will attempt to take a fresh view of the basic plan of God and try to clarify the plausible possibilities.

Therefore, we shall take an imaginable glimpse into the future regarding the possibilities as to what our future life will be like. Let us therefore begin from the proposition that there are no limitations to God's Master Plan.

Let us begin our imaginary glimpse into the future with what we do know from scripture to draw some kind of hypothesis as we try to answer the question: *"who will the Family of God rule over, and how will it expand throughout eternity?"*

Throughout this four volume study on the *types*, we have examined the importance to God regarding a family relationship. Husbands and wives, Christ to His Church. However, there remains one final question to which answers may be attempted: *"How is God going to expand His Family throughout eternity?"*

We will try to be objective as possible in our quest for answers to this very important question without any emphatic position.

Let us begin by asking some pertinent questions realizing that we cannot fully understand the sovereign mind of Almighty God. However, we do know God created the billions of stars long before He ever made man. Why was that? Was it ever God's intended purpose to create man in the first place?

We have read how God's plan was to create mankind in His "image" and "likeness" as He began to instill His character on the earth in bringing many Sons and Daughters into His FAMILY.

We have also read how these spiritual family members would be *rulers* in His Kingdom. If God's government is to increase forever in His Kingdom according to scripture, then these family members will help Him rule it!

How then will God REPRODUCE His character throughout the vast universe? We can only speculate as to the possibilities!

A Physical Creation

Will there be physical human beings in the "New Heavens"

and "New Earth?" The argument here revolves around whether God will create anything physical again after the "New Heavens" and "New Earth" is made (Rev. 21:1).

Some have thought the "New Heavens" and "New Earth" will be entirely made of spiritual material. However, the scriptures do not say this explicitly. God does not reveal what the exact composition will be, but He uses physical terminology to describe it. Precious jewels, metals and stones are listed in physical terms, but there is indication that these could be of spiritual composition since gold is listed as being "transparent" as glass (Rev. 21:21).

Those who believe the "New Universe" to be a *spiritual* creation only, base their understanding on (Revelation 21:4) which says: **"...God shall wipe away all tears from their eyes, and there shall be no more death; neither sorrow, nor crying, neither shall there be any more pain, for the former things are passed away."**

The reasoning here is that physical beings would see death, sorrow, crying and pain. But the rebuttal to this scripture is that Satan is the one who has caused all of the tears, death, sorrow, crying and pain in the world, and he won't be around any longer.

Furthermore, this scripture could apply only to the 7000 year dispensation of God's plan when all tears, crying, pain and death would finally cease, since all will become spirit beings. This coincides with Christ being the Alpha and Omega (the beginning and the end—Rev. 1:11). But are we to suppose that this will be the end of God's plan?

Adherents of the physical creation philosophy cite the following scriptures which indicate that nations will be on earth after the Millennium and will have a progeny, need healing for sickness, and have wicked sinners who will not be permitted to enter the gates of the holy city:

> **For, behold, I create *new heavens and a new earth*: and the former shall not be remembered, nor come into mind. But be ye glad and rejoice for ever in that which I create: for, behold, I create Jerusalem a rejoicing, and her people a joy. And I will rejoice in Jerusalem, and joy in my people: and the voice of weeping shall be no more heard in her, nor the voice of crying.**

> **There shall be no more thence an infant of days, nor an old man that hath not filled his days:** *for the child shall die an hundred years old*, **but the** *sinner* **being an hundred years old shall be accursed (Isa. 65:17-20).**

Some hold this verse to apply to the time just after the Millennium known as the Great White Throne Judgment, and believe this verse is speaking of a 100 year period of time (Rev. 20:11).

Adherents of this belief maintain that all those who have ever lived and did not have the chance to understand God's laws, will be resurrected at this time and given a first time opportunity for eternal life for the duration of 100 years.

It is believed by those of this persuasion, that this is a millennial setting as the wolf and the lamb shall feed together, and the lion shall eat straw (vs. 25).

It is also believed that children will not be born during this centennial period of time. However, this is not conclusive based upon where one places the comma in this verse. By eliminating the comma after "days" we have: **"There shall be no more thence an infant of days nor an old man that hath not filled his days: for the child shall die an hundred years old; but the sinner being an hundred years old shall be accursed."** In other words, every human being will live to be one hundred years old, not that human reproduction would cease! The *J.F.B.* states of this verse, **"none shall die without attaining a full old age."**

The thought of this thinking is that if God did not eliminate reproduction during this time, someone would surely be pregnant during the 100th year, and the cycle would have to start all over again. This would be convincing proof for a resurrection period to judgment.

However, if infants are in fact to be born, this would be convincing proof that this time period could not be referring to the Great White Throne Judgment, but rather the "New Heavens and New Earth" after the Millennium. It is also very possible that this verse could apply to both the Millennium and the "New Heaven and New Earth" as the Millennium is a *type* of the "New Heaven and New Earth."

Let's read the 66th chapter of Isaiah:

> For as the *new heavens and the new earth*, which I will make, shall remain before me, saith the LORD, *so shall your seed and your name remain* (Isa. 66:22).

Let's now read (Revelation 21) for some additional verses on this subject:

> And *the nations of them which are saved* shall walk in the light of it: and the *kings of the earth* do bring their glory and honour into it (Holy Jerusalem). And the gates of it shall not be shut at all by day: for there shall be no night there. And they shall bring the glory and honour of *the nations* into it. And *there shall in no wise enter into it any thing that defileth*, neither whatsoever worketh abomination, or maketh a lie: but they which are written in the Lamb's book of life (Rev. 21:24-27).

William R. Newel, in defending the position of this plausibility, writes on the interpretation of "the nations" into eternity in Revelation 21:24-26:

> In chapter 21:3, where we read that the tabernacle of God is at last with men, we also read that 'they shall be his peoples' (Greek *laoi*). It is amazing to find discerning men apparently almost wilfully translating the plural *laoi*, as if it were *laos*...The Revised Version...translates truly and plainly, 'They shall be his *peoples*,' and thus prepares us to avoid the impossible assumption that 21:9 to 22:5 is a passage that reverts to millennial scenes (William R. Newell, *The Book of Revelation*, pp. 343-45).

For a final scripture we read Revelation 22:2:

> In the midst of the street of it, and on either side of the river, was there *the tree of life*,

> which bare twelve manner of fruits, and yielded her fruit every month: and *the leaves of the tree were for the healing of the nations.*

From these scriptures speaking of the "New Heavens" and the "New Earth", it indicates that children and men will live to be 100 years old, and will need healing for sickness during the course of that lifetime. Also, the fact that sinners will not be permitted into the holy city is indicative of a physical creation, similar to the Millennium! See also (Revelation 21:3), where it speaks of God the Father tabernacling [dwelling] with men!

Some may argue that these scriptures are in reference to the Millennium, rather than the "New Heaven" and "New Earth", but these scriptures appear to be in the context of the "New Heaven" and "New Earth."

To Keep the Law Eternally

It appears that the nation of Israel will be one of many nations on the newly created earth (Isa. 66:22). Now we will discover that the *law of God* must be in CONTINUAL existence in order to govern these nations.

Concerning the eternal existence of the nation of Israel, coinciding with God's 10 Commandment Law, Jeremiah writes: **"If those ordinances depart from me, saith the LORD, then the seed of Israel also shall cease from being a nation before me** *for ever."*

True, this scripture could be rendered, "age lasting" or "till the dispensation be fulfilled," instead of "for ever" meaning eternally. But what of the other scriptures that indicate God's Law to be in existence for all ETERNITY?

Paul put it very succinctly when he wrote: **"For we know the law is spiritual..." (Rom. 7:14).** Now that which is spiritual is eternal isn't it, ask "physical creation" advocates?

Certainly, if the 10 Commandments are to be in effect for all eternity—there would have to be children born—for several of the Commandments revolve around the family, inclusive of children. Notice the fifth commandment: **"Honour thy father and thy mother"** would have to include the birth of children.

Not only that, but these *generations* of families would continue to keep God's law for a **"thousand generations" (Deut.**

7:9). If a generation is considered to be roughly 30 years, this would mean God's law to be in existence for at least 30,000 years (30 x 1000). Therefore, God's law would last at least 23,000 years beyond the Millennium (7,000 - 30,000 = 23,000).

And what about the laws of Moses?—will they be carried out for all eternity? There is indication that animal sacrifices will exist during the Millennium as "symbolic" reminders—not that they will actually remove sin.

Let us therefore summarize this "physical creation" concept of reproduction. Scriptural indications point to God's 10 Commandment law centered around family life and children, to be existent for generations beyond this 7000 year plan for mankind.

Many scriptures seem to indicate that there will be physical beings, comprising nations that will be of need of healing *after* the "New Heavens" and "New Earth" are created.

WHAT A GLORIOUS PLAN OF GOD THAT AWAITS US!

www.ingramcontent.com/pod-product-compliance
Lightning Source LLC
Chambersburg PA
CBHW070545010526
44118CB00012B/1233